HULL SPEEDWAY 1930-81

HULL SPEEDWAY 1930-81

ROGER HULBERT

TEMPUS

First published 2004

Tempus Publishing Ltd
The Mill, Brimscombe Port
Stroud, Gloucestershire GL5 2QG
www.tempus-publishing.com

British Library Cataloguing in Publication Data.
A catalogue record for this book is available from the British Library.

ISBN 0 7524 3200 1

Typesetting and origination by Tempus Publishing.
Printed and bound in Great Britain.

CONTENTS

INTRODUCTION

Speedway in Hull has had a chequered history. At the time of writing, the sport is being staged at Craven Park, the fourth venue to stage speedway in the area. This somewhat nomadic existence has not generally been the fault of speedway itself. The first venue at White City was an open-licence track that ran for a few years in the 1930s, a time of depression. The second venue at Hedon, eight miles from the city centre lasted less than two years and initially attracted good crowds, but struggled, not only because of a lack of on-track success, but because of its location and a reliance on public transport in an era when few owned cars. Also, punitive levels of Entertainment Tax in the immediate post-war years caused the track to acquire the unwanted record of being the first post-war speedway to close mid-season. Transplanted into the modern era, the venue would have undoubtedly succeeded.

The third, and to date most successful attempt to establish the sport in Hull was the eleven-year tenure of the Boulevard. The stadium, although in a built-up area was accessible, in speedway terms well appointed, and attracted good support right to the end in 1981 when the lease was terminated by a rugby club whose success convinced them that they no longer needed tenants in their stadium. Modern environmental regulations ruled out a return to this venue in 1995.

The latest venue at Craven Park again sees speedway as tenants, this time of the rival rugby club who have hit on hard times in recent years. The Craven Park era will be covered in the second volume of this history.

In the light of what I have described above, being a speedway supporter in Hull has been something of a roller-coaster ride, ranging from the heights of the Ivan Mauger/Kelly Moran/Dennis Sigalos era and the cup-winning years of 2000/2001 to the despair of closure in 1981 and the numerous closure threats in the current era, notably 1997, 2000 and 2002. For all that, it has never been dull, and the club enjoys a perhaps modest but loyal support. The tenacity of the club is a credit in a city dominated by rugby league tradition and rivalry, and now boasting a brand-new super stadium which inevitably grabs most of the limelight.

This book documents the first fifteen recorded years of speedway racing in Hull, and it is hoped that it will prove informative and also bring back memories of the teams and riders of those years, some well known, others less so, all of whom have entertained us.

ACKNOWLEDGEMENTS

This book has been the best part of seven years in the making, and after my initial desktop-published statistical work of five years ago and one update, I did not anticipate any further literary efforts. However, the excellent range of speedway books published by Tempus prompted me to the view that a history of Hull speedway should have a place in that range.

In the course of the research for this volume I have received much help in the way of materials given and loaned by many very generous people, and without the help of the people listed this book would never have happened.

Chris Benham, Colin Cheeseman, the late Ray Cooper, Judy Davis (aka Hipflask), Brian Gray, Mike Greenwood, John Horsley, Innes Photographers, Matt Jackson, Mike Kemp, Dave Lofthouse, Wendy Mills, Trevor Nicholson, Mark Oliver (aka Marko), Mike Patrick, R. Peacock, Speedway Researcher, Steve Radge, Barry Stephenson, Ian Ward.

I should also like to thank Speedway Star magazine for allowing me to use material from their publication.

Also, I should like to thank Robert Bamford for his advice and encouragement during the course of the project.

If I have omitted anybody from the above list, please accept my apologies; your assistance has not been overlooked, it's just that my memory isn't as good as it was!

About the Author

Roger has been a supporter of Hull Speedway since 1974, when his family moved from their Midlands origins to Hull. He first saw speedway at Coventry in 1962 after being persuaded by a schoolfriend to go, and was bitten by the bug. He followed the sport at Brandon, Birmingham, Cradley Heath and Wolverhampton in the '60s and early '70s. Since 1974, he has been a regular at both the Boulevard and Craven Park and remains as strong an enthusiast for the sport as he was in his younger days. Roger is married to a Hull lady, and has recently celebrated his Silver Wedding anniversary.

He is currently employed by the local authority in the Education department.

HULL SPEEDWAY VENUES 1930–1981

1. White City Stadium, Hull

Years of Operation: 1930–1933 (Open Licence)

2. Hedon Stadium, Staithes Lane, Hedon, near Hull, East Yorkshire

Years of Operation: 1948–1949 (National League)
Race Day: Saturday 7.15 p.m.
Track Length: 443 yards
Track Record: 82.4 seconds, Billy Bales (Yarmouth), 14 May 1949
Promoters: Capt F. Archer, Mrs V.C. Carberry, Brig. D.H.M. Carberry, Capt. E.C. Aylott, P.J.C. West

3. Boulevard Stadium, Airlie Street, Hull, East Yorkshire

Years of Operation: 1971–1981 (British League)
Race Day: Wednesday 7.30 p.m.
Track Length: 415 yards
Track Record: 68.6 seconds, Dennis Sigalos (Hull), 23 July 1980
Promoters: Ian Thomas (1971–1981), Wally Mawdsley (1971–1975), Brian Larner (1976–1981), Ernie Park (1978)

CLUB HONOURS AND RECORDS

Club Honours – Team

Winners:
Inter-Divisional Knock-Out Cup: 1976
Inter-League Four-Team Championship: 1979
Yorkshire Cup: 1976, 1978, 1979, 1981
Best Performances (League): 2nd, British League 1979

Club Honours – Individual (won while a Hull rider)

Winner: World Championship: Ivan Mauger, 1979
World Team Cup: Ivan Mauger, 1979 (with New Zealand)
Grand Prix: Dennis Sigalos, 1980
Northern Riders Championship: Ivan Mauger, 1980

Club Records (these records include League and KO Cup matches)

Biggest Win:
Home: 81-25 v. Sheffield (K.O. Cup) 1 June 1979.
Away: 52-26 v. Wolverhampton (League) 5 October 1979.
Heaviest Defeat:
Home: 42-66 v. Cradley Heath (K.O. Cup) 1 May 1948.
Away: 29-78 v. Cradley Heath (K.O. Cup) 7 May 1948.
Most Appearances: 279 (Bobby Beaton, 1974-1981).
Most Races: 1209 (Bobby Beaton, 1974-1981).
Most Race Points: 2012.5 (Bobby Beaton, 1974-1981).
Most Bonus Points: 237 (Frank Auffret, 1976-1981).
Most Total Points: 2228.5 (Bobby Beaton, 1974-1981).
Most Maximums: 29 (24 FM, 5 PM, Ivan Mauger, 1978-1981).

1
WHITE CITY STADIUM 1930–1933

The sport of speedway, which originated in Australia, was introduced to Britain in the 1920s. Although there were some earlier meetings, it is acknowledged that the first major dirt-track meeting was staged at High Beech, Essex, in February 1928.

Dirt-track racing caught on rapidly and tracks sprung up all over the country, some standing the test of time while others came and went quickly. The sport was introduced to the Hull area when in July 1929, a London-based syndicate secured an agreement to convert eleven acres at the rear of the skating rink in the White City amusement park, situated in Anlaby Road and Calvert Lane, roughly a mile to the west of the Boulevard stadium, into a track. The circuit was modelled on the existing track at Sheffield, which was the only Australian-type track in the country.

WHITE CITY

DIRT TRACK

NO RACING TO-NIGHT (Thursday)

LIGHT NOT FAVOURABLE.

SATURDAY NEXT

GIGANTIC PROGRAMME at 3

NEEDLE MATCH RACE

BINGHAM v. DOWSE

OTHER WELL-KNOWN RIDERS WILL APPEAR.

Poster advising of a postponed White City meeting.

An open licence was granted and the first meeting was staged on 3 May 1930. Regular meetings were staged throughout the summer of 1930, and these meetings were well reported in the local press. In the pioneering spirit, riders rejoiced in names like 'Tear A Long' of Thorne, 'Broadside' Gatley, and 'Hurricane' Dowse. Meetings were mainly staged on Saturday afternoons and were well attended.

Team racing was not totally absent as a team representing Hull met and defeated teams from Leicester and Middlesbrough.

In August, there was a dispute between riders and management regarding payments which led to new management taking over and improvements to the stadium being carried out. Meetings ceased in late August 1930 to avoid clashes with football and rugby matches, as of course there was no floodlighting and sport on a Sunday was several decades away.

It is believed that some meetings took place between 1931 and 1933 but no records of any such meetings have come to light. The stadium was destroyed by fire in 1938 and was rebuilt, only to collapse under the weight of snow in the bad winter of 1947-48. Eventually, in 1965 the site was redeveloped and high-rise flats were built, which are known locally as the White City flats.

Saturday 3 May 1930

Little is known about the first meeting at White City. The Hall Cross Trophy was presented to the winner by Mr A. Fogg on behalf of the trophy donor (Mrs Fogg).

Result
Hall Cross Trophy: Winner: E. Johnston (Hull).
Crowd: 7,000

Saturday 17 May 1930

The second meeting at White City was held in excellent weather, and the 3,000 crowd enjoyed some fine racing. The star of the meeting was 'Skid' Fenton of Thorne, who set up a new track record of 77.4 seconds. Two unsuccessful attempts were made to break the lap record.

Results
Successful track record attempt by 'Skid' Fenton: New record time: 77.4 seconds.
White City Scratch Race: Heat Winners: A. Young (no time), N. Cox (95 seconds), 'Skid' Fenton (94.6 seconds), G. Samson (109 seconds), H. Brook (115 seconds). Final: 'Skid' Fenton (86.2 seconds), N. Cox, G. Samson.
Whirlwind Four: Heat Winners: 'Broadside' Gatley (87.4 seconds), M. Bennett (109 seconds), G. Samson (110 seconds). Final: Winner: 'Broadside' Gatley (96.2 seconds).

Speedway Trophy Handicap: Heat Winners: 'Broadside' Gatley (97.2 seconds), I. Barwood (100.2 seconds), H. Hall (98.6 seconds), A. Drabble (100.8 seconds), S. Worthington (98 seconds). Final: 'Broadside' Gatley (92 seconds), S. Worthington, I. Barwood.

Unsuccessful attempt of 25.2 seconds on the lap record by I. Barwood. D. Adams' record of 22.4 seconds stands.

Crowd: 3,000.

Saturday 24 May 1930

A crowd of 3,000 witnessed another entertaining afternoon of racing, which started with Holmes of Thorne breaking 'Skid' Fenton's week-old track record, establishing a new time of 76.8 seconds. Fenton gained compensation by setting a new lap record with a time of 19.8 seconds.

A spectacular spill occurred in a sidecar race when one of the sidecars overturned on a bend. However, neither driver nor passenger were seriously hurt.

Results

Successful track record attempt by I. Holmes: New record time: 76.8 seconds.

Successful attempt of 19.8 seconds on the lap record by 'Skid' Fenton.

White City Scratch Race: Heat Winners: Tear A Long (98 seconds), H. Hall (82.4 seconds), N. Barwood (103 seconds), I. Holmes (97 seconds). Final: Holmes (88 seconds), Tear A Long, Barwood.

Match Races: Heat Winners: G. Samson (108.4 seconds), I. Holmes (97.4 seconds), Tear A Long (No Time). Final: Holmes (85.6 seconds), Tear A Long.

Speedway Trophy Handicap: Heat Winners: I. Holmes (96 seconds), N. Barwood (101 seconds), H. Hall (99 seconds), G. Samson (101 seconds). Final: Barwood (91 seconds), Holmes, Samson.

Crowd: 3,000.

Saturday 31 May 1930

Another reported crowd of 3,000 at the White City were disappointed to learn that the star attraction, 'Smoky' Stratton was unable to attend. There were many close finishes and some spills although no serious accidents occurred.

Results

Unsuccessful track record attempt by A. Bingham.

White City Scratch Race: Heat Winners: E.W. Greenwood (87.4 seconds), I. Holmes (89.2 seconds), S. Worthington (105 seconds), A. Bingham (102 seconds). Final: Bingham (85 seconds), Greenwood, Holmes.

Match Races: Greenwood (89.2 seconds) beat Bingham, Holmes (85.4 seconds) beat H. Dowse, Greenwood (No Time) beat H. Hall.
Speedway Trophy Handicap: Heat Winners: 'Broadside' Gatley (94.8 seconds), Bingham (88.2 seconds), Jud Heath (93.2 seconds). Final: Heath (92.2 seconds), Gatley, Greenwood.
Unsuccessful attempt on the lap record by H. Hall.
Crowd: 3,000.

Thursday 12 June 1930

Another large crowd saw a close finish to the White City Scratch Race final with Archie Bingham beating Tommy Bateman by a third of a wheel after a tremendous race with three competitors racing neck and neck for three laps.

Results
Unsuccessful track record attempt of 79 seconds by T. Bateman. A. Bingham's record of 74 seconds stands.
Unsuccessful attempt on the lap record by Al Brown, falling 0.6 seconds short of A. Bingham's record.
White City Scratch Race: Heat Winners: N. Cox (125 seconds), E.W. Greenwood (84.8 seconds), T. Bateman (88 seconds), A. Bingham (82.2 seconds). Final: Bingham (81 seconds), Bateman, Greenwood.
Junior Handicap: E. Johnston (94 seconds), L. Robinson, G.T. Grant.
Match Races: Bingham (78 seconds) beat F. Ledger, 'Hurricane' Dowse (79.2 seconds) beat 'Twister' Holmes, Bateman (80.2 seconds) beat Greenwood.
Speedway Trophy Handicap: Heat Winners: Bingham (83.2 seconds), Johnston (95.6 seconds), Dowse (88 seconds), H. Hall (87.4 seconds). Final: Bingham (77.2 seconds), Dowse, Hall.

Saturday 14 June 1930

A new lap record of 17.4 seconds was established by Archie Bingham in front of 4,000 fans, but Bingham finished the meeting with a spectacular spill in the final of the Speedway Trophy Handicap. Unscheduled entertainment was provided when an aeroplane gave a display of stunts above the stadium. An unusual incident happened during the last lap of the second heat of the White City Trophy Handicap when a flywheel came off one of the machines and flew into the crowd. It stuck a spectator who was a police sergeant, inflicting a leg wound inches long. The spectator was treated in hospital, while the machine carried on its way, the rider finishing second in the race!

Results

White City Scratch Race: Heat Winners: T. Bateman (90 seconds), A. Bingham (77.4 seconds, including new lap record of 17.4 seconds), J. Heath (91 seconds), E.W. Greenwood (89 seconds). Final: Bingham, Bateman, Greenwood (77 seconds).

Junior Handicap: S. Worthington (103.2 seconds), G.T. Grant.

Match Races: B. Elmore (No Time) beat A. Bingham, E.W. Greenwood (84.6 seconds) beat R. Lucas.

Speedway Trophy Handicap: Heat Winners: Bateman (85 seconds), H. Dowse (85.2 seconds), Heath (88.2 seconds), N. Cox (91.8 seconds). Final: Dowse (83.2 seconds), Heath, Cox.

Crowd: 4,000.

Saturday 21 June 1930

Another close finish to the White City Scratch Race final with only twenty yards separating all four riders entertained 2,500 people at White City. The non-appearance of Archie Bingham was a disappointment, but the riding of local rider Harry Hall offered some compensation.

Results

Unsuccessful track record attempt of 74 seconds by B. Styring. A. Bingham's record of 76 seconds stands.

White City Scratch Race: Heat Winners: E.W. Greenwood (82 seconds), Al Brown (86 seconds), B. Styring (89 seconds), H. Hall (86 seconds). Final: Styring (83 seconds), Brown, Hall.

Big-Six Match Races: Heat Winners: Styring (83.2 seconds) beat G. Seddon, Brown (81.2 seconds) beat R. Lucas, T. Bateman (82 seconds) beat 'Twister' Holmes, Greenwood (82 seconds) beat Unknown. Final: Brown (79 seconds), Styring, Bateman.

Speedway Trophy Handicap: Heat Winners: Hall (87 seconds), Bateman (90.4 seconds), Greenwood (89.6 seconds). Fastest Second: R. Lucas. Final: Hall (86.2 seconds), Bateman, Greenwood.

Crowd: 2,500.

Saturday 28 June 1930

The Hull City Police Charity Cup was presented to the winner, Al Brown by Mrs Howden, wife of the chief constable. Brown intended to do a lap of honour on his machine, but the bike would not start, so instead he ran round the track displaying the trophy to the crowd.

Results

Hull City Police Charity Cup: Heat Winners: A. Bingham (82.4 seconds), Al Brown (87.2 seconds), Tear A Long (95 seconds), 'Cyclone' Smith (95 seconds). Final: Brown (No Time), Bingham, Smith.

Match Races: Bingham (87.6 seconds) beat Smith, T. Bateman (89.6 seconds) beat E. Greenwood.

Saturday 5 July 1930

The first evening meeting at White City attracted a good crowd, who were treated to a successful track record attempt by Archie Bingham, who shaved 2.4 seconds off the previous best time.

Results

White City Scratch Race: Heat Winners: Holmes (93 seconds), L. Greenwood (88.4 seconds), L. Dowse (78 seconds), A. Bingham (84.2 seconds). Semi-finals: Holmes (88 seconds), Worthington; Bingham (84 seconds), Frowe. Final: Holmes (No Time), Frowe, Bingham (nf), Worthington (nf).

Flying-Two Race: Heat Winners: Brown (82.4 seconds), Dowse (83 seconds), Bateman (86 seconds), Frowe (87 seconds). Final: Details unknown.

Speedway Trophy Handicap: Heat Winners: Heath (95 seconds), Bellhouse (92 seconds), Holmes (93.8 seconds), Bateman (95 seconds). Semi-finals: Holmes (95.6 seconds), Bateman; Heath (90 seconds), Frowe. Final: Heath (89.6 seconds), Frowe, Bateman, Holmes (nf).

Saturday 12 July 1930

Team racing came to White City for the first time as Hull took on a team from Leicester, although Hull ran out comfortable winners, the Midlanders only tracking two riders.

Results

Challenge

Hull 25 Leicester 11

HULL						
H. Dowse	3	2	2	2.5	9.5	1
A. Bingham	3	3	–	–	6	0
T. Bateman	2	1	2.5	–	5.5	2
E.W. Greenwood	2	2	–	–	4	1
LEICESTER						
H. Smith	1	3	1	3	8	0
N. Wolloff	1	1	1	–	3	0

		Hull	Leics
Heat 1	Bingham (82.4 seconds), Bateman, Smith	5	1
Heat 2	Dowse (85 seconds), Greenwood, Wolloff	10	2
Heat 3	Smith (84.2 seconds), Dowse, Bateman	13	5
Heat 4	Bingham (84 seconds), Dowse, Smith	18	6
Heat 5	Dowse and Bateman (dead heat, 84.4 seconds), Wolloff	23	7
Heat 6	Smith (85 seconds), Greenwood, Wolloff	25	11

Yorkshire Show Handicap: Heat Winners: G. Brown (98 seconds), T. Grant (97 seconds), Jud Heath (No Time). Final: Brown (94.2 seconds), Heath.
Speedway Trophy Handicap: Heat Winners: E.W. Greenwood (90 seconds), A. Bingham (97 seconds), Worthington (94 seconds), Jud Heath (92.4 seconds). Semi-finals: Greenwood (91.4 seconds), Brown; Heath (93 seconds), Bateman.
Final: Heath (93.4 seconds), Brown, Bateman.

Thursday 17 July 1930

This meeting reverted to the usual format, the highlight being a challenge race between Archie Bingham and 'Hurricane' Dowse, which was won by Dowse in a new track-record time of 76.8 seconds. Dowse also distinguished himself in the first semi-final of the Yorkshire Show Scratch Race, with a victory despite racing the last three laps with a flat tyre, and still recording a time only 1.2 seconds outside the track record.

Results
Attempt on the lap record by F. Hatton equalled the record of 19 seconds.
Attempt on the track record by A. Brown failed by 3 seconds.
Yorkshire Show Scratch Race: Heat Winners: A. Bingham (82 seconds), H. Dowse (83 seconds), T. Allott (88.4 seconds), A. Brown (85.8 seconds). Semi-finals: Dowse (79.2 seconds), J. Heath; Brown (81.4 seconds), Allott. Final: Brown (79 seconds), Allott, Heath.
Special Challenge Race: Dowse (76.8 seconds, new track record) beat Bingham.
Match Races: Allott (79.6 seconds) beat Greenwood, Brow (81.2 seconds) beat F. Hatton.
Great Yorkshire Show Handicap: Heat Winners: N. Cox (90.8 seconds), T. Bateman (91 seconds), H. Hall (91.4 seconds), S. Worthington (94.4 seconds). Semi-finals: Cox (89 seconds) R. Shaw; Hall (88.2 seconds), A. Brown. Final: Brown (88.8 seconds), Hall, Cox.
Special Challenge Race: Worthington (92.4 seconds) beat Cox.

Saturday 19 July 1930

The White City track records again took a battering as the lap record was equalled by Harry Frowe and the four-lap record was broken by 'Hurricane' Dowse, the new fastest time being 74.5 seconds. This was all the more remarkable as the track was extremely heavy owing to a downpour of rain.

Results

Successful attempt on the track record by H. Dowse. New record time 75.5 seconds.

White City Scratch Race: Heat Winners: N. Cox (88 seconds), J. Heath (89.2 seconds), A. Bingham (88 seconds), E.W. Greenwood (87.8 seconds). Semi-finals: Heath (88 seconds), F. Franks; H. Frowe (94 seconds), Greenwood. Final: Frowe (84.4 seconds), Heath, Greenwood.

Devil Takes The Hindmost: Heat Winners: W. Bellhouse, H. Frowe, A. Bingham (No Times). Final: Bingham (No Time), Frowe.

Speedway Trophy Handicap: Heat Winners: T. Holmes (96 seconds), E.W. Greenwood (88.6 seconds), A. Bingham (86.8 seconds), H. Frowe (93.4 seconds). Final: Holmes (87.4 seconds), Bingham, Frowe.

Thursday 24 July 1930

This meeting was seriously rain affected and only went ahead after considerable effort from the track staff. Not surprisingly, no track records were broken.

Results

Unsuccessful track record attempt of 78.6 seconds by H. Frowe. Existing record of 77.6 stands.

Unsuccessful attempt of 19.4 seconds on the lap record by E.W. Greenwood. Existing record of 19 seconds stands.

White City Scratch Race: Heat Winners: Frowe (81.4 seconds), Bateman (85 seconds), Bingham (84.8 seconds), Dowse (93 seconds). Semi-finals: Greenwood (No Time), Frowe; Bingham (80.4 seconds), Heath. Final: Frowe (80.6 seconds), Greenwood, Heath.

Speedway Trophy Handicap: Heat Winners: G.T. Grant (89.8 seconds), Dowse (84.4 seconds), Bingham (84 seconds), Bateman (95 seconds). Semi-finals: Grant (92.8 seconds), Dowse; Bingham (82 seconds), Frowe. Final: Frowe (84.6 seconds), Grant, Dowse.

Junior Challenge Race: Grant (90 seconds) beat F. Franks.

Saturday 26 July 1930

A second team fixture again resulted in a victory for the home side, despite Hull's 'Hurricane' Dowse suffering two flat tyres in his heats. The visitors were handicapped by losing Bill Carins who crashed and damaged his machine.

Results

Challenge: Hull 22 Middlesbrough 14 (heat details not available)

Match Race: H. Hall (82.4 seconds) beat E.W. Greenwood.

Speedway Trophy Handicap: Heat Winners: W. Bellhouse (93 seconds), A. Bingham (84 seconds), 'Indian' Allen (No Time), R. Shaw (No Time). Semi-finals: Bingham (82.2 seconds), Bellhouse; H. Hall (89.2 seconds), E. Davies. Final: Bingham (86 seconds), Bellhouse, Davies.

Crowd: 3,000.

Saturday 2 August 1930

This meeting was delayed for an hour while discussions took place to decide if the track, which had been subjected to heavy rain, was fit to race on. Racing did commence, but had to be abandoned after a further shower. There was also a disagreement between riders and management over pay, after which the riders were informed that the track was being taken over by a syndicate who proposed to carry out improvements. No results for this meeting are available.

Saturday 9 August 1930

The first meeting under new management took place in perfect conditions. Improvements to the track had been carried out, notably added banking on the bends, with the promise of track lighting to enable evening meetings to take place. Times were not particularly fast as the riders were adjusting to the improved track.

Results

Junior Match Race: S. Worthington (86 seconds) beat F. Franks.

Senior Match Race: A. Bingham (78.4 seconds) beat H. Frowe.

Handicap Race: Heat Winners: J. Heath (93 seconds), Franks (88 seconds), Bingham (79.4 seconds), H. Hall (87.6 seconds). Semi-finals: W. Bellhouse (87 seconds), Heath; Bingham (80.2 seconds), Worthington. Final: Bingham (78.4 seconds), Heath, Bellhouse.

Track Championship: Bingham (82.4 seconds), Heath.

Saturday 16 August 1930

The crowd were disappointed when six Sheffield riders who were booked to appear failed to turn up. Nevertheless the entertainment served up was still good, despite the track being dry and dusty.

Results

White City Scratch Race: Final: T. White (No Time), H. Frowe, H. Dowse.

Match Races: A. Bingham (77.2 seconds) beat Dowse, Bingham (77.2 seconds) beat Dowse, H. Hall (85 seconds) beat H. Frowe, S. Worthington (85.4 seconds) beat T. Holmes, Frowe (85 seconds) beat White, F. Franks (92 seconds) beat G. Shaw.

Handicap Race: Heat Winners: Bingham (82 seconds), Hall (88.4 seconds), White (86 seconds). Final: Bingham (77.2 seconds), G. Shaw, Hall.

2
HULL SPEEDWAY 1948–1981

Hedon Stadium

After six years of war, sport enjoyed a boom as a war-weary public looked for entertainment. Speedway played its part and new tracks opened up and down the country. A group of potential promoters, Captain F. Archer, Brigadier D.H.M. Carberry, Captain E.C. Aylott, Mrs V.C. Carberry and P.J.C. West had tried to open a track at Ipswich, but when that project fell through they turned their attention to the Hull area. A potential site was identified at the Hedon aerodrome, several miles to the east of Hull city centre. An application for the site to be used for speedway racing was considered by the Hull Aerodrome Committee in June 1947, when it emerged that the committee were already in negotiation with a syndicate wishing to use the site as a racecourse. The committee chairman pointed out that neither sport would interfere with the other, and the promoters would work together. The site would have parking for 2,000 cars.

Initial hopes that the application would be granted were dashed when Hull appeared on a Home Office list of industrial areas where permits for new tracks were not to be granted. This was a blow as £8,000-£10,000 had already been spent on building the track and a supporters' club already boasted 300 members. Some team building had already been undertaken and practice sessions at the track were underway. The Speedway Control Board in the person of Major W.W. Fearnley had already inspected the track. Dan Smith, chairman of the supporters club, was baffled by the ban, stating that it was never intended that the track should interfere with local industry, as meetings were planned for Saturday evenings. Hull Corporation had expressed their support for the venture and had promised to lay on public transport to and from the track, and the railway authorities had agreed to consider establishing a halt near the stadium.

Fortunately, common sense prevailed and the track was sanctioned not long before the 1948 season was due to start. It was announced that the new team, to be known as the Angels, would be a member of the National League Division Three, and that negotiations were underway to bring riders to Hull. Serious practice was to begin on 1 March with the first meeting scheduled for Easter Saturday, 27 March.

The track itself was 442 yards in length, cinder surfaced, and would have an unusual shape with a bulge on one of the straights which was almost like a fifth bend. This would offer the Hull riders a considerable home advantage.

Racing at Hedon Stadium.

A halt on the Hull–Withernsea railway line was built to allow spectators to travel to meetings by train.

Following the closure of the speedway track in August 1949, the stadium was used for other events for several years, and the site is still used for junior motorcycling. Evidence can still be seen of the track and banking, as the site is still undeveloped.

1948 – National League Division Three

Any new track faces the problem of building a team from scratch and Hull Angels were no exception. The team was largely composed of junior riders with little or no league experience. Experience came in the form of Mick Mitchell who came from New Cross, and George Craig arriving from Bristol a month into the season. Alf Webster, a Belle Vue junior, was recruited and given the captain's role which he held briefly until he was injured when Mick Mitchell took over the role and never relinquished it. Bob Baker had been practising at the Rye House training school, signed for New Cross and was promptly loaned to Hull, making his debut in early May. Dick Shepherd, who when not racing speedway performed for Kirby's Flying Ballet Pantomime, arrived after an undistinguished season at Plymouth. After Wigan closed, eighteen-year-old Derek Glover had a trial and became an Angel. Odsal juniors' Johnny White, who cost a £50 transfer fee and loanee Al Allison joined the squad and the line-up was completed by Alan Nicholson and Norman Johnson, two juniors from the North-East.

The Angels, still without Mitchell, Craig and Baker who had yet to sign, tracked an under-strength side on their challenge match debut at Hanley and were sunk without trace, managing only 16 points, with Derek Glover and stand-in Stan Pennell the only Angels to achieve a second-place heat finish. Two days later, the Hedon track was officially opened by the Lord and Lady Mayoress of Hedon. A crowd of 6,000 saw Angels once again lose in the return leg with Hanley, skipper Alf Webster top scoring with 7 points and also coming away as the initial track record holder with a time of 87.2 seconds. The following Saturday saw the first victory, a 45-38 challenge success against a combined Cradley Heath and Tamworth side. Alf Webster improved his own track record to 85.4 seconds in a match which saw Mick Mitchell make his debut with a 6-point return. Seven days later, the winning ways continued with a 52-32 win against a Halifax Nomads team, Mick Mitchell scoring the first of what was to be many maximums as an Angel.

The following week saw the league programme open at Hedon with the return visit of Hanley and once again the Potters ran out victors. Although Mick Mitchell, newly installed as captain in the injury absence of Alf Webster, ran unbeaten for a second week in a row and Alan Nicholson also hit double figures, the back-up was poor and no match for Hanley's strength in depth. Times were poor in a meeting affected throughout by torrential rain.

George Craig made his debut the following Saturday in the best possible way with a maximum as the Angels secured their first league points at the expense of Yarmouth, and two days later Hull made the long trip to Devon for the first away match for league points at Exeter. Numerous machine problems contributed to a 23-60 reverse, Mitchell's two heat successes being the only wins achieved. Angels had drawn Cradley Heath in the first round of the National Trophy. The Cubs were too strong at Hedon and ran out 66-42 winners over a Hull side missing Webster, Mitchell and Nicholson through injury. Sandwiched between the two legs of the Cup tie was a comprehensive 19-65 loss at Poole, Dick Shepherd's 5-point tally being the best offering from an Angel. Al Allison made a stunning 12-point debut in the second leg of the Cup tie at Cradley Heath but could not prevent a heavy defeat and an early exit from the Knock-Out Tournament.

Mitchell returned the following night with his injured wrist in plaster and inspired another league win at Hedon, this time over Hastings, the Saxons relying on Wally Green and Jock Grierson for 24 of their 39 points. Angels were beginning to use Hedon's home advantage to win matches. Success away from Hedon would prove elusive and a further defeat ensued at Yarmouth. A 4,500 crowd saw Hull put up a much better display than before on their travels but still go down 35-48.

In a break from league racing Hull entertained Division Two Newcastle, putting up a good fight before losing 35-48. Alf Webster's track record was beaten, Newcastle's Ken Le Breton posting a new best time of 84.8 seconds. Two days later, on Whit Monday, Hedon played host to a qualifying round of the Speedway Riders' Championship. This competition was a substitute for the World Championship, which would not resume until the following year. Southampton's Alf Bottoms ran through the card for a 15-point maximum, while Angels' best was George Craig with a disappointing 3 points.

Later that same week Hull travelled across to the West Riding for the first of four Yorkshire derbies with the Wombwell Colliers. Angels came away from this encounter

Hull Angels 1948 – Left to right: Captain F. Archer (Promoter), Bob Baker, Al Allison, Norman Johnson, Dick Shepherd, Mick Mitchell (on machine), George Craig, Johnny White, Alan Nicholson, Derek Glover, Wilf Skinner (staff), Betty Radge (staff).

on the wrong end of a 31-53 scoreline, unable to cope with Colliers' strength in depth. Fellow first-year club Coventry were next up at Hedon. Alf Webster returned from injury, and Angels edged home 44-39 thanks to a best-yet 10-point return from Derek Glover. Revenge over Wombwell was gained with a 47-31 success at home, and then Cradley Heath took their second victory at Hedon. Just when Angels were able to track a full-strength side, Al Allison was sidelined with a broken arm after a heat 2 crash in the Cradley match. The second league visit to Poole produced a slightly better result than the first time, but Angels still crashed 24-59. Mick Mitchell was the only visitor to win a race.

The team travelled along the coast for the second match of a southern tour and suffered an almost identical fate at Southampton, and then two days later again conceded 59 points, this time at the hands of Plymouth. The team broke the journey back to Hull with a league match at Cradley Heath and fared slightly better, managing 30 points. The season was settling into a pattern where Angels were largely uncompetitive away from home but at Hedon the home advantage offered by the unusual shape of the track was most often good enough to secure the points. This was clearly illustrated when Yarmouth came to Hedon on the Saturday following the southern tour and were comfortably beaten 51-33, only Billy Bales for the Bloaters putting up much resistance. Bales was denied his maximum in a thrilling heat 10, losing by a wheel to Derek Glover.

1948 programme cover.

Seven days later, in the second of five consecutive home fixtures, Hull just got the better of Tamworth 43-38. Johnny White found his best form and raced to a maximum, but the Angels reserves did not manage a single point. Next week Hanley once again showed their liking for the Hedon track to record their third success and second league win in East Yorkshire. Mick Mitchell was missing through injury and the rest of the team could not successfully cover for his absence. The skipper returned to the team for the next fixture when Hull gained revenge for two heavy defeats in Dorset with a 58-24 hammering of the Poole Pirates, both Dick Shepherd and Johnny White recording full maximums. The track record was reclaimed by a home rider in this meeting when Bob Baker cut the best time to 84.6 seconds in heat 1. In the last of the sequence of home matches, Plymouth were well beaten with Dick Shepherd again getting a full house, this time being joined by Mick Mitchell on the maximum mark.

Hull gave their best away performance so far in front of a large travelling support at Wombwell. Angels were eight points up after seven heats, the Colliers staged a tremendous recovery and the scores were level going into the final race. Unfortunately Mick Mitchell's machine chose this race to give up the ghost and Wombwell took the 5-1 and the match. The following night back at Hedon, Exeter were demolished 63-21, with a paid maximum from Mick Mitchell who also equalled Bob Baker's track record. Dick Shepherd was unbeaten by an opponent the following week as the Angels sent Coventry packing 56-28. Shepherd also featured strongly in the next home match against Tamworth, equalling the track record and only being denied a maximum by a heat 9 tapes exclusion, in a match comfortably won by the Angels.

Two days later, on Bank Holiday Monday, Division One Odsal sent a junior side to Hedon. Although this team contained such names as Norman Price and Arthur Forrest, Price provided the visitors' only heat winner in the opening race, slicing 0.8 of a second off the track record. Angels were easy winners, by a 61-23 margin. The next visitors to East Yorkshire were Plymouth who were demolished 58-26, Norman Johnson returning a rare double figure score. Al Allison returned 10 paid 11 from reserve, deputising for Derek Glover who was unable to take his first three rides. The team then took to the road, firstly travelling to the South Coast to take on Southampton. The result was only slightly better than on the previous visit to Banister Court, Mick Mitchell's 10 points providing Angels' only serious resistance. Mitchell's good form continued two nights later along the coast at Plymouth, this time a full 12-point maximum was to no avail, the rest of the team only managing 19 between them. The Angels skipper came away from this meeting with the track record, having taken one second off the previous best time.

The Saints put up a good fight in the next match at Hedon, going down by 6 points, despite providing nine out of fourteen heat winners, a solid team display earning the home side the points. Seven days later, Hull met Yarmouth in the semi-final of the North v. South Cup, a competition for Division Three teams. The match took place in appalling conditions: the track resembled a quagmire. Yarmouth's protests to the steward fell on deaf ears; unsurprisingly Angels won by a large margin, 68-28, virtually ensuring a final place even before the second leg was raced.

On 25 August, Angels visited Hastings for the first time, putting on a fine display, only going down by 3 points. Hull were never in front but went into the last heat 1 point in arrears but the Saxons' best two riders of the night, Jock Grierson and Ken Middleditch,

Dick Shepherd and Derek Glover in action.

Mick Mitchell and Gil Blake after Mitchell's Bronze Helmet victory.

secured the match winning 4-2 over Mick Mitchell and Dick Shepherd. Norman Johnson suffered a shaking after colliding with the fence in heat 9. This was the last match in Angels colours for Al Allison who had been recalled by parent club Odsal. Defeat at Cradley Heath was followed by yet another home reverse to Hanley, this time in a challenge match. On 31 August, Hull travelled to Tamworth for their debut at Deer Park, and but for an uncharacteristic 6-point return from Mick Mitchell and a blank from Bob Baker might even have won instead of suffering a 10-point reverse.

An uneventful match on a heavy track at Hanley saw Hull go down to their usual crushing defeat before returning to Hedon to take it out on Wombwell 58-26, Dick Shepherd and Johnny White being unbeaten by a Collier. Four days later it was Mick Mitchell's turn to bag the lot as Angels put up another creditable show at Hastings. An 11-point defeat of Poole at Hedon was followed by a second home challenge against Division Two Newcastle. Full revenge was extracted by Angels with a 57-26 victory, Dick Shepherd unbeaten. Two days later the good form was maintained with a decisive win over high-flying Cradley Heath, once again Dick Shepherd led the way with a maximum. Then followed the second leg of the North v. South Cup semi-final, Angels completing the job in style with a 56-40 success at Caister Road, booking a final place against Southampton.

The first ever visit to Coventry's Brandon Stadium produced a heavy 29-55 defeat, only George Craig with 10 points offering any resistance. Unusually, while this match was taking place, a meeting was staged at Hedon with Division Two Sheffield narrowly edging out a Division Three Stars team 42-41 in a closely fought match. A revitalised Yarmouth reversed the result of seven days previous taking the league points by a 50-33 margin. On 2 October, a last-heat Shepherd-Mitchell 5-1 earned a challenge victory over a combined Hanley/Cradley Heath side. Immediately before the match, Mick Mitchell became the holder of the Bronze Helmet, defeating Hanley's Gil Blake in two straight races, equalling the track record in the first.

Two consecutive clashes with Southampton followed. The first, a league encounter at Hedon went the way of Hull, 47-36, the inspiration being a Mick Mitchell maximum. The second was the final of the North v. South Cup which was raced on 15 October at neutral Cradley Heath. Hull led in the early stages, but the Saints, led by 15-point maximum man Alf Bottoms were not to be denied and ran out trophy winners with a 53-43 scoreline in a match watched by a small crowd owing to the Cradley Heath side being in action at Wombwell on the same night. Angels soon overcame their disappointment as twenty-four hours later champions-to-be Exeter were sent packing from Hedon on the wrong end of a 50-34 scoreline. Falcons' Don Hardy suffered a broken collarbone after a heat 7 crash.

With the season drawing to a close, Angels were busy, travelling to Tamworth where Mitchell, Craig and Shepherd scored 27 of a 30-point total. The final meeting of the season at Hedon resulted in the biggest league win of the campaign, 64-20 over Hastings. Four Angels, Mitchell, Baker, White and Shepherd signed off in unbeaten style. Angels wound up proceedings with three away engagements, predictably all resulting in defeats, trouncings at Exeter and Hanley with a better showing in the last one at Coventry on 30 October.

The first season at Hedon was, overall, a success. Crowds at Hedon were satisfactory, and although the team was largely uncompetitive on their travels, most matches were won at home, visitors finding the Hedon track difficult to master. Mick Mitchell proved a superb leader after taking over the captaincy from Alf Webster, and he received good back up from George Craig, these two often bearing the brunt of the scoring in away matches. Dick Shepherd excelled at Hedon while finding the away tracks more challenging. Al Allison was a capable performer until his recall by Odsal, with Johnny White rather like Dick Shepherd, scoring freely at Hedon but struggling away. The bottom end of the team was largely inexperienced but Derek Glover and Bob Baker improved as the season progressed and promised much for the future. Alf Webster's season was interrupted with injury but he showed enough to indicate he was worth persevering with. Norman Johnson followed the pattern of doing virtually all his scoring at home, and was mainly ineffective in away matches.

Highlights of the season were reaching the final of the North v. South Cup and Mick Mitchell finishing the season as the Bronze Helmet Holder.

1948 National League Division Three – Final Table

		M	Home W	D	L	F	A	Away W	D	L	F	A	Pts
1	Exeter	44	21	0	1	1273	569	11	1	10	877	954	65
2	Cradley Heath	44	20	1	1	1181.5	663.5	9	1	12	798	1039	60
3	Southampton	44	21	0	1	1227.5	610.5	8	0	14	886	958	58
4	Tamworth	44	19	1	2	1152.5	688.5	4	3	15	802	1037	50
5	Hanley	44	19	0	3	1138	703	5	1	16	787	1048	49
6	Hastings	44	18	0	4	1074	763	4	0	18	682	1161	44
7	Plymouth	44	18	1	3	1113	721	3	0	19	748.5	1089.5	43
8	Coventry	44	16	1	5	1004	830	3	0	19	666.5	1168.5	39
9	**HULL**	**44**	**19**	**0**	**3**	**1104**	**724**	**0**	**0**	**22**	**653**	**1185**	**38**
10	Poole	44	16	0	6	1069.5	768.5	1	0	21	691	1148	34
11	Yarmouth	44	13	1	8	984.5	844.5	0	0	22	622	1214	27
12	Wombwell	44	10	1	11	933	907	0	0	22	581.5	1248.5	21

Final Averages (League and National Trophy matches)

	M	R	1st	2nd	3rd	Unp	Pts	BP	Tot	Avg	Max F	Max P
Mick Mitchell	42	166	78	49	23	16	355	16	371	8.94	6	3
Alan Nicholson	3	12	3	5	2	2	21	3	24	8.00	0	0
Dick Shepherd	41	165	51	39	38	37	269	27	296	7.18	4	2
George Craig	44	179	49	52	36	42	287	24	311	6.95	2	1
Al Allison	23	65	17	20	12	16	103	9	112	6.89	0	0
Johnny White	45	171	45	29	47	50	240	27	267	6.25	2	2
Bob Baker	35	128	15	35	45	33	160	32	192	6.00	0	2
Derek Glover	43	136	18	23	44	51	144	30	174	5.12	0	0
Norman Johnson	43	159	17	39	40	63	169	25	194	4.88	0	0
Ray Muir	7	18	2	2	6	8	16	1	17	3.78	0	0
Brian Gorman	12	35	2	4	13	16	27	2	29	3.31	0	0
Alf Webster	21	48	0	7	18	23	32	9	41	3.42	0	0
Bill Worgan	2	4	0	0	2	2	2	0	2	2.00	0	0
Phil Dargue	1	2	0	0	1	1	1	0	1	2.00	0	0
Peter Dodds	5	10	0	0	2	8	2	0	2	0.80	0	0
Tom Coggins	1	2	0	0	0	2	0	0	0	0.00	0	0

1949 – National League Division Three

Most of the team that represented the Angels in 1948 were back for 1949. Mick Mitchell, George Craig, Bob Baker, Derek Glover and Norman Johnson all signed up for another season at Hedon. Of the class of 1948, Dick Shepherd moved to Walthamstow, as he wished to cut down on his travelling owing to poor health, and Johnny White signed for Division Three rivals Yarmouth, preferring a smaller track as a home base. Al Allison was loaned by Odsal to Division Three newcomers Halifax. By way of replacements, Angels signed Johnny Green and Jack Watts, who were juniors, Ken Allick arrived from Wombwell, Mike Wood also arrived from Exeter. The team did not on paper seem as strong as in 1948, and much would depend on the youngsters progressing if Angels were not to be cellar dwellers.

Unlike 1948 when several challenge matches preceded the league programme, there was no preamble and the first meeting was a league visit from Hanley. Lack of consistency and motor troubles cost Hull the match 40-43, although Angels led for six heats in the middle of the match. Each Hull rider had at least one pointless ride. The return league fixture at Hanley took place five days later on 7 April, and Angels' fate was exactly as in 1948, a severe beating! Norman Johnson was the only Angel to win a heat in a 20-point tally, even Mick Mitchell only managed two points. Division Three newcomers Leicester Hunters were next up at Hedon in the first round of the National Trophy. Lack of experience, particularly of the Hedon circuit, meant that the tie was virtually decided after one leg, Angels running out easy winners 77-31. Bob Baker posted a stunning 18-point maximum, the first full maximum of his career, and skipper Mick Mitchell was also unbeaten by a visitor. The return leg at Blackbird Road on 15 April was pretty much a formality, but a 12,000 crowd turned out to see a much closer match, although Angels were never headed throughout. Ron Wilson and Harwood Pike managed 30 out of Hunters' 49 points, with Bob Baker and George Craig heading the visitors' score chart with 13 apiece. Unusually, Mick Mitchell suffered two machine failures, preventing a larger victory margin.

League racing returned to Hedon the following night, with Tamworth providing the opposition. An exciting match in which the lead changed hands several times was eventually settled in Angels' favour, courtesy of a last-heat Mick Mitchell-Bob Baker 4-2. The skipper slotted back into the maximum groove, and with much improved form from Alf Webster and a continuation of the splendid start to the season by Bob Baker, there was cause for optimism.

The following match was Angels' first visit to another new team to the league, the Rayleigh Rockets. The home side were not seriously troubled and posted a 52-31 success, the smaller Weir track being vastly different from Hedon's wide-open spaces. Mick Mitchell did, however, push Rockets' heat leader Ron Howes into setting a new track record in the opening heat. The next match at Hedon on 23 April saw a quick return visit from Leicester, this time in league action. Maximums from Bob Baker (full) and Mick Mitchell (paid) saw Angels home by a 53-30 margin. Unusually, for the Hunters Pedlar Palmer won both his heats from the reserve berth, while Norman Johnson scored three for Hull despite riding with two fractured ribs in plaster following a crash in the match at Rayleigh.

Bob Baker on the way to another win.

Angels' next encounter was at Tamworth in the National Trophy second round. The visitors, Mitchell and Baker apart, were never at ease on the small Deer Park track and a 70-38 reverse left a mountain to climb in the second leg. Angels' cause was not helped by a spate of mechanical troubles and an accident to George Craig in heat 2 when he reared at the start and his machine fell on him. Once again, Mick Mitchell was involved in a track record, this time pushing homester Harry Saunders into equalling the record in heat 5. Three days later, Hull managed to win the second leg 61-47 but never looked like making up the deficit, and the cup dream was over. Mitchell and Baker once again led the way with 17 and 12 respectively, and the skipper equalled the Hedon best time of 83.2 seconds in heat 1.

Another new Division Three team, Oxford, played host to the Angels on 5 May and the Yorkshire team recorded a historic first away league victory, by a 51-32 margin to boot, maximum-man Mick Mitchell leading by example, backed up by solid scores from Derek Glover (7+2), and both Alf Webster and Bob Baker with 9+2.

As they had done in 1948, Angels invited a Division Two team to Hedon for a challenge match, this time Walthamstow providing the opposition on 7 May. The visitors fought back from a poor start to earn a 42-42 draw, Bob Baker's 10 points being Angels' best, while Wilf Jay and Dick Geary each managed 9 for the Wolves. Seven days later Yarmouth were the visitors, and after a ding-dong tussle with never more than four points separating the teams, honours were even for the second week running. Former Angel Johnny White scored a useful 8 points for the visitors but the meeting belonged to Bloaters' young star Billy Bales, who not only recorded an immaculate maximum but smashed the Hedon track record, posting a time of 82.4 seconds. This new record was destined never to be equalled.

On 21 May, individual racing took pride of place as Hedon played host to a qualifying round in the reinstated World Championship. The round was won by Bristol's Billy Hole who raced unbeaten, but special mention must be made of the performance of Hull's Derek Glover who finished equal-second with 12 points. In only his second year of league racing, it demonstrated the progress he had made. Johnny White, back on his old stamping ground for the second week running, finished with a creditable 11 points. Two days later, Angels resumed their league campaign with a visit to the fourth newcomer to the league, Liverpool. Angels led for the early part of the match, but the Chads rallied strongly to secure the points with a 48-34 scoreline. Jack Watts suffered a nasty injury when his chain came off and wrapped itself round his ankle, inflicting a deep cut which needed hospital treatment. Forty-eight hours later the final new team was crossed off the list as Hull paid their first visit to the Shay at Halifax. The Dukes had three riders unbeaten, including a full house from ex-Angel Al Allison and ran riot 57-26 over an Angels team whose top scorer was Alf Webster with a mere 7-point tally.

Plymouth were the next callers at Hedon, and although Angels were never headed, the Devils made the home side work hard for their 44-40 win, Bob Baker coming within 0.4 seconds of the track record in the last heat of the match. Mitchell and Baker were again the Angels' stalwarts with 10 apiece. Two days later after a long trip to the South Coast, Angels put up a tremendous performance at Poole, going down by only 4. A solid team showing was led by skipper Mitchell whose only defeat was at the hands of Fred Pawson in the opening heat. Mick was, however, able to take his revenge on the Pirate with a heat 14 win. A further two days on saw Angels fulfil a league fixture at Tamworth, where the Hounds once again comfortably defeated a Hull side in front of a small crowd on a treacherously wet track which was responsible for several falls and machine failures. Mick Mitchell's first-heat tumble restricted his total to an uncharacteristic 3, with Norman Johnson, who also suffered a fall, showing up best for the visitors with 7 points.

Hedon proved a happier hunting ground as Poole were beaten 54-30 by an all-round team performance on 4 June. The dynamic duo of Baker (full max) and Mitchell (paid max) once again topped the home score chart. A Whit Monday home fixture was Rayleigh's first visit to Hedon, and they failed to get to grips with the track, suffering a 62-22 defeat. Apart from Mitchell and Baker, Alf Webster recorded a paid maximum, while the Rockets' top scorer was Pat Clarke with 5. Two away matches ensued, the long haul to Devon providing no reward whatsoever in a 25-59 trouncing by Plymouth, Mick Mitchell's 9 points providing the only resistance, while Bob Baker failed to score. The following night the team put up a better show in a 35-49 reverse at Leicester's Blackbird Road. Bob Baker recovered his form to record 10 points, while Mick Mitchell posted a paid maximum, finishing second to Baker in an Angels heat 14 5-1. For the second away match in succession, Angels came up against a home side with a reserve scoring a two-ride maximum. George Gower was Leicester's reserve in question, while Ivan Kessell performed the feat for Plymouth.

Hastings made the long trek from the Sussex coast to East Yorkshire on 11 June and gave Angels a good battle before finally losing 37-47. Mick Mitchell suffered mechanical problems and was restricted to a 6-point tally, but Derek Glover stepped magnificently

1949 programme cover.

into the breech with a first ever full house. Halifax were the next up at Hedon, with Angels looking for revenge over their Yorkshire rivals after the Shay trouncing. Alas it was not to be: the Dukes adapted well to Hedon's wide-open spaces, and ran out 46-37 winners. Five falls or retirements contributed to the defeat, Mick Mitchell failing to finish twice. Bob Baker was best for the home side, only losing out to Arthur Forrest in heat 9.

The South Coast was the next stopping-off point for the Angels. The match against Exeter took place after a tribute to Exeter rider Stan Hodson who had recently died after an short illness, and was something of an anti-climax, Angels putting in their best performance at the County Ground in a 36-48 defeat. Further along the coast, Angels again rode well but were always chasing the match against Hastings and eventually lost 39-45, with the improved Alf Webster top man with 9+1. Returning to the Hedon raceway on 25 June, Oxford paid their first (and last) visit and the Cheetahs journeyed back to Cowley with their tails firmly between their legs following a 60-24 thumping. Mitchell, Glover and Baker were all unbeaten while Bert Croucher was Oxford's pick with 6 points.

The second league visit to Merseyside was next up and the score was much as before, 48-36 for the Chads. Mick Mitchell was off the pace with 6, while Bob Baker was Angels' best on 10, running unbeaten after a third place first time out. The return fixture at Hedon on 2 July was the Chads' first visit and Hull exacted full revenge, coming out on top 53-31. Mitchell and Baker were as usual unbeaten, and were joined by Alf Webster, maintaining his good form, in not having his colours lowered by a Chad. A clear week saw Rayleigh arrive at Hedon seven days later, and although the Rockets did a little better they were still grounded 52-32. The skipper had a torrid night, finishing only one race, his last for 3 points, Bob Baker fell in his last race, but George Craig came good with a full maximum, and Alf Webster kept it going with another superb paid maximum performance.

Angels' next fixture was at the Shay in a challenge against the Halifax Jumbos, the junior version of the Dukes. The West Riding youngsters proved far too good for a Hull side missing only Bob Baker and earned a 51-33 success. Disappointingly, only Mick Mitchell was a Hull race winner, taking the chequered flag twice. There was no meeting at Hedon on 16 July, Angels had an open date and because of a spell of extremely dry weather and lack of available water, the management did not feel they would be able to prepare a safe track. The enforced break did not help as Angels slumped to their worst defeat of the season on 21 July, an 18-66 reverse at Yarmouth. The Bloaters provided all fourteen heat winners, and only shared the spoils in the opening heat when home rider Bill Carruthers fell.

Back at Hedon, Exeter took the points in a match where Hull were 10 points down with only three races to go, but left it far too late and could only pull back 6 of them. Mechanical problems and inconsistent performances, particularly a disappointing 1-point return from George Craig were largely responsible, not to take away from a solid Falcons team showing. No joy was forthcoming at Cowley, where Angels could not repeat their earlier Cup success and gave best to the Cheetahs 54-29. Both Mick Mitchell and Bob Baker had off nights, scoring 4 and 2 respectively. Angels then once again found Halifax too strong and the Dukes completed a Hedon double with a 45-39

Hull Angels 1949 – Left to right: Norman Johnson, Mike Wood, George Craig, Les Godwin, Alf Webster, Jack Watts, Johnnie Green, Harold Bottoms, Derek Glover, Don Wilkinson, Bob Baker. On machine – Mick Mitchell.

win, Arthur Forrest and Dick Seers remaining unbeaten by an Angel, while George Craig and Derek Glover, each with 9, were Hull's best.

Next on the Hedon agenda were track specialists Hanley, and perversely Angels recovered the winning touch with a much-improved showing led by a back-to-form maximum for the skipper. Success was short lived though as seven days later Tamworth took the points back to Staffordshire with a 46-37 victory. Angels got off to the worst possible start, losing the opening race 0-5, after George Craig retired with engine trouble and Mick Mitchell fell. Hull never recovered and were well beaten by a solid all-round Hounds' team performance, Bob Baker's paid 11 being Angels' best. The next visitors to East Yorkshire were Poole, and some pride was restored with a 49-35 win over a Pirates crew for whom only Cyril Quick (11) and Alan Chambers (9) put up much resistance. Chambers was the only Pirate to lower Mick Mitchell's colours. Angels looked a much more solid outfit with special mention due to Jack Watts for his seven points from reserve.

Another poor performance at Yarmouth with a 24-60 thrashing was compounded when the Bloaters came to Hedon four days later and did the double with a 49-35 success. The victory margin disguises what was a tremendous match. Track record holder Billy Bales was only denied a maximum by an opening heat fall, and former Angel Johnny White used his track knowledge to score 9 points, while Mick Mitchell's 8 points, which included a retirement, was Hull's best offering.

It had been apparent for some time that the Angels were in some trouble financially. The track was reported to be losing £200 per week. The novelty of the first season had worn off and the fans had seen, arguably, a poorer team on view in 1949, and certainly no improvement in the league position. The track's location was also proving a problem, situated several miles away from the city centre. In an era when most people worked on Saturday mornings and relied on public transport, the track was not the easiest to get to. With this in mind the promoters approached Hull FC and noise tests were carried out at the Boulevard, but nothing came of it, and as a last throw it was proposed that a track be constructed on the site of Hull City's old ground on Anlaby Road (this site is now the new KC Stadium). However the football board rejected the idea, so the 27 August home league fixture with Liverpool at Hedon was the last ever Angels home fixture. Angels ended at home with a 54-29 win, and fittingly Mick Mitchell scored a maximum, and his Hedon Scratch Race success made him the winner of the track's last ever race.

It is worth mentioning the rumours circulating that a wealthy Hedon resident was in the process of making an official complaint about the noise of the racing, so it can only be speculation as to how long the track would have lasted even if the financial problems had not existed.

Angels had not quite finished business, and made their last track appearance on 31 August at Halifax and a 22-62 defeat finally drew down the curtain on their brief existence. Hedon acquired the unwanted record of being the first post-war venue to close during the season. Ambitious open-licence track Swindon took over Hull's remaining fixtures, and four Angels transferred to Blunsdon. Mick Mitchell, far and away the leading Angel and George Craig, whose scores had dipped somewhat in 1949, accompanied Alf Webster and Derek Glover, both of whom had shown great improvement in their second year at Hedon to Wiltshire. Eric Mason reverted to his parent club Halifax, while Norman Johnson had a few meetings for Ashfield. The star of 1949, Bob Baker, reverted to his parent track New Cross, and finally linked with Oxford until his retirement during 1956. The final Angel to see track action was Don Wilkinson who rode for Newcastle in 1961 and 1962.

1949 National League Division Three – Final Table

			Home					Away					
		M	**W**	**D**	**L**	**F**	**A**	**W**	**D**	**L**	**F**	**A**	**Pts**
1	Hanley	48	23	0	1	1327	674	12	1	11	1009	1000	71
2	Yarmouth	48	22	0	2	1335	666	13	1	10	995	1010	71
3	Tamworth	48	23	0	1	1351.5	657.5	10	0	14	942.5	1064.5	66
4	Halifax	48	20	0	4	1307	696	8	2	14	905	1096	58
5	Plymouth	48	19	1	4	1181	826	9	1	14	915	1091	58
6	Poole	48	19	0	5	1120	888	8	0	16	842.5	1165.5	54
7	Exeter	48	20	0	4	1194	811	4	0	20	844	1162	48
8	Hastings	48	18	1	5	1191.5	816.5	3	0	21	744.5	1263.5	43
9	Liverpool	48	16	0	8	1101	909	3	0	21	741	1263	38
10	Leicester	48	13	1	10	1088	924	4	0	20	790	1216	35
11	**HULL / Swindon**	**48**	**14**	**1**	**9**	**1096**	**913**	**1**	**0**	**23**	**713**	**1294**	**31**
12	Rayleigh	48	14	0	10	1017	985	0	0	24	691	1310	28
13	Oxford	48	10	1	13	952.5	1051.5	1	0	23	685	1326	23

Final Averages (League and K.O. Cup matches)

											Max	
	M	**R**	**1st**	**2nd**	**3rd**	**Unp**	**Pts**	**BP**	**Tot**	**Avg**	**F**	**P**
Bob Baker	39	160	67	46	34	13	327	24	351	8.78	5	3
Mick Mitchell	39	160	79	41	14	26	333	15	348	8.70	6	5
Alf Webster	36	148	33	39	49	27	226	39	265	7.16	0	3
Derek Glover	35	138	34	34	41	29	211	24	235	6.81	2	0
George Craig	38	153	26	42	34	51	196	24	220	5.75	1	0
Eric Mason	8	17	1	3	5	8	14	6	20	4.71	0	0
Johnny Green	17	47	4	11	12	20	46	8	54	4.60	0	0
Norman Johnson	37	143	17	32	33	61	148	16	164	4.59	0	0
Jack Watts	34	92	4	24	29	35	89	16	105	4.57	0	0
Ken Allick	11	26	0	2	11	13	15	1	16	2.46	0	0
Don Wilkinson	5	13	0	0	5	8	5	2	7	2.15	0	0
Les Godwin	1	2	0	0	1	1	1	0	1	2.00	0	0
Mike Wood	8	19	0	2	3	14	7	1	8	1.68	0	0
Bob Newell	1	2	0	0	0	2	0	0	0	0.00	0	0
Harold Bottoms	1	2	0	0	0	2	0	0	0	0.00	0	0
Ron Stringer	2	3	0	0	0	3	0	0	0	0.00	0	0

The Boulevard

Speedway underwent a major reorganisation prior to the 1965 season which resulted in the Provincial and National Leagues amalgamating to form the British League. These changes gave the sport a much-needed boost, and heralded a twenty-year boom in popularity and interest.

The Hull area had not heard the roar of speedway engines since August 1949, when Hedon Stadium closed its doors. In 1966, Asset Speedway Enterprises (fronted by Dave Lanning of World of Sport and later Reading fame) approached Hull Rugby League Club with a view to staging speedway at their Boulevard Stadium. The club, who were not enjoying a very successful period in their history, were interested in the project, but Hull's Planning Committee rejected the application on the grounds of noise, as the Boulevard is situated in a densely populated area.

The idea of bringing the sport to Hull resurfaced in 1970, when Workington promoter Ian Thomas and multi-track boss Wally Mawdsley gained the interest of the Boulevard bosses. After noise tests were taken, and much deliberation, the Council gave the go ahead for the sport to commence in 1971, although there was some opposition from local residents, and one or two of the more diehard members of the rugby club board vowed to fight speedway's introduction, although it was pointed out to them that compromise was required, as the club was strapped for cash.

The club was admitted to Division Two and Messrs Thomas and Mawdsley set about installing the track, which was no mean feat, as floodlights had to be moved in time for the start of the season. The construction work was the responsibility of Colin Tucker who was assisted by other members of the team, including Robin Amundson and Peter Baldock. The track was 423 yards in length, and was fairly narrow because of space restrictions. The opening date was set for 7th April, 1971. All that remained was to put a team together and select a nickname for the team.

Some people wanted to retain the Angels nickname from the Hedon days, but it was felt that the name Hull Angels sounded too much like Hell's Angels, and did not reflect speedway's family sport image. The local paper organised a vote, and the name Kestrels came out as winner. The two fans who suggested this name were presented with season passes, only to be disappointed at the last minute when the Vikings nickname was selected. It is hoped that the two young supporters kept their passes, although this is not recorded!

After the cessation of speedway in 1981, the stadium was used solely for rugby league until 2003 when Hull FC moved into the newly built KC Stadium on the other side of Anlaby Road. At the time of writing, greyhound racing which has recently ceased at Craven Park, is set to commence at the Boulevard.

Three views of the Boulevard.

1971 – British League Division Two

The newly formed Vikings needed to put a team together fairly quickly, and a potential number one rider was found at Hull's sister track Workington, when Sheffield asset Reg Wilson, fourth in the Comets averages, but with masses of promise, made the move back to his home county. Even the most optimistic fans could not have realised what a success Reg was to be at the Boulevard.

Further heat-leader strength was obtained when Tony Childs, who rode for Crayford in 1970 and was left trackless when the Highwaymen closed at the end of that season, was signed. Tony came to the Boulevard having never missed a league match in Division Two since it started in 1968. This was surprising as Tony was certainly a character who kept himself busy during the winter with a bit of part-time motor dealing, and was involved in more than his fair share of on-track controversy. However, Ian Thomas made him captain, and he became a massive favourite with the Boulevard faithful.

Joining Tony on the road from Kent to Hull was another Crayford heat-leader, George Devonport. George was highly rated, came with a seven-point average, but his season was to come to an early end when he suffered a back injury.

The middle order of the team was made up of Colin Tucker, a New Zealander who rode for Crewe for half of 1970, fell out with them, and ended the year at Long Eaton.

1971 programme cover.

Colin was also a noted track man and before building the Boulevard track was responsible for the track at Crewe. Yorkshireman Dennis Wasden from Sheffield was snapped up when Doncaster closed at the end of 1970. Tucker was not a consistent scorer, but was capable of double-figure scores, whereas Wasden was steadier without scaling the heights or plumbing the depths.

Also signed was Peter Baldock, an Aussie, who had a few meetings for Glasgow in Division One the previous year, then moved on to Berwick and broke his wrist after a few meetings. He was nevertheless considered a very promising rider. His first job on arrival at Hull was to help to prepare the stadium ready for opening night.

Hull then took a gamble on another Aussie, Robin Amundson. Robin also came with a promising tag. He would have arrived in Britain in 1969, but was called up by the Australian Army to do his National Service. He failed the medical but by then it was too late to come for the 1969 season. Robin worked during the 1970 season to save the money to come to the UK in 1971. It was worth the effort, as in his first British season, his form well exceeded expectations. Like Peter Baldock, Robin kept in condition with stadium preparation work prior to opening night.

The new Vikings first took to the track with a challenge match at Bradford's Odsal Stadium. The starting line-up was Wilson, Childs, Devonport, Amundson, Tucker, Baldock and local grass-tracker Alan Bradley. Bradley did not last one match, suffering head and back injuries in a crash, and didn't ride again in 1971. The Boulevard opened its doors to speedway on Wednesday 7 April with a challenge match against Sunderland. To maintain a link with the 1940s Hull Angels, Ian Thomas invited former Angels captain Mick Mitchell to be guest of honour. Five thousand people turned up to see the Vikings win comfortably 47-25. Ian Thomas explained to the crowd that times would get faster when the track settled. Work on the track had only finished a few days earlier, and unsurprisingly caused the riders numerous problems. Sunderland's Russ Dent was the first track-record holder with a time of 76.4 seconds.

Vikings ran a series of challenge matches which enabled the riders to find their way around the Boulevard circuit, all of which were won, the first league match taking place on April 28 against sister track Workington. Vikings got off to a winning start 43-33, in a meeting where the track record was broken in the last race of the night, Workington's Mal Mackay setting a new fastest time of 75.8 seconds.

The team then raced both legs of their first round K.O. Cup tie with Rochdale. Sandwiched between these fixtures, Vikings were the first visitors to open-licence Scunthorpe's Quibell Park track, going down 39-38 to the Saints. An unusual incident at the start of heat 3 saw George Devonport's clutch fly off and shoot down the track as the tapes went up. In the Cup, Vikings lost 31-47 in a wet meeting at Rochdale, the Hornets completing the double with a 39-38 win at the Boulevard, Hull's first home defeat. Strongly influential in the first-round exit was Hornets' young reserve Peter Collins, who scored double figures in both legs, despite missing his first ride at the Boulevard, as he arrived late, coming directly from college in Manchester.

Vikings staged their first individual meeting at the Boulevard on 12 May, home favourite Reg Wilson racing to a 15-point maximum to win the inaugural Hull Open Championship. George Devonport scored his only 12-point maximum for Hull on

Left: *Programme for the first ever meeting at Scunthorpe's Quibell Park.*

Opposite: *Hull Vikings 1971 – Left to right: Robin Amundson, Alan Bradley, Wally Mawdsley (co-promoter), George Devonport, Colin Tucker, Ian Thomas (co-promoter), Peter Baldock. On machine – Tony Childs.*

19 May in Vikings 55-23 rout of Teesside. Poor George was injury plagued, and his season finally came to an end on 7 July at the Boulevard when he crashed, and suffered spinal injuries. Vikings covered his absence with Rider Replacement for the rest of the season.

The Boulevard track record found its way into home hands on 26 May, Tony Childs flying round in 75.0 seconds, and four days later, the first away win was recorded in a narrow 40-38 success at Sunderland. Tony Childs was involved in controversy at Romford on 3 June when he was excluded for unfair riding, the referee having originally excluded Romford's Brian Foote, then changing his decision. Childs stormed the referee's box, but failed to change the referee's mind.

The first team change of the season occurred in June when before the home match with Canterbury, Ian Thomas announced the signing of Crewe's Bradford-born Ian Bottomley who came out of retirement to link up with the Vikings. Bottomley raced at No. 8 in the Canterbury match, which was to be Peter Baldock's last match in Hull colours. The young Aussie had not lived up to expectations, and never raced in Britain again. A novel feature of that Canterbury meeting was the interval attraction which was sixty-five-year-old stuntman Stanley Lindberg who performed a sixty-five-foot death dive into six feet of water!

Vikings performed creditably to only go down 38-40 at Rochdale, but came away with some consolation as Reg Wilson took the Silver Helmet, albeit on default from Alan Wilkinson, who had been injured the previous night. Reg did not successfully defend the Helmet, as he was beaten by Ipswich's John Louis at Hull, but was constantly

topping the Vikings score chart. It was clear to see he was due a big future in the sport. Bradford staged a tremendous comeback in their league visit to the Boulevard on 31 May, coming back from 10 points down to draw. Indeed, only a Wilson-Tucker 4-2 in heat 13 prevented Northern taking both points.

Hull's first-ever visit to Crewe resulted in a 32-46 defeat, but the meeting saw the Earle Street track record broken three times, Reg Wilson holding the record for four races, before Kings' Barry Meeks lowered it further. Berwick's Doug Wyer relieved Tony Childs of the track record, setting a new fastest time of 74.8 seconds on 30 June, in the Boulevard leg of the Northern Fours, which featured Hull, Berwick, Workington and Teesside. After all four rounds, Vikings had won their first trophy, edging out a five-point win over second-place Workington.

The first home defeat in the league came on 7 July when a strong Ipswich team overpowered a Vikings side who suffered injuries to both George Devonport and Dennis Wasden. Devonport crashed when his throttle jammed open, and suffered back injuries. He was out for the rest of the season. The Witches led from start to finish and to add insult to injury, John Louis relieved Reg Wilson of the Silver Helmet. Vikings rallied well and won both their next two home matches, against Eastbourne (champions that season) and Crewe, lost narrowly at Birmingham before once again losing at home, this time to Boston in a tempestuous match. Tony Childs attempted to overtake Boston's Jim Ryman in heat 10, and brought both of them off. Childs tried to remount his machine when Ryman grabbed his handlebars, and Childs accelerated to free

1971 top man Reg Wilson.

himself, then when he started his last lap, Boston team manager Cyril Crane and a rider rushed on to the track to try to stop him completing the race. They did not succeed, but after the race, Childs was confronted by angry Boston riders. The referee excluded him for unfair riding.

On 4 August against Rayleigh, Hull gave a debut to lanky Aussie Pete Boston, who legend has it came to Britain to ride for Boston, could not find a place there, and landed a spot at the Boulevard. Pete was in and out of the side, was used as No. 8, but proved a useful squad rider. Pete had unusual accommodation – he lived in a van! No doubt this saved on expenses.

At this point, Hull were comfortably winning their home matches. Sunderland, Romford and Rochdale in the League and Bradford in a Challenge were despatched, with an away League success at Workington. In the Rochdale match, Peter Collins received no support from his teammates in a 51-27 Vikings win, scoring 14 points, only being beaten by Reg Wilson. Hull lost a tremendous meeting 37-41 at title-chasing Bradford, only losing to an Alf Wells-Alan Knapkin 5-1 in heat 13. Another narrow away defeat followed at Boston, Robin Amundson taking an ambulance ride to hospital after a crash which cost him two teeth, including a gold filling! The team rallied to cover Amundson's absence the following Wednesday and defeated Peterborough, and the following week gained some revenge for a league defeat with a narrow 40-38 challenge victory over Ipswich. The victory was clinched by guest Taffy Owen with a thrilling heat 13 win over John Louis. Back-to-back away wins followed; a depleted Peterborough were beaten at Alwalton, the highlight being a four-lap wheel-to-wheel tussle in heat 4 between Richard Greer and Reg Wilson, Reg just getting the win on the line. Next in line, Canterbury were beaten, and more controversy with Tony Childs, who appeared to fence Graeme Stapleton in heat 11. Ted Hubbard laid his machine down to avoid the carnage, but the referee allowed the race to continue, despite there being track officials and ambulance men on the track, and Childs appearing to have crossed the white line. A home point was salvaged against Birmingham, on a night when Hull were forced to track Ian Bottomley and Dennis Wasden, neither of whom were fully fit.

The league programme was rounded off with a 32-46 defeat away to champions Eastbourne, and the season was rounded off with several challenge matches. The first of these was home to Boston, and once again Hull v. Boston meant trouble involving Tony Childs. Boston's Carl Glover was left at the start in heat 5, and incensed by this, parked his bike sideways across the track to block the other riders. After the race was over, Childs chased Glover round the track and rammed him against the fence. Childs was fined for dangerous riding, and was pulled out of the meeting by Hull co-promoter Wally Mawdsley to avoid him being suspended by the referee. Childs did not escape unscathed in the return leg at Boston, being carried off after a first-bend pile up in heat 10.

The season was concluded with a 38-40 reverse to a Stars of the League team, but the overall verdict on speedway's return to Hull was a great success. Crowds were very good, and the team finished sixth in the League. Reg Wilson and Tony Childs formed a formidable twin spearhead, there never being a dull moment when Tony was around, with solid backing from Colin Tucker, first-year man Robin Amundson and Dennis Wasden. It is only for speculation what might have been if George Devonport had escaped injury and lived up to his 1970 average.

Left: *Rider, track curator and later team manager Colin Tucker.*
Right: *Lanky Pete Boston in action.*

Individually, Reg Wilson was capped three times for England v. Czechoslovakia, and also represented the Vikings in the Division Two Riders Championship at Hackney, scoring 6 points. Both Reg and George Devonport entered the World Championship, neither progressing past the British qualifying rounds.

1971 British League Division Two – Final Table

			Home					Away					
		M	W	D	L	F	A	W	D	L	F	A	Pts
1	Eastbourrne	32	15	0	1	800	438	7	3	6	594	649	47
2	Bradford	32	16	0	0	778	468	5	1	10	592	651	43
3	Ipswich	32	14	1	1	746	495	6	2	8	599	646	43
4	Boston	32	15	0	1	744	503	3	3	10	568	670	39
5	Rayleigh	32	12	2	2	688	555	6	0	10	589	654	38
6	**HULL**	**32**	**12**	**2**	**2**	**703**	**542**	**4**	**0**	**12**	**589**	**657**	**34**
7	Crewe	32	15	1	0	826	418	1	0	15	475	766	33
8	Berwick	32	16	0	0	784.5	461.5	0	0	16	500	747	32
9	Rochdale	32	14	0	2	700	544	2	0	14	477	767	32
10	Long Eaton	32	13	2	1	690	555	0	1	15	505	735	29
11	Birmingham	32	13	1	2	704	541	0	2	14	477	771	29
12	Romford	32	12	0	4	700	542	1	0	15	522.5	721.5	26
13	Teesside	32	12	0	4	707.5	536.5	1	0	15	483.5	762.5	26
14	Canterbury	32	12	2	2	702	543	0	0	16	458	789	26
15	Workington	32	11	0	5	701	547	1	1	14	533	703	25
16	Peterborough	32	11	1	4	691	553	0	0	16	482	764	23
17	Sunderland	32	9	1	6	635	600	0	0	16	398	847	19

Final Averages (League and K.O. Cup matches)

	M	R	1st	2nd	3rd	Unp	Pts	BP	Tot	Avg	FM	PM
Reg Wilson	33	163	88	55	13	7	387	8	395	9.69	5	1
Tony Childs	34	167	77	59	23	8	372	13	385	9.22	4	0
George Devonport	6	14	6	2	3	3	25	1	26	7.43	1	0
Colin Tucker	32	122	18	32	37	35	155	34	189	6.20	0	0
Robin Amundson	31	126	12	38	36	40	148	39	187	5.94	0	0
Dennis Wasden	34	138	11	29	57	41	148	33	181	5.25	0	0
Pete Boston	11	34	3	4	14	13	31	7	38	4.47	0	0
Ian Bottomley	21	71	7	14	16	34	65	13	78	4.39	0	0
Peter Baldock	12	34	1	3	11	19	20	8	28	3.29	0	0
George Beaton	1	4	0	0	0	4	0	0	0	0.00	0	0
Tony Armstrong	1	2	0	0	0	2	0	0	0	0.00	0	0
Mike Glover	1	2	0	0	0	2	0	0	0	0.00	0	0
Also Rode												
Geoff Bouchard	1	4	2	0	0	2	6	0	6	6.00	0	0
Jim Ryman	1	4	0	0	4	0	4	2	6	6.00	0	0

1972 – British League Division Two

The nature of speedway being what it is, it is rare – if almost unheard of – for any track to start a season with the same line-up that finished the previous campaign. However, in the case of the 1972 Vikings, the starting line-up showed relatively few changes from the team that enjoyed a successful Boulevard debut season in 1971.

Reg Wilson, as expected, had been recalled by parent club Sheffield to race in Division One, and Hull faced a mammoth task to replace him. As they had done in 1971, Vikings looked to Australia, and came up with what turned out to be an inspired capture in Dave Mills, who had raced at Liverpool NSW. Mills was an instant success, whose arrival in the UK was somewhat overshadowed by the rise to Division Two stardom of one Phil Crump.

Captain Tony Childs lined up once more, as did now heat leader Robin Amundson. Also returning for another season were Colin Tucker (for part of the season, until he took over team manager duties), Dennis Wasden, Pete Boston and Ian Bottomley, who rode three early season matches before disappearing off the scene. George Devonport, having recovered from his 1971 injuries also lined up for another season. As in 1971, Alan Bradley rode in the first match of the season, coincidentally also at Bradford, but did not appear again, preferring to concentrate on grass-track racing.

Spectacular action from Dave Mills.

Programme for the last ever meeting at West Ham's Custom House.

Mills started as he meant to go on with paid 13 on his debut at Odsal, but the team made a slow start with a North-Eastern Trophy defeat by Berwick in the first home match, in which Mills injured his hand, coupled with a few heavy challenge match defeats on the road. The Trophy win over Sunderland at the Boulevard was punctuated by fisticuffs. Sunderland's Jack Millen was excluded for bringing Colin Tucker down. Millen's teammate Graeme Smith tried to take Millen's now-vacated gate position, but was prevented from doing so after a protest. When the rerun got underway Smith and Tucker collided with Tucker ending up in the fence. He was unhurt, and headed straight to confront Smith. Punches were thrown before the riders were separated.

Mills was proving to be a tremendous asset in these early matches, operating from the reserve berth, as he had not yet raced enough matches to acquire a proper average. Pete Boston scored a maximum in the home match against Teesside, but sadly it was not a sign of things to come. Vikings finished third out of four in the North-Eastern Trophy which was won by Berwick.

The league programme commenced with a home win over a fancied Birmingham side, with a match-winning 13 from Dave Mills, which was as well, because George Devonport was struggling for confidence, and only appeared in a few league matches before slipping out of the side. Mills recorded maximums in successive matches as Vikings completed the double over league newcomers and local rivals Scunthorpe. However, Vikings' lack of strength in depth was exposed when Peterborough won

43-35 at the Boulevard on 17 May. Vikings created a bit of history the following week, being the last ever visitors to West Ham's Custom House track. Vikings even won the match 40-38 with a maximum from Tony Childs.

The second Hull Open Championship was raced in May, and was won by Phil Crump with a faultless maximum. The trophy was presented by Coronation Street actress Pat Phoenix. The nearest home challengers were Dave Mills and Robin Amundson who tied for fifth place with 11 points each. This meeting saw the home debut of Aussie Bryan Loakes, who took the place of George Devonport. Loakes, who hailed from Brisbane, rode a second half at Halifax, but Hull beat the West Riding club to his signature. Additionally, Colin Tucker had decided to take up the speedway manager's duties as well as continuing to be the track curator, and to replace him Hull signed Dennis Gavros on loan from Division One Halifax. Gavros had not raced in Britain since 1969 and was running a garage in the Halifax area. This created a furore as it was thought in some quarters that he should have been offered to another Division One club. Gavros's signing was eventually ratified, but not before it cost Hull their place in the Knock-Out Cup. Vikings were adjudged to have used Gavros illegally in both legs of the tie with Teesside, and deducting his points gave the tie to the Teessiders. These signings stabilized the side, and the next three home league matches were won, including a narrow scrape against Sunderland, when a last heat 5-1 from Mills and Amundson rescued the points, and a 41-36 success over the season's champions Crewe.

The good run, however, came to a shuddering halt the following week when Boston came to the Boulevard and demolished the Vikings 49-29. Hull were without Dennis

Hull Vikings 1972 – Left to right: George Devonport, Robin Amundson, Dennis Wasden, Colin Tucker, Dave Mills, Peter Boston. On machine – Tony Childs.

Gavros, Dave Mills and Robin Amundson, all injured. Gavros sustained an injury against Crewe at the Boulevard, Mills and Amundson at Halifax in an individual meeting. Mills missed three and Amundson four league matches, all of which were lost. Bernie Hornby, who had been restricted to second-halves at Workington came in for a few matches but made little impact, and the promising Clark Facey arrived on loan from Exeter. Facey was capable of some big scores but was inconsistent, also missing some matches in order to complete his engineering apprenticeship.

Despite the injuries, Vikings only went down 36-41 at Rayleigh on 22 July. Childs was unbeaten until his final race when he was excluded for unfair riding, the referee ignoring his vehement protests. Clark Facey failed to score on his debut but he put that right the following day at Boston, scoring 11 in a 33-45 reverse. Only 12 from Tony Childs challenged the home team's dominance.

On 26 July Vikings took on Danish touring team Fredericia at the Boulevard and raced to a comfortable 55-23 win. Malcolm Mackay, guesting for Robin Amundson, was top scorer with 12 but injury struck again as Bryan Loakes suffered torn muscles following a heat 6 crash. The match at Berwick was decided by two tremendous final heats. Hull looked to have guaranteed a draw when Dave Mills and Clark Facey led heat 12 but were passed by Bandits' Doug Templeton. Tony Childs could only manage second place in the last race and Vikings went down by two points.

Hull returned to winning ways with a 44-34 win over Ellesmere Port on 2 August. Robin Amundson's comeback lasted three races before he crashed again, while Clark Facey continued his impressive form with 10 points from reserve. Teesside's Cleveland Park was never a happy hunting ground for the Vikings and they went down 31-47 the following night, Tony Childs being the only Viking to put up any resistance with 12 points which included Hull's only two heat wins.

Another new signing in the form of veteran Stan Stevens followed. Stan had raced for West Ham and had moved with the team to Barrow, but the travelling plus a desire to give the youngsters a chance saw him make his Vikings debut on 9 August against Rayleigh. He scored 5 points in a 44-34 win, achieved with a solid team display. Hull visited Ellesmere Port next and benefitted from Gunners losing Paul Tyrer with a first-heat injury. A ding-dong encounter saw Vikings edge home 40-38 courtesy of a Tony Childs-Dennis Gavros 4-2 in heat 13. Dave Mills also acquired the Silver Helmet by default from holder Paul Tyrer.

A gap in the fixture list was filled with a challenge match against a Stars of the League side which finished in a 39-39 draw, and then Vikings went down by ten points in a full-blooded encounter at Birmingham, new boy Stan Stevens leading the way with 12 paid 13.

Dave Mills was not able to successfully defend the Silver Helmet, losing out to Birmingham's Arthur Browning. Hull then won three in a row, including a 43-35 success at Canterbury and a thumping 53-24 challenge victory over Bradford, new boy Stevens providing excellent back-up for the heat leaders. A 24-53 reverse to strong-in-depth Eastbourne at Arlington brought the run to an end, in a meeting where Robin Amundson sustained an injury which caused him to miss two league matches plus the Anglian Fours. Hard work was made of completing the double over Canterbury, Vikings only clinching a 41-37 win in the last race.

1972 programme cover.

A few days break from league racing saw Vikings comfortably win the Anglian Fours, scoring 124 points in the four rounds. Boston were second with 96 points, Peterborough finishing third with Scunthorpe taking the wooden spoon.

A uncharacteristic 1-point return from Tony Childs due to mechanical problems cost Vikings a 38-40 home reverse to Workington, despite yet another Mills full house, and the league programme was completed with a 46-32 home success over Teesside, this time Childs scoring a maximum.

The season drew to a close with a few challenge matches, including the customary clash with Boston. Radio 1 DJ and speedway fan David Hamilton was the guest announcer for this meeting. The final meeting was an uncharacteristic Saturday meeting, the Supreme Individual Open Trophy for the Lord Mayor's Charity. This meeting was won by Boston's Jim Ryman, with Tony Childs's 10 and 9 from Stan Stevens being Hull's nearest challengers. The staging of this meeting went some way to ensuring that Vikings' lease to operate at the Boulevard was extended.

On the individual front, Dave Mills and Robin Amundson received 3 caps and 1 cap respectively for Australia v. England, and Tony Childs earned 1 cap for England in the same series. It's probably fair to say that the Hull contingent did not cover themselves with glory in these Tests.

Tony Childs, Robin Amundson and Clark Facey entered the World Championship, all being eliminated in the Preliminary Round.

Dennis Gavros, mid-season signing.

Tony Childs represented the club at Wimbledon in the Division Two Riders' Championship, scoring 2 points.

Although a glance at the league table shows that Vikings dropped two places to eighth, the usual crop of injuries and changes of team line-up prevented a much better showing. Tony Childs once again led by example, and was ever present, but the big success was Dave Mills, who was outstanding from the start, and after only one season was being chased by more than one Division One club. Robin Amundson progressed to just under 8 points a match, while Messrs Stevens, Gavros, Loakes and Boston were a solid middle order, even if none of them rode the full season. To have made an impact at the top of the table, Hull really lacked a steady third heat-leader to back up Childs and Mills, and also, of course, an injury-free run.

1972 British League Division Two – Final Table

		M	Home W	D	L	F	A	Away W	D	L	F	A	Pts
1	Crewe	32	15	0	1	834	413	7	1	8	610	628	45
2	Boston	32	16	0	0	785	461	5	1	10	580	666	43
3	Peterborough	32	14	0	2	738	508	7	0	9	574	671	42
4	Rayleigh	32	15	1	0	771	474	2	3	11	562	686	38
5	Eastbourne	32	15	1	0	771	469	3	1	12	552.5	691.5	38
6	Birmingham	32	15	1	0	782	462	3	0	13	547	695	37
7	Workington	32	15	0	1	777	468	3	0	13	531	715	36
8	**HULL**	**32**	**12**	**0**	**4**	**673**	**574**	**4**	**0**	**12**	**550**	**695**	**32**
9	W Ham / Barrow	32	13	0	3	712	532	2	1	13	548	698	31
10	Teesside	32	14	1	1	728	516	0	2	14	490	754	31
11	Bradford	32	13	0	3	710	530	2	0	14	517	729	30
12	Sunderland	32	13	1	2	702	541	0	1	15	478	765	28
13	Canterbury	32	11	0	5	717	526	2	1	13	512	734	27
14	Berwick	32	11	3	2	671	575	1	0	15	486	755	27
15	Ellesmere Port	32	11	0	5	667	575	1	0	15	489	754	24
16	Long Eaton	32	10	2	4	655	589	1	0	15	449	796	24
17	Scunthorpe	32	5	1	10	580.5	663.5	0	0	16	402	841	11

1972 North Eastern Trophy – Final Table

		M	Home W	D	L	F	A	Away W	D	L	F	A	Pts
1	Berwick	6	3	0	0	142	91	1	1	1	118	115	9
2	Teesside	6	3	0	0	137	96	0	1	2	98	136	7
3	**HULL**	**6**	**2**	**0**	**1**	**128**	**104**	**0**	**1**	**2**	**97**	**137**	**5**
4	Sunderland	6	0	3	0	117	117	0	0	3	95	136	3

Final Averages (League and K.O. Cup matches)

	M	R	1st	2nd	3rd	Unpl	Pts	BP	Tot	Avge	FM	PM
Tony Childs	34	151	62	57	22	10	322	19	341	9.03	3	1
Dave Mills	31	136	55	44	21	16	274	18	292	8.59	5	2
Robin Amundson	27	105	30	39	23	9	191	12	203	7.73	0	0
Stan Stevens	11	45	12	10	11	12	67	9	76	6.76	0	0
Dennis Gavros	13	49	11	8	15	15	64	6	70	5.71	0	0
Bryan Loakes	22	94	14	16	34	30	108	19	127	5.40	0	0
Pete Boston	27	91	11	14	31	35	92	23	115	5.05	0	0
Clark Facey	12	52	10	7	10	25	54	5	59	4.54	0	0
Dennis Wasden	28	89	7	20	24	38	85	11	96	4.31	0	0
Colin Tucker	9	27	1	4	10	12	21	7	28	4.15	0	0
Bernie Hornby	8	23	0	1	7	15	9	1	10	1.74	0	0
George Devonport	5	12	0	0	4	8	4	0	4	1.33	0	0
Nicky Allott	2	6	0	0	2	4	2	0	2	1.33	0	0
Doug Underwood	1	2	0	0	0	2	0	0	0	0.00	0	0
Shane Hearty	1	1	0	0	0	1	0	0	0	0.00	0	0

1973 – British League Division Two

Before the start of the 1973 season, there were renewed doubts over the continuation of the sport at the Boulevard. There were still objections on the grounds of noise and public health, but Hull City Council decided that these were not sufficient to close the track, and a two-year extension was granted, to commence in 1974.

Meanwhile, the Vikings team for the 1973 campaign did not show too many changes from 1972. Stan Stevens was released and Bryan Loakes had personal problems in Australia which prevented him making the trip. Clark Facey returned to the Boulevard, and brought his brother Glyn on loan from Exeter, but Glyn broke his ankle in early April and never returned. George Devonport had basically retired, although he turned out a couple of times for Chesterton during the season. Aussie Dave O'Connor, on loan from Newport, tried his hand at the start of the season, but only raced four matches and was gone. The remainder of the faces were the same, in particular the heat-leader trio of Childs-Mills-Amundson.

Vikings fans were saddened to hear of the death during the close season of popular Starting Marshal Charlie Parkinson.

Left: *1973 programme cover.*

Right: *Robin Amundson, who left the club mid-season.*

The season got under way with Ian Thomas controversially taking the captaincy away from Tony Childs and giving it to Dennis Gavros. The reason given was to allow Tony to concentrate on his racing, but it was not a popular decision with the fans.

As a sign of the injury problems to come, in only the second home match against Teesside, Tony Childs was absent owing to an ankle injury sustained in the first home meeting and Glyn Facey broke his ankle. Dennis Gavros crashed but luckily was not badly injured and did not miss a match. Unsurprisingly, Vikings lost the match 36-42; the strong Teesside outfit would go on to win the early season North-Eastern Trophy. Dave Mills was carrying on exactly where he left off at the end of 1972, and Clark Facey was looking distinctly promising, making up for the slow start made by Robin Amundson.

The league campaign got off to a disappointing start with a 37-41 home defeat by league newcomers Chesterton, on a track that curator Colin Tucker admitted he had overwatered. A six-point return from Dave Mills was his poorest of the season to date. The following Wednesday, Vikings squeezed home courtesy of a heat 13 Mills-Amundson 5-1 against Ellesmere Port. Hull had to draft in Aussie junior Peter Thompson in place of Clark Facey who did not arrive due to motorway delays. The team then once again showed their liking for the Ellesmere track, in a solid performance, winning by a larger margin than at home! A close win over Scunthorpe was followed by another home defeat to the strong-looking Peterborough side. Vikings were without Dave Mills who was at the World Championship, his guest replacement Mitch Graham of Workington could only manage two points. The following night, Mills' guest replacement Mal Mackay scored nine in a Vikings 42-36 win at Long Eaton. The top-scoring Viking Robin Amundson was, however, unsuccessful in his attempt to wrest the Silver Helmet from Long Eaton's Roger Mills.

A third home defeat was inflicted by the Brummies from Birmingham, Facey was again missing, this time in hospital with nerve trouble. Roger Austin was drafted in, and rode a total of ten matches, only managing a 2.80 average. The local derby at Scunthorpe was lost 35-43, Saints' Jack Bywater being injured in a first-heat crash involving Tony Childs, a repeat of an incident in the first meeting between the sides at the Boulevard.

Vikings drew Rayleigh Rockets in the Knock-Out Cup, and once again failed to make any progress, losing 75-80, Tony Childs scoring his first maximum of the season at the Boulevard. At this meeting Vikings fans were entertained by a guest appearance of comedian Charlie Williams. Sandwiched between the two Cup ties was the third and final staging of the Hull Open Championship. It was a Hull 1-2 with Dave Mills taking the trophy with 14 points from Tony Childs who scored 12. Robin Amundson with 10, Dennis Gavros 9, Pete Boston 8 and Clark Facey who scored 7 made it a good night for local riders.

Clark Facey rode his last match for Hull on 20 June, retiring due to ill health, and the travelling to Hull from the South-West. He was replaced by Alan Cowland who doubled up with riding for a German team. This was uncommon in 1973. Tony Childs required a police escort after the 33-45 defeat at Workington, several on-track clashes with Comets' Mal Mackay angered the crowd. Childs won the second half but did not wait

Hull Vikings 1973 – Left to right: Peter Boston, Clark Facey, Robin Amundson, Dave O'Connor, Dave Mills, Dennis Gavros, Tony Childs.

to collect his trophy, making a hasty departure for his own safety. Hull then did the double over Berwick: a crushing 60-18 win at the Boulevard, the best performance of the season so far, the team scoring solidly throughout. The good form continued with two consecutive away draws, at Chesterton and Rayleigh. Tony Childs relieved Mike Broadbanks of the Silver Helmet at Chesterton, but lost it to Peter Moore at Rayleigh. Alan Cowland was settling in well and producing heat-leader scores which was just as well, because Robin Amundson quit Vikings after the Rayleigh match. He claimed he was fed up of racing in Division Two and wanted to ride in Division One. Hull's management fixed him up with a place with a Division One side, but Robin turned this down and returned to Australia. Perhaps a break from league matches was called for, and on 4 July Hull staged its first ever Test Match when England took on Poland. A tremendous match where the lead changed hands several times finally went the way of the Poles 55-53. Tony Childs represented the Vikings for England and scored 9 paid 10.

Vikings were given permission to use Rider Replacement for Robin Amundson who was deemed to be withholding his services and then proceeded to win their next five home matches, including a 43-34 win over champions-to-be Boston. A challenge match with Birmingham saw Tony Childs involved in incidents with a couple of the Brummies, but the meeting ended up with Childs in hospital with a broken ankle after a first-bend crash in the Rider of the Night final. Thus ended Tony's record of never having missed a Division Two match. Lou Sansom of Workington guested for Childs the following week against Ellesmere Port, who tracked a sixteen-year-old Chris Morton at reserve. Roger Austin, a New Zealander more famous on the scrambles circuit, came from Ellesmere Port to fill a gap, rode ten matches but did not look the part; Mike Vernam was signed from Eastbourne but only rode three matches, failing to make an impact. Manchester junior Grahame Dawson was promoted from No. 8 and looked to have potential. At one point, Hull seemed to be signing a rider a week! On 22 August, Barrow visited the Boulevard and gained a 39-39 draw, in a match which introduced Vikings fans to Joe Owen, who was to play a big part for Hull in the years to come, and also saw the first of six matches for Chris Blythe, who had raced a few times for Ellesmere Port earlier in the season.

Team Manager and track man Colin Tucker was responsible for a story that caused a little amusement, when it was revealed that he had been tunneling at the Boulevard. Colin was not trying to escape, he was constructing a tunnel under the terracing to allow a more direct route from the pits to the track.

Another on the way out was Dennis Wasden, who retired for financial reasons. Heading in the other direction was King's Lynn junior Kelvin Mullarkey, gaining his first team place of what was to be a successful career. Yet another newcomer was Aussie Eddie Argall, son of former rider Ted, who had been second-halfing at Halifax. The team was bearing little relation to the side that started the season. Cowland and Mills were shouldering most of the burden, and the team, who were now feeling the absence of Amundson and Childs were struggling to win at home and losing away. The heaviest defeat of the season was suffered on 11 September with the 20-57 loss at Barrow, only Alan Cowland putting up any resistance.

The Boulevard staged its second Test Match of the season on 12 September, when Australasia cruised to a 64-44 win over England. Dave Mills and Dennis Gavros

Ever-popular former captain, Tony Childs.

Left: *1973 signing Alan Cowland.*

Below: *West Countryman Clark Facey leads the way.*

represented the Anzacs, scoring 11 and 3 respectively, while Alan Cowland had two races at reserve for England, failing to score.

Tony Childs returned to the team on 26 September and helped the Vikings to their first win since 27 August, a 42-35 success over Workington, but in reality had returned too soon, and his ankle injury was to give him trouble throughout the winter. Two weeks later despite Childs, Mills and Cowland scoring 32 points between them, the remaining Vikings could only manage 6, and the last home match in the league was lost 38-40 to Teesside. Kelvin Mullarkey returned 13 paid 14 to top score in a 33-45 defeat at Sunderland. Missing from this match was Tony Childs who had aggravated his ankle injury the previous week. Mullarkey earned himself the nickname 'Mudlark' the following week when the riders went ahead with a challenge match against Barrow on a track that was more like a swimming pool. Kelvin scored 14 paid 15 in a 40-37 win.

The following week, the Boulevard bade farewell to one of its favourites. Colin Tucker had decided not to return in 1974, owing to problems with immigration regarding a work permit. A farewell meeting was staged, which was won by skipper Dennis Gavros with a 15-point maximum, Alan Cowland taking the runner-up slot with 12. Over 2,000 fans turned out, despite the counter attraction of an England v. Poland World Cup football match live on TV. After four postponements, the league visit to Bradford rounded off the Division Two programme. A makeshift Hull side, with Mills already having departed back to Australia, were well beaten 25-53. Mills departed making noises to the effect that with a new addition to his family, he might not return in 1974. As it turned out, Hull could sure have used him in 1974. A challenge victory over Boston pulled the curtain down on a season perhaps best forgotten, a settled side was never achieved, due to injuries, retirements, and a walkout, and the team slipped further down the table to twelfth.

Not much success was achieved on the individual front either, although Dave Mills did reach the Division One rounds of the World Championship, scoring 1 point at Sheffield and 5 at Cradley Heath. Tony Childs and Robin Amundson were eliminated at the Division Two stage. Mills was the Vikings representative in the Division Two Riders Championship at Wimbledon on 6 October, but could only manage 1 point.

The tribulations of 1973 were soon forgotten during the winter with news that ushered in a new era of speedway at the Boulevard.

1973 North Eastern Trophy – Final Table

			Home					Away					
		M	**W**	**D**	**L**	**F**	**A**	**W**	**D**	**L**	**F**	**A**	**Pts**
1	Teesside	6	3	0	0	137	97	2	1	0	125	109	11
2	Sunderland	6	2	1	0	124	109	0	0	3	106	126	5
3	**HULL**	**6**	**2**	**0**	**1**	**124**	**109**	**0**	**0**	**3**	**109**	**125**	**4**
4	Berwick	6	2	0	1	120	112	0	0	3	87	146	4

1973 British League Division Two – Final Table

			Home					Away					
		M	**W**	**D**	**L**	**F**	**A**	**W**	**D**	**L**	**F**	**A**	**Pts**
1	Boston	34	17	0	0	853	471	12	0	5	689	629	58
2	Workington	34	16	1	0	841	481	5	1	11	634	690	44
3	Eastbourne	34	17	0	0	791	532	2	2	13	588	762	40
4	Peterborough	34	16	0	1	813	509	3	1	13	592	731	39
5	Birmingham	34	16	0	1	867	456	3	0	14	585	734	38
6	Teesside	34	16	0	1	827	499	3	0	14	562	763	38
7	Bradford	34	16	0	1	805	519	2	0	15	553	770	36
8	Crewe	34	17	0	0	785.5	538.5	0	1	16	503	820	35
9	Long Eaton	34	15	0	2	782	535	2	1	14	493	831	35
10	Barrow	34	15	0	2	822	499	0	2	15	533	769	32
11	Sunderland	34	15	1	1	777	548	0	1	16	499	824	32
12	**HULL**	**34**	**10**	**3**	**4**	**707**	**613**	**3**	**2**	**12**	**550**	**775**	**31**
13	Chesterton	34	11	1	5	711	611	3	0	14	540	784	29
14	Ellesmere Port	34	11	0	6	737	586	3	0	14	543	781	28
15	Canterbury	34	11	1	5	718	603	2	1	14	526	797	28
16	Scunthorpe	34	12	1	4	727	598	0	0	17	485	837	25
17	Berwick	34	11	1	5	713	609	0	0	17	435	890	23
18	Rayleigh	34	9	3	5	733.5	592.5	0	0	17	500	823	21

Final Averages (League and K.O. Cup matches)

	M	**R**	**1st**	**2nd**	**3rd**	**Unpl**	**Pts**	**BP**	**Tot**	**Avge**	**FM**	**PM**
Dave Mills	32	152	75	44	22	11	335	18	353	9.29	4	2
Tony Childs	25	114	41	40	21	12	224	18	242	8.49	1	2
Alan Cowland	23	107	38	33	16	20	196	9	205	7.66	0	1
Robin Amundson	16	60	13	22	17	8	100	14	114	7.60	0	1
Dennis Gavros	34	139	30	22	43	44	177	16	193	5.55	0	0
Pete Boston	24	82	10	15	22	35	82	13	95	4.63	0	0
Dennis Wasden	20	66	6	12	20	28	62	11	73	4.42	0	0
Kelvin Mullarkey	10	39	4	6	13	16	37	5	42	4.31	0	0
Clark Facey	9	28	4	4	5	15	25	3	28	4.00	0	0
Grahame Dawson	14	53	4	3	18	28	36	6	42	3.17	0	0
Roger Austin	10	30	2	2	9	17	19	2	21	2.80	0	0
Mike Vernam	2	8	1	0	1	6	4	1	5	2.50	0	0
Peter Thompson	2	5	1	0	0	4	3	0	3	2.40	0	0
Eddie Argall	9	33	1	3	7	22	16	0	16	1.94	0	0
Chris Blythe	6	14	0	0	4	12	4	1	5	1.43	0	0
Dave O'Connor	1	2	0	0	0	0	0	0	0	0.00	0	0
Also Rode												
Mitch Graham	1	4	0	1	0	3	2	0	2	2.00	0	0
Mal Mackay	1	4	1	3	0	0	9	1	10	10.00	0	0

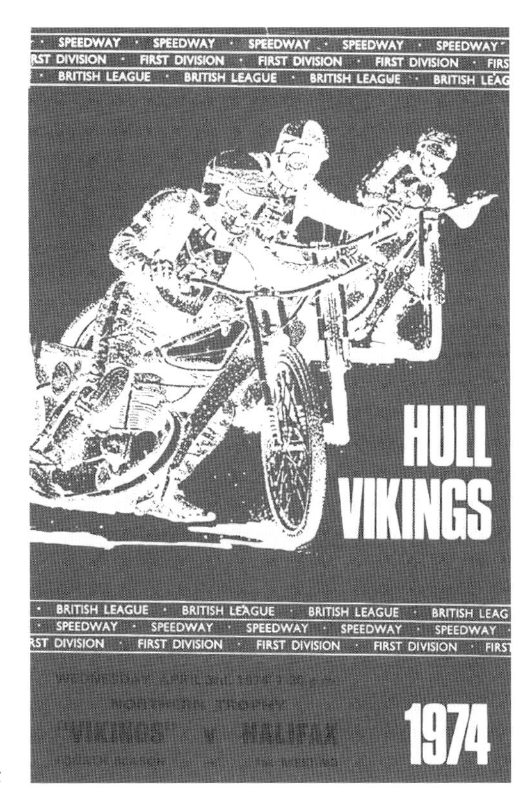

1974 programme cover.

1974 – British League Division One

As the 1973 season finished, there was no indication that Hull would do other than take their place in Division Two for 1974. But ambitious promoter Ian Thomas had other ideas, and when Division One Coatbridge indicated that they favoured dropping into Division Two, Ian Thomas quickly did a deal, bought their Division One licence, and took the Vikings into the top flight for the first time in their history.

The mammoth task then was to find a team. As part of the Coatbridge deal, Tigers' Scottish duo of Jim McMillan and Bobby Beaton transferred to Hull, and Dave Gifford opted to stay in Scotland but double up at the Boulevard. From the 1973 Vikings, Tony Childs decided to try his luck in Division One. By this time, 1973 star Dave Mills had made it clear he was stopping in Aussie. Hull signed promising Ellesmere Port youngster Robbie Gardner, and ambitious American Steve Gresham, who came on the back of Scott Autrey's success in 1973. The starting line-up was completed by Norwegian Stein Pedersen, who got an early chance as first-choice German Jurgen Hehlert was injured. Nos 8 and 9 in the squad were Workington's Mitch Graham and Barrow's Tom Owen, both of whom were loaned back to their Division Two tracks. Former Ellesmere Port track man Derek Tattersall took over from the departed Colin Tucker.

The season started with the mini league Northern Trophy, with Vikings taking on Belle Vue, Halifax and Sheffield. More than 6,000 fans saw Hull's first senior home match, and found a new hero in Jim McMillan, who scored a 15-point maximum on his Vikings debut to earn a point in a 39-39 draw against Halifax. It was clear, though, that the team had little strength in depth, and the first casualty was Pedersen after two matches, followed by his replacement Hehlert after only one. Vikings lost all their remaining Northern Trophy matches, including a 28-49 home defeat by Sheffield in which former Viking Reg Wilson scored a maximum, but had persuaded German long-track star Josef Angermuller, who rode for Reading in 1971, to sign. However "Seppi" was to miss a number of matches as he juggled his Continental commitments.

The league campaign got underway with a 37-41 loss at home to Cradley United. Hull had persuaded veteran Tommy Roper to come out of retirement for one last season, and although he struggled on his debut, he was to score over 150 points in Hull colours, mainly in home matches. Gresham was struggling to get into the side, Hull often preferring Mitch Graham.

In a break from team matches, Hull staged a World Championship Qualifying Round on 1 May. This was won by Cradley's John Boulger with an immaculate 15-point maximum, in a meeting that saw Jim McMillan equal Phil Crump's two-year-old track record of 73.4 seconds. The following week, Vikings took their first league win, 40-38 over Oxford, in a match which would be the subject of appeal and counter-appeal about the make up of the Vikings team and ultimately allow Hull to avoid the wooden spoon. After this match, Hull parted company with Tony Childs, the last link with Division Two days. Tony was struggling to keep up at the top level and with controversy to the last he was accused by the promoters of not giving 100% and not having the temperament for Division One. Tony linked up with Division Two Scunthorpe later in the season. Sheffield were the opposition in the Knock-Out Cup, and Hull made their usual early exit, losing 64-92. A best-so-far 51-27 win over Newport saw the track record equalled twice, by Mitch Graham and Newport's Reidar Eide, and then reduced to 73 seconds by Jim McMillan in the second half. The following Wednesday 6,328 fans turned out to see Ivan Mauger's first visit to Hull. The greater strength in depth of his Exeter side took the match 44-34. Falcons were to be the 1974 champions. No. 9 Tom Owen made his first appearance at Swindon in a 29-49 defeat to cover another of Josef Angermuller's absences.

Vikings were without Angermuller for three more league matches in June, after he broke his collarbone in a World Championship semi-final meeting, despite dispensation to use a guest, all three were lost. On 12 June, Hull staged the Inter-Continental Best Pairs, which was won by Norwegians Reidar Eide and Dag Lovaas. During this meeting, the track record was equalled or broken five times. Scott Autrey having the final say with a new time of 71.4 seconds. Mechanical failures for McMillan and Beaton cost a 37-41 defeat by Ole Olsen inspired Wolverhampton, and in Hull's Northern Riders Championship Qualifying Round, Peter Collins sailed home with a 15-point maximum.

Some success came on a dusty track in a Four-Team Tournament at Division Two Barrow, but a fortnight later home colours were again lowered, this time by Wimbledon, led by Barry Briggs, establishing the popularity he would always enjoy at Hull, both as a visitor and as a Hull rider.

The fourth out of a seven-match Test series against Poland was staged at the Boulevard on 17 July. This was a comfortable 69-39 win for England, although there was

1974 captain and No. 1 Jim McMillan.

no Vikings representation in the match. Back in the league, Tom Owen came in and scored 12 from reserve at Newport, on a track which in 1975 would be his home track. His sterling effort could not prevent a 33-45 defeat.

Steve Gresham, who had struggled to get a regular team slot, walked out on the club the following week. The problems were apparently financial, and he went back to the States, not to resurface in Britain until 1975, when he linked up with Newport.

On 31 July, Belle Vue visited the Boulevard for a league match. The track, which was very wet after two days of rain, was inspected by the referee and declared rideable. Belle Vue raced four heats under protest, and then decided they had had enough and walked out, accompanied by Hull's Dave Gifford. Hull completed the remaining nine heats uncontested for a 60-9 win, a result which was ultimately allowed to stand. Gifford was sacked immediately after the meeting.

The Hull promoters were still trying to strengthen the team. Among others, Aussies Greg Kentwell and Jim Airey, both former Division One stars, turned down substantial offers to race the rest of the season at Hull. Vikings also made a bid for Steve Reinke, who ended up at Exeter, former World Champion Ronnie Moore, and even made an

Dave Gifford, sacked after walking out with Belle Vue.

audacious £2,500 bid to Sheffield for former Viking Reg Wilson. The next two home league matches were both won 58-20 against Coventry and Poole, two of 1974's weaker teams, with three of the four away matches in the same period lost 36-42. One of these defeats, at Sheffield, included a four-ride maximum from Jim McMillan, despite missing his first race due to arriving late at Owlerton. Among all these league encounters, in a scoop for Hull, they persuaded Yorkshire Television to sponsor the first YTV Trophy individual meeting. Viewers were asked to vote for the riders they wanted and the meeting was staged on 21 August in front of a Boulevard record crowd of 7,500. Viewers were treated to a last-heat decider between Phil Crump and Ole Olsen who both had 11 points from their first four rides. At the first attempt Olsen broke the tapes and was penalised 20 yards in the rerun. At the second attempt, Olsen quickly overtook Mitch Graham, and had a titanic four-lap battle with Crump, but the Aussie hung on to win the trophy.

Championship-chasing Ipswich demolished the Vikings 46-31 at the Boulevard, and the league programme was completed with a comfortable 45-33 win over Sheffield.

Hull Vikings 1974 – Left to right: Robbie Gardner, Tom Owen, Josef Angermuller, Tommy Roper, Dave Gifford, Derek Tattersall (team manager), Bobby Beaton. On machine – Jim McMillan.

Veteran Tommy Roper spent his last season at Hull.

'Seppi' Angermuller.

Vikings lost the Yorkshire Cup to Halifax 70-85, after a 37-41 home loss on a rain-soaked Boulevard track. The season came to an end with a four-team tournament won by Briggo's All Stars, but the show was stolen by World Champion Anders Michanek, making his first visit to Hull. He beat Barry Briggs in a match race, and, guesting for Hull, was only deprived of a maximum by a mechanical problem in his final race. Overall, despite only lifting themselves off the bottom of the league after an appeal, Vikings' first season in the top flight was a success. The East Yorkshire public patronized the Boulevard in great numbers to the tune of an average crowd of over 5,000 per meeting and enjoyed seeing speedway's top riders, even if their own team struggled with an under-strength side. How much would today's promoters give for a 7,500 crowd as witnessed the YTV Trophy?

Jim McMillan and Bobby Beaton were both successful and popular, while Robbie Gardner improved as the season went on. Tommy Roper posted some good scores at home, and if Seppi Angermuller had been able to fit more matches in he would have been approaching third-heat-leader standard. Mitch Graham showed a lot of promise, but the rest of the team was somewhat patchwork with several riders not completing a full season for various reasons.

Individually, Jim McMillan reached the European final of the World Championship as reserve, scoring 2 points. He also reached the final of the World Long Track Championship, finishing fifth. Jim represented Scotland in the World Team Cup and World Pairs Championships, earned 7 caps for Great Britain in Australia, and was Hull's representative in the BLRC at Belle Vue scoring 6 points. Nearer to home, he scored 8 points in the Northern Riders' Championship final at Sheffield.

Bobby Beaton reached the British semi-final of the World Championship, scoring 8 points at Sheffield. Bobby also represented the Scots in the World Team Cup, and returned 7 points in the Northern Riders Championship.

No other Hull rider progressed beyond the World Championship preliminaries, or reached the final of the Northern Riders' Championship.

1974 British League Division One – Final Table

			Home					Away					
		M	**W**	**D**	**L**	**F**	**A**	**W**	**D**	**L**	**F**	**A**	**Pts**
1	Exeter	32	16	0	0	760	485	9	1	6	615	632	51
2	Belle Vue	32	16	0	0	795	453	7	0	9	585	653	46
3	Ipswich	32	15	0	1	741	505	7	1	8	623	623	45
4	Sheffield	32	16	0	0	824	424	5	0	11	602	643	42
5	Kings Lynn	32	14	1	1	713	535	6	0	10	568	675	41
6	Newport	32	15	0	1	742	506	2	3	11	557	691	37
7	Halifax	32	13	1	2	694	554	1	2	13	515	732	31
8	Wimbledon	32	13	1	2	731	509	1	0	15	469	778	29
9	Hackney	32	10	1	5	670	574	3	1	12	548	699	28
10	Leicester	32	11	1	4	676	572	2	0	14	534	710	27
11	Wolverhampton	32	9	1	6	633.5	609.5	4	0	12	524	723	27
12	Swindon	32	11	2	3	674	574	1	0	15	505	742	26
13	Cradley Heath	32	8	1	7	648	598	4	0	12	523	724	25
14	Poole	32	12	0	4	665	580	0	1	15	482	764	25
15	Coventry	32	10	0	6	636	607	2	0	14	511	735	24
16	**HULL**	**32**	**10**	**0**	**6**	**708**	**530**	**0**	**0**	**16**	**504**	**739**	**20**
17	Oxford	32	8	0	8	651.5	594.5	2	0	14	507	659	20

1974 Northern Trophy – Final Table

			Home					Away					
		M	**W**	**D**	**L**	**F**	**A**	**W**	**D**	**L**	**F**	**A**	**Pts**
1	Sheffield	6	3	0	0	148	86	2	0	1	127	105	10
2	Belle Vue	6	3	0	0	140	93	1	0	2	109	124	8
3	Halifax	6	2	0	1	127	105	0	1	2	103	131	5
4	**HULL**	**6**	**0**	**1**	**2**	**105**	**128**	**0**	**0**	**3**	**74**	**159**	**1**

The Northern Trophy was won by the team scoring the most race points

Final Averages (League and K.O. Cup matches)

	M	R	1st	2nd	3rd	Unpl	Pts	BP	Tot	Avge	FM	PM
Jim McMillan	33	147	74	53	13	7	341	16	357	9.71	3	3
Bobby Beaton	33	142	34	57	39	12	255	21	276	7.77	3	0
Mitch Graham	24	90	12	22	31	25	111	18	129	5.73	0	0
Tommy Roper	32	121	26	23	32	40	156	11	167	5.52	1	1
Tom Owen	16	49	4	11	18	16	52	11	63	5.14	0	0
Josef Angermuller	20	72	7	19	16	30	75	17	92	5.11	0	1
Robbie Gardner	34	117	16	23	27	51	121	28	149	5.09	0	1
Tony Childs	2	9	1	2	2	4	9	1	10	4.44	0	0
Steve Gresham	6	23	0	6	7	10	19	5	24	4.17	0	0
Dave Gifford	19	57	4	11	15	27	49	10	59	4.14	0	0
Also Rode												
Alan Cowland	2	7	0	1	4	2	6	0	6	3.43	0	0
Phil Crump	1	5	4	1	0	0	14	0	14	11.20	0	0
Ricky Day	1	5	1	1	2	1	7	2	9	7.20	0	0
Cyril Francis	1	2	0	0	0	2	0	0	0	0.00	0	0
Paul Gachet	1	3	0	0	1	2	1	1	2	2.67	0	0
Richard Greer	1	4	1	2	1	0	8	1	9	9.00	0	0
Alan Guest	1	2	0	0	0	2	0	0	0	0.00	0	0
Arnold Haley	1	4	0	3	0	1	6	3	9	9.00	0	0
John Harrhy	1	3	1	0	0	2	3	0	3	4.00	0	0
Alan Jay	1	4	0	1	1	2	3	0	3	3.00	0	0
Tony Lomas	1	5	3	1	0	1	11	0	11	8.80	0	0
Richard May	2	9	4	4	1	0	21	0	21	9.33	0	0
Arthur Price	1	3	0	0	1	2	1	0	1	1.33	0	0
Graeme Stapleton	1	3	0	1	1	1	3	2	5	6.67	0	0
Neil Street	2	8	0	1	1	6	3	0	3	1.50	0	0
Ian Turner	1	3	0	0	1	2	1	1	2	2.67	0	0

1975 – British League

After the difficulties of the initial season in the top flight, Hull were looking to put a team together that would build on 1974 and consolidate the Vikings' Division One status. This proved to be a much harder task than could have been envisaged. From the 1974 line-up, Jim McMillan and Bobby Beaton were back, together with Mitch Graham and Robbie Gardner. Former Vikings from the Division Two days Robin Amundson and Alan Cowland returned, and the starting line-up for the first match, a Northern Trophy fixture at Halifax, was completed by Swede Tommy Johansson, 1974 World Finalist, formerly with Ipswich, who was expected to occupy a heat-leader role. Also signed was another former Viking Bryan Loakes, but he was injured riding for Australia against Poland, and returned home without turning a wheel in Vikings colours. Of the riders who turned out in 1974, Tommy Roper retired, Josef Angermuller decided to stick to

Hull Vikings 1975 – Left to right: Bobby Beaton, Mitch Graham, Derek Tattersall (team manager), Alan Cowland, Tommy Johansson, Robin Amundson. On machine – Jim McMillan.

racing on the Continent, Tom Owen and Steve Gresham signed for Newport, while Dave Gifford and Tony Childs remained in Division Two. The leagues were, in fact renamed for 1975, with Gulf Oil sponsoring the British League, and the former Division Two opting for a degree of independence as the New National League.

A piece of good news before the season started was that Vikings had agreed a four-year deal with Hull Rugby Club and the council, so speedway was safe until the end of 1978.

Vikings made their usual slow start to the season, and lost all six Northern Trophy matches, finishing rock bottom of the table. After the second match of the season, the opening League match at Leicester, Robbie Gardner decided he had lost confidence in racing at the top level and opted for National League Workington. Hull borrowed fellow Comet Lou Sansom to temporarily fill the gap. The visit of Belle Vue on 9 April was, as usual, eventful with Aces' Alan Wilkinson and Vikings' Robin Amundson both ending up in hospital after two separate crashes. Fortunately, both escaped serious injury. The gloom was broken on 19 April when Vikings won their first league match away from home in the top flight with a 41-37 success at King's Lynn. A Jim McMillan-Tommy Johansson 5-1 in heat 13 gave Hull the lead for the first time in the match. This win was followed up by a 42-36 home success over Coventry, and on 28 April, Vikings were the first visitors to Reading's newly opened Smallmead Stadium. Jim McMillan came away as the first track-record holder at the new venue, but the match was lost 30-48.

Tommy Johansson was missing for the home match with Hackney on 30 April because of a racing commitment in Sweden. This was the first of many such absences which was to have a detrimental effect on Vikings' season. The following week, Hull

Left: *Programme from Reading's Smallmead opener.*
Right: *Programme from Hull's first ever match overseas.*

would have ended Belle Vue's unbeaten league record but for a Tommy Johansson engine failure. The match was drawn. The improved away form continued with a creditable 39-39 draw at Coventry. This match marked the first appearance in Hull colours of Joe Owen. Joe was racing for Hull's sister track, National League Newcastle, and started off what would turn out to be a long and eventful Vikings career with a tremendous 8-point score. Hull's World Championship round was won for the second year running by a Cradley rider, this year Bruce Cribb taking the meeting with 14 points. Viking Jim McMillan was runner-up with 12 points.

Another away draw was earned at Halifax, with good performances from McMillan, Beaton and Graham, who was occupying the third heat-leader role owing to Johansson's many absences. but the good work was undone by successive home defeats by Sheffield and King's Lynn. Hull had signed Kym Amundson, brother of Robin, from Workington, to replace fellow Comet Sansom, and Amundson Junior made his debut in the King's Lynn match, scoring 6 from the reserve berth. Kym rode for both Hull and Workington during June before assuming full-time duties at the Boulevard. Vikings made their by now customary first round exit from the Knock-Out Cup despite a 46-32 win over Swindon in the Boulevard leg. McMillan and Beaton were the only Vikings to put up any resistance as the team slumped to a 31-47 reverse at Blunsdon.

On 22 June, Vikings made club history by racing abroad for the first time. They travelled to Denmark to take on Randers, who turned out to be pretty much the Danish national team. Bolstered by guests Richard Greer and Craig Pendlebury, Vikings went down narrowly in a close match by 38-40, Bobby Beaton scoring 11, only being beaten by Ole Olsen. Home form continued to be poor with Exeter and Reading taking both points home with Ivan Mauger and Anders Michanek remaining unbeaten by a Viking, and Halifax recovering a 10-point deficit to earn a draw. Young Joe Owen showed what great potential he had in the Reading match, scoring 7 points.

Robin Amundson rode his last ever match in Hull colours on 16 July. In an uncanny repeat of 1973, a disagreement with the management resulted in him packing his bags and disappearing back to Australia. In that 16 July meeting Ian Thomas booked seventy-one-year-old Henry Lamothe, on tour with the Evel Knievel road show to perform a spectacular 45-feet death dive into 14 inches of water as an interval attraction! Meanwhile Hull won a four-team tournament at Workington, and then staged an England v. Rest of the World Test Match, part of the Daily Mirror International Tournament. A massive 7,131 crowd saw England win the match 41-37 despite a scintillating 15-point maximum from Ivan Mauger, who then went on to win the Yorkshire TV Trophy, which was staged as a knock-out second half to the Test.

Hull came second to the hosts in a four-team tournament held on a boiling hot Sunday afternoon at Bradford's Odsal Stadium, and then once again were second-best at home, this time to title-chasing Newport. Six points up after three heats, Vikings were well beaten in the end, only Jim McMillan and Joe Owen offering serious

Action from Lou Sansom.

Left: *1975 programme cover.*

Below: *Long-serving Scot Bobby Beaton.*

resistance. By then, Joe had been signed as a Hull asset, and loaned back to Newcastle. On 6 August, Amundson minor rode his last match for Hull. He dislocated his arm and tore ligaments in a spectacular crash, and when he was fit to travel, followed his brother home. The following week was the Northern Riders' Championship Qualifying Round. Due to injuries and absenteeism there were more National League than British League riders. Ian Thomas's anger at this situation led to the qualifying rounds being scrapped in future years, and the finalists being nominated by the British League clubs.

Once again Joe Owen rescued Hull from a heavy defeat, with his best-ever British League score of 11 points in a 37-41 defeat at Hackney. Tommy Johansson was rarely available in these weeks and in fact made his final appearance on 20 August in the 47-31 win over Cradley United, which was held as the best team performance of the season, Joe Owen going one better scoring 12 paid 14. The first ever afternoon meeting was staged at the Boulevard on August Bank Holiday Monday, when Poole were the visitors in the clash of the Wednesday tracks. An oddity occurred on 3 September when Leicester were beaten 43-35, and the Lions managed to use eight riders, not strictly in accordance with the rules!

Controversy seemed to follow Belle Vue to the Boulevard, and the Challenge Match visit on 10 September followed the pattern, with the Aces riders retiring on the first bend of the last two heats following a dispute over the operation of the green light. Vikings were unable to wrest the Yorkshire Cup from Halifax's grip, losing 72-84 to the Dukes. A seven-match unbeaten run at home was brought to an end by champions-to-be Ipswich, who went away 41-37 winners. An off night for Bobby Beaton, and poor returns from the lesser lights contributed to this defeat.

The final league match of the season was on 11 October when a patched-up Vikings lost 36-42 at Swindon, and the season was rounded off with a four-team tournament in which Hull finished third to winners Hackney.

A final league position of fourteenth out of eighteen was an improvement on 1974, but could have been much better, but for Tommy Johansson only racing 11 League and Cup matches out of 36, Robbie Gardner dropping out early season and the Amundson brothers' disappearing act.

The management could not be faulted for trying to put out a successful side. The fact that thirty-four riders were called upon in League and Cup matches tells its own story. On the positive side, Jim McMillan was an outstanding No. 1, Bobby Beaton was steady although he dropped his average a little, but the star of the show was Joe Owen. A 7.29 average in his first thirteen British League matches was sensational, and held out some hope that the next few seasons might hold better things in store.

Away from team duties, Vikings riders had a busy season. Jim McMillan reached the British final of the World Championship, scoring 5 points at Coventry. He also represented Scotland in the World Team Cup, received 4 caps for the Rest of the World in various Test series, plus 2 caps for England (!) in Poland. Jim represented Hull in the British League Riders' Championship at Belle Vue, scoring 4 points. He was also placed fourth in the Northern Riders Championship final at Sheffield with 12 points.

Bobby Beaton reached the British semi-final of the World Championship, being eliminated with a 6-point score. He also represented Scotland in the World Team Cup, and received one cap for the Rest of the World v. England at the Boulevard. He scored 3 points in the Northern Riders' final.

Tommy Johansson was eliminated from the World Championship at Gothenburg's Inter-Continental final with an 8-point return. He raced for Sweden in the World Team Cup Qualifying Round, and earned 7 caps for Sweden in Tests against England in both countries. Mitch Graham reached the Sheffield semi-final of the World Championship British rounds, scoring 4 points. He also scored 10 points in the Northern Riders' final.

1975 British League – Final Table

			Home					Away					
		M	**W**	**D**	**L**	**F**	**A**	**W**	**D**	**L**	**F**	**A**	**Pts**
1	Ipswich	34	17	0	0	802	522	9	1	7	656	670	53
2	Belle Vue	34	17	0	0	819	507	8	2	7	669	657	52
3	Newport	34	17	0	0	883	442	7	1	9	655	670	49
4	Exeter	34	14	0	3	762	564	6	3	8	648	676	43
5	Sheffield	34	15	0	2	760	564	6	0	11	608	717	42
6	Reading	34	16	0	1	754	571	5	0	12	588	737	42
7	Oxford	34	14	0	3	757	563	4	0	13	613	711	36
8	Leicester	34	14	1	2	733	593	2	3	12	615	710	36
9	Wimbledon	34	13	1	3	728	596	3	1	13	589	735	34
10	Halifax	34	12	2	3	707	618	3	1	13	582	744	33
11	Cradley Heath	34	12	2	3	736	588	3	0	14	552	768	32
12	Kings Lynn	34	10	2	5	716	609	4	1	12	579	746	31
13	Wolverhampton	34	11	1	5	691	635	2	0	15	546	779	27
14	**HULL**	**34**	**9**	**2**	**6**	**691**	**634**	**1**	**2**	**14**	**567**	**759**	**24**
15	Poole	34	9	2	6	691	635	1	1	15	549	776	23
16	Coventry	34	8	2	7	673.5	651.5	1	0	16	503	822	20
17	Hackney	34	8	1	8	685	641	1	0	16	536.5	788.5	19
18	Swindon	34	8	0	9	652	672	0	0	17	550	775	16

1975 Northern Trophy – Final Table

			Home					Away					
		M	**W**	**D**	**L**	**F**	**A**	**W**	**D**	**L**	**F**	**A**	**Pts**
1	Belle Vue	6	3	0	0	137	97	2	0	1	120	114	10
2	Sheffield	6	3	0	0	137	97	1	0	2	114	120	8
3	Halifax	6	2	0	1	127	107	1	0	2	98	135	6
4	**HULL**	**6**	**0**	**0**	**3**	**110**	**123**	**0**	**0**	**3**	**92**	**142**	**0**

The Northern Trophy was won by the team scoring the most race points

Final Averages (League and K.O. Cup matches)

	M	R	1st	2nd	3rd	Unpl	Pts	BP	Tot	Avge	FM	PM
Jim McMillan	36	168	84	65	13	6	395	12	407	9.69	2	0
Joe Owen	13	62	15	19	17	11	100	13	113	7.29	0	0
Bobby Beaton	36	150	41	41	40	28	245	25	270	7.20	1	1
Mitch Graham	35	151	36	47	31	37	233	15	248	6.57	0	0
Tommy Johansson	11	44	5	16	14	9	61	12	73	6.64	0	0
Lou Sansom	9	36	5	6	11	14	38	9	47	5.22	0	0
Brian Havelock	9	28	2	8	5	13	27	9	36	5.14	0	0
Kym Amundson	13	40	6	7	11	17	43	8	51	5.10	0	0
Ron Henderson	1	5	0	1	1	3	3	1	4	3.20	0	0
Alan Cowland	35	111	4	15	33	59	75	22	97	3.50	0	0
Robin Amundson	18	51	3	7	13	28	36	8	44	3.45	0	0
Robbie Gardner	1	2	0	0	0	2	0	0	0	0.00	0	0
Also Rode												
Keith Anderson	1	2	0	0	0	2	0	0	0	0.00	0	0
Phil Bass	1	2	0	0	0	2	0	0	0	0.00	0	0
Dave Baugh	1	2	0	1	0	1	2	1	3	6.00	0	0
Arthur Browning	1	5	0	0	4	1	4	1	5	4.00	0	0
Brian Clark	1	2	0	0	0	2	0	0	0	0.00	0	0
Graham Drury	4	20	4	3	7	6	25	2	27	5.40	0	0
Carl Glover	2	8	0	1	7	0	9	2	11	5.50	0	0
Alan Grahame	1	3	0	0	0	3	0	0	0	0.00	0	0
Richard Greer	2	9	1	1	6	1	11	3	14	6.22	0	0
Vic Harding	1	2	0	0	0	2	0	0	0	0.00	0	0
Phil Herne	1	4	1	0	0	3	3	0	3	3.00	0	0
Rob Hollingworth	1	2	0	0	0	2	0	0	0	0.00	0	0
Norman Hunter	1	3	0	0	0	3	0	0	0	0.00	0	0
Tony Lomas	1	5	0	1	3	1	5	0	5	4.00	0	0
Tom Owen	3	12	0	4	4	4	12	4	16	5.33	0	0
Colin Richardson	1	4	0	0	2	2	2	1	3	3.00	0	0
Mike Sampson	1	3	0	1	1	1	3	0	3	4.00	0	0
Sid Sheldrick	3	6	0	0	0	6	0	0	0	0.00	0	0
Nigel Wasley	2	6	0	0	1	5	1	0	1	0.67	0	0
Steve Weatherley	1	3	0	0	2	1	2	0	2	2.67	0	0
Pete Wigley	1	2	0	0	0	2	0	0	0	0.00	0	0

1976 – British League

The winter of 1975-76 was for Hull Speedway dominated by the 'Ole Olsen' affair. The Rider Control Committee had allocated Olsen to Hull, and as part of the deal, Jim McMillan and Tommy Johansson moved to Olsen's club Wolverhampton. Then, Olsen indicated that he would not ride for Hull, but would only link up with Coventry. No amount of persuasion would change the rider's mind, so with only a few weeks before the start of the new season, Vikings were left in an extremely precarious position over team strength. Promoters Ian Thomas and Brian Larner (a Bradford businessman who

1976 programme cover.

had taken over from Wally Mawdsley as co-promoter) set about raising a team almost from scratch. Bobby Beaton was persuaded to forget about talk of retirement and Mitch Graham was talked out of a transfer request. From the class of 1975, Alan Cowland moved into the National League with Peterborough, both Amundson brothers stayed put in Australia, and Joe Owen indicated that he preferred to remain as Hull's No. 8 and continue to race for Newcastle.

Vikings snapped up Frank Auffret from Leicester and signed Graham Drury from now-defunct National League Crewe. Graham had made a few guest appearances for Hull at the back end of 1975, impressing favourably. On the recommendation of Ivan Mauger and Barry Briggs, promising American Mike Curoso was engaged, and additionally Vikings were allocated Kazimierz Adamczak, one of four young Poles released to ride in Britain. It was also reported that negotiations were being conducted to bring young American Bruce Penhall to Hull. If only that had come off!

Initially, Hull had dispensation to use a guest up to Olsen's average, but Messrs Thomas and Larner were not prepared to put up with that situation for long, and after considerable effort one week into the season announced that they had persuaded four-times World Champion Barry Briggs to spend one last season at Hull. The deal involved Vikings preparing Barry's machinery, and organizing his transport to and from the Continent, where he was living.

As usual the season got underway with the Northern Trophy, and Hull kept up their tradition of finishing bottom without winning a match, although because of a rain-off the home match with Belle Vue was not raced until 30 June when the two sides raced for League points as well. Briggo made his debut on 7 April, but his 10-point return, together with a 12-point maximum from Bobby Beaton and an 11-point score from reserve Frank Auffret could not prevent a 38-40 defeat by Sheffield. Mike Curoso and Kaz Adamczak were struggling to settle, and before April was out, the latter was released, Hull opting to fill the gap with Newcastle riders.

The league campaign started with a 45-32 win over Leicester, stand-in Brian Havelock recording 9 points. Briggo scored 14 points in a 36-42 defeat at Reading, and recorded a paid maximum in the 46-32 defeat of Wimbledon, a match which saw Joe Owen's first appearance of the season, scoring 9 points.

The first home league defeat of the season was inflicted by Swindon on 5 May, Bobby Beaton recording a rare 1-point score. The following week, Briggo got his first full maximum against King's Lynn, a back-to-form Bobby Beaton defeating Terry Betts in a thrilling heat 13 to ensure both points for Hull. Joe Owen scored 12 at Hackney in a meeting Barry Briggs missed, but Vikings were already showing that they were a much more competitive outfit than before.

The 19 May clash with Exeter produced controversy. In a match that Hull won comfortably 45-33, a heat 13 incident where Ivan Mauger appeared to force Bobby Beaton out and into the fence caused a storm when referee Vic Harris excluded Beaton, who was taken to hospital and was fortunate to get away with bruising. Ian Thomas

Speedway legend Barry Briggs ended his career at the Boulevard.

protested angrily, and clashed with his former co-promoter Wally Mawdsley, in charge of Exeter. Thomas also had an angry confrontation with Mr Harris after which he announced to the crowd that Mr Harris would not be welcome again at the Boulevard. Fortunately, tempers cooled and Messrs Thomas and Mawdsley ended the meeting still talking to each other!

On a different note, team manager Derek Tattersall resigned in May. He cited travelling as a reason, also he had never been popular with the fans, and had been receiving criticism from a section of the crowd. His duties were taken up by promoters Thomas and Larner.

Newport were defeated 40-36 on 26 May in a match where visitor Phil Herne was taken to hospital after a horror crash. Fortunately, he was back in action a month later. Vikings then won two away matches in successive days, winning 44.5-33.5 at White City and 46-32 at Leicester, and completing the double over White City the following day. Briggo led the way with three double-figure scores in solid team displays. Hull had now aspired to second place in the League.

Knock-out Cup time saw Hull drawn against Yorkshire rivals Halifax, and the home leg was won 44.5-33.5 with Joe Owen scoring his second-consecutive full maximum. The ever-enterprising Hull management arranged for showbusiness star Max Bygraves to make a guest appearance at this match. However, Vikings could not progress, losing at the Shay 32-46. Mitch Graham scored a full house the following week as Hackney were beaten 46-32, but Ipswich then came calling and took away both points, Hull looking weak at reserve with Mike Curoso still struggling to make an impact.

Then, out of the blue, Vikings pulled off a coup. Barry Briggs persuaded Continental Champion Egon Muller to join Hull. Muller had qualified for the World Final and sought some experience on conventional speedway tracks, as he mainly rode the long track circuit. He made his debut on 28 June at Birmingham and helped his new team to a 44-34 win, only dropping 1 point from four rides. His 8 points on his Boulevard debut could not prevent the Aces winning 42-36; ironically Briggo had one of his poorest matches, scoring only 5.

A couple of new tournaments made their bow in July. The Inter-Divisional Knock-out Cup which had actually made its bow in 1975 without Vikings taking part, included teams from the National League who were given home advantage in the first round. Vikings were drawn at Berwick in the first round and negotiated a tricky tie successfully, winning 43-35. Also the Grand Prix tournament was launched. Not to be confused with the current Grand Prix which determines the World Champion, this competition was for British League riders, and consisted of qualifying rounds and a final, using the traditional sixteen-riders twenty-heat format. Points were awarded for finishing position in a round, and qualifying points were carried into the final. Hull's round was staged on 7 July and was won by Peter Collins with five undefeated rides. Mitch Graham and Bobby Beaton were the best-placed Vikings, each scoring 7 points.

A depleted Sheffield were beaten 43-35 on 14 July. Mike Curoso had obtained one of the Neil Street four-valve conversions and responded with a best-so-far score of 7 paid 9. Egon Muller recorded a low score of 4. Vikings then lost 36-42 on the difficult-to-master Newport track, Muller scoring 9, as did track specialist Tom Owen, drafted in for

There were eight matches in Vikings colours for Egon Muller, seen team riding with Bobby Beaton.

the match. The following day, Hull were edged out 39-38 at Cradley United when Barry Briggs was pushed into third place as Bruce Cribb and Arthur Price recorded a match-winning heat 13 5-1. Mike Curoso again impressed with 7 points.

The third annual YTV Trophy was staged at the Boulevard on 21 July, resulting in a win for Reading's Dave Jessup with a five-ride maximum. Hull's Bobby Beaton was runner-up, dropping his only points to Jessup and third-placed Terry Betts. Joe Owen scored an excellent 7 in a strong field, while Briggo could only manage 3 points.

After British League newcomers Birmingham were swept aside 52-26, Vikings lost 37-41 at Ole Olsen-inspired Coventry, Egon Muller top-scoring with 13. Vikings then rode a challenge match against sister track Newcastle, who were programmed as 'The Diamonds' as National League teams were not allowed to race challenge matches on British League tracks!

Hull then raced at Halifax on 7 August. An exciting match was lost in heat 13 when Briggo kept Chris Pusey at bay for three laps only for the Halifax rider to squeeze past on the last bend to win the match 40-38 for the Dukes. Egon Muller scored 12 points in a pulsating performance, but it was to be his last match for the Vikings as he quit the club amid recriminations over what deal had actually been agreed, the rider claiming he was sick of the travelling and could make more money on the Continent, and the club maintaining they had shaken hands on a deal for the entire season.

Tom Owen was drafted in as a replacement, and did the team proud with 8 points as Vikings advanced to the semi-final of the Inter-Divisional Knock-Out Cup with a 50-27 success over depleted Newport. A rare home defeat was sustained one week later at the

Hull Vikings 1976 – Back row, left to right: Ian Thomas (co-promoter), Mitch Graham, Graham Drury, Mike Curoso, Phil Michelides, Brian Larner (co-promoter). Front row, left to right: Frank Auffret, Barry Briggs (on machine), Bobby Beaton.

hands of Cradley United, off-form displays from Frank Auffret and Mitch Graham being contributory. Bobby Beaton broke down on route to Wimbledon the following day, Vikings losing out 33-45. Over the years Bobby seemed jinxed when it came to arriving at Plough Lane.

Two more away defeats followed at King's Lynn and Exeter, although Vikings were producing great entertainment on their travels, largely due to the Briggs influence on the team. A welcome return to form then produced home successes against Reading and Poole. As a precursor to the Bank Holiday meeting against Poole, Hull staged the deciding leg of the Golden Helmet Match Race Championship between Malcolm Simmons and Chris Morton. Simmons won 2-0. Two days later Vikings lost the return against Poole at Wimborne Road 37-41 thanks to an Eric Broadbelt/Kevin Holden 4-2 in heat 13. Twenty-four hours later, despite a mechanically troubled 3-point return from Briggo, Hull then triumphed 42-36 at Sheffield in their third match in three days, Bobby Beaton and Mitch Graham each mustering 10 points.

From 8 September Hull started using Rider Replacement for Egon Muller, who was deemed as withholding his services, and this inspired them to a 45-33 success over Halifax with a solid team performance. Seven days on, Wolverhampton were demolished 57-21, Mitch Graham romping to a 15-point maximum against a side for whom only former Viking Jim McMillan's 12 points offered any resistance. A four-team challenge at Coatbridge was won, Mitch Graham maintaining his good form, dropping his only point to Peter Collins.

More all-round teamwork produced a sweet 51-27 win over Coventry in the final home league match, despite Ole Olsen's 15-point maximum. The last four road league fixtures were all lost, although they ran Belle Vue to a last heat decider at Hyde Road. Sandwiched between these matches was the one-leg home semi-final of the Inter-Divisional Knock-Out Cup against National League Workington who had beaten British League Ipswich and King's Lynn on their way to the penultimate stage. However the Comets, who were without Steve Lawson and Taffy Owen were no match for the Vikings who ran out easy winners 54-23 to qualify for their first final since 1948!

At the third time of asking Vikings annexed the Yorkshire Cup with an 88-68 defeat of Halifax, including a 43-35 win at the Shay. On 20 October Hull virtually sealed their first ever national trophy by hammering Wolverhampton 57-21 in the first leg of the Inter-Divisional Knock-Out Cup final on an extremely wet track made worse by rugby players training on it the day before! Two days later on a similar lake of a track at Monmore Green, Vikings completed the job with a 39-39 draw in a match they led 27-15 after heat 7. Graham Drury for one ploughed through the mud for 10 points in each leg, Mike Curoso also scoring well to give the strength in depth Wolves could not match.

The season concluded with a Farewell to Barry Briggs challenge, but opponents Belle Vue once again threatened to walk out because of track conditions and although they were persuaded to continue, they rather spoiled what should have been a celebration with their lack of effort.

American Mike Curoso, who raced two seasons for Hull.

Programme cover for the Inter-Divisional Knock-Out Cup final.

What threatened to be a catastrophe turned out to be the best year yet at the Boulevard. Vikings finally got a side together to make the fans proud, with a World Champion as leader, the brief exciting stay of Egon Muller, and a couple of trophies to show for it. Bobby Beaton improved his average, and Mitch Graham showed some great form. Of the newcomers, Graham Drury benefitted from the Briggs influence, while Frank Auffret's early season form in particular made him a great crowd favourite. Mike Curoso showed great improvement after a slow start, when he upgraded his machinery. The Newcastle contingent stood in with great success, in particular Joe Owen who proved he was ready to step up into the big league.

On the individual front, Barry Briggs was eliminated from the World Championship at the Australasian final, while Frank Auffret and Tom Owen reached the British semi-finals. Briggo reached the World Long Track final scoring 7 points and represented his country in the World Pairs final with a 7-point return. The New Zealander gained one cap for the Rest of the World v. England at Vojens and represented Vikings in the BLRC at Belle Vue managing 6 points.

Bobby Beaton represented Scotland in the World Team Cup at Ipswich, while no Hull rider progressed to the final of the new Grand Prix competition.

Viking riders did not distinguish themselves in the Northern Riders Championship at Sheffield, Bobby Beaton being the best of the bunch with 5 points.

1976 British League – Final Table

			Home					Away					
		M	**W**	**D**	**L**	**F**	**A**	**W**	**D**	**L**	**F**	**A**	**Pts**
1	Ipswich	36	18	0	0	853	550	9	1	8	702	702	55
2	Belle Vue	36	15	1	2	833	570	8	1	9	682	719	48
3	Exeter	36	18	0	0	792	607	5	2	11	668	731	48
4	Coventry	36	18	0	0	829.5	573.5	3	2	13	616.5	784.5	44
5	Swindon	36	15	3	0	828	574	4	1	13	634	769	42
6	Reading	36	14	2	2	795	609	5	1	12	682	716	41
7	Hackney	36	16	0	2	761	636	4	0	14	631	768	40
8	Newport	36	18	0	0	841.5	559.5	1	1	16	595	807	39
9	Cradley Heath	36	16	1	1	772	631	3	0	15	625	777	39
10	Poole	36	15	0	3	808	593	3	1	14	583	819	37
11	Wolverhampton	36	12	0	6	738	663	6	1	11	609	793	37
12	**HULL**	**36**	**14**	**0**	**4**	**797**	**602**	**4**	**0**	**14**	**672.5**	**729.5**	**36**
13	White City	36	13	1	4	794.5	609.5	3	2	13	643	758	35
14	Kings Lynn	36	14	2	2	798	602	2	1	15	628	773	35
15	Halifax	36	14	1	3	771.5	630.5	0	0	18	533	870	29
16	Wimbledon	36	11	2	5	756	645	1	1	16	604.5	798.5	27
17	Sheffield	36	13	1	4	745	658	0	0	18	576	825	27
18	Birmingham	36	7	0	11	658	741	0	0	18	538.5	862.5	14
19	Leicester	36	5	1	12	683	719	0	0	18	550	852	11

1976 Northern Trophy – Final Table

			Home					Away					
		M	**W**	**D**	**L**	**F**	**A**	**W**	**D**	**L**	**F**	**A**	**Pts**
1	Belle Vue	6	2	1	0	138	96	3	0	0	123	111	11
2	Sheffield	6	2	0	1	139	95	1	0	2	105	129	6
3	Halifax	6	2	0	1	117	117	0	2	1	101	133	6
4	**HULL**	**6**	**0**	**1**	**2**	**113**	**121**	**0**	**0**	**3**	**100**	**134**	**1**

The Northern Trophy was won by the team scoring the most race points

Final Averages (League and K.O. Cup matches)

											Max	
	M	**R**	**1st**	**2nd**	**3rd**	**Unp**	**Pts**	**BP**	**Tot**	**Avg**	**F**	**P**
Barry Briggs	34	136	58	51	17	10	293	11	304	8.94	1	1
Joe Owen	10	42	17	13	9	3	86	7	93	8.86	2	0
Egon Muller	8	32	14	11	2	6	66	4	70	8.75	0	0
Mitch Graham	38	149	47.5	48.5	24	29	263.5	16	279.5	7.50	3	0
Bobby Beaton	36	152	43	49	37	24	264	23	287	7.55	0	0
Frank Auffret	37	145	17	33.5	57.5	52	175.5	48	223.5	6.17	0	0
Mike Curoso	33	116	14	23	48	31	136	41	177	6.10	0	0
Graham Drury	37	134	12	35	48	39	154	43	197	5.88	0	1
Tom Owen	6	27	2	8	10	7	32	5	37	5.48	0	0
Brian Havelock	2	9	4	0	1	4	13	1	14	6.22	0	0
Phil Michelides	2	7	0	2	2	3	6	0	6	3.43	0	0
Ron Henderson	2	8	0	1	0	7	2	0	2	1.00	0	0
Kaz Adamczak	1	2	0	0	0	2	0	0	0	0.00	0	0

	M	R	1st	2nd	3rd	Unp	Pts	BP	Tot	Avg	Max F	Max P
Also Rode												
Ray Bales	1	4	0	3	0	1	6	1	7	7.00	0	0
Geoff Bouchard	1	5	1	0	2	2	5	1	6	4.80	0	0
Graeme Dawson	1	4	1	0	2	1	5	0	5	5.00	0	0
Colin Farquharson	1	3	0	0	1	2	1	1	2	2.67	0	0
Dave Gooderham	1	3	0	1	2	0	4	2	6	8.00	0	0
Brian Havelock	1	4	0	0	2	2	2	1	3	3.00	0	0
Kevin Holden	1	3	0	2	0	1	4	0	4	5.33	0	0
Craig Pendlebury	2	7	0	2	3	2	7	2	9	5.14	0	0
Brendan Shilleto	1	2	0	0	1	1	1	1	2	4.00	0	0
Paul Tyrer	1	3	1	2	0	0	7	2	9	12.00	0	0
Doug Wyer	1	5	3	2	0	0	13	0	13	10.40	0	0

1977 – British League

The team that took to the track for the start of the 1977 season was largely the same that represented Vikings in 1976 with only a couple of exceptions, although they were significant. Hull were not able to persuade Barry Briggs to delay his retirement from league racing for just one more year, neither did they get near a deal to bring Egon Muller back for a longer stint in the British League. To partially compensate, Joe Owen decided to move up to top-flight racing full-time. Bobby Beaton, who was given the captaincy in succession to Barry Briggs, Mitch Graham, Frank Auffret, Graham Drury and Mike Curoso, who had just won a big meeting staged at the Houston Astrodome all returned for another term and local junior Phil Kynman was given the No. 8 slot and loaned to Newcastle. Hull were given dispensation to use Rider Replacement in the absence of Muller.

As a result of certain complaints regarding the Boulevard track in 1976, considerable work was carried out over the winter months. New drainage was installed, and a complete new surface was laid. Much of this work was done by Mitch Graham.

The season opened up as usual with the Northern Trophy, and Hull broke new ground on two counts. They actually managed to get in the win column; in fact, two home matches were won, and also finished third out of four, Halifax occupying the cellar spot. The away match at Belle Vue was not raced owing to adverse weather. The opening night saw a 51-27 win over Halifax with Tom Owen, deputising for not-yet-arrived Mike Curoso, scoring 11 points and Graham Drury showing signs of the form which would produce his best season in the sport with a 9-point return. Curoso arrived back in the UK the following week, turning up at the Boulevard midway through the Sheffield match, his two Rider Replacement wins from the No. 8 berth helping Hull to a 46-32 victory.

Vikings finished one point behind Sheffield in third place in a Good Friday Triangular Tournament at Belle Vue, and three days later on Easter Monday morning were trounced 54-24 at White City with Bobby Beaton's 9 points the only serious resistance.

1977 programme cover.

The lack of top-end strength was causing problems, but Hull found a way round it the following Wednesday when Graham Drury rattled in a 12-point maximum from the reserve berth in the 44-33 defeat of Coventry. Joe Owen, not a natural gater, was finding it difficult to adjust to top-flight racing, particularly in the No. 1 race jacket, but was battling to find his feet. It was the Drury-Beaton duo who kept the score down to 35-43 at Leicester, but they could not prevent the first home defeat of the season on 20 April when Belle Vue won 42-36, preventing Hull from posting a 100% home record in the Northern Trophy. Machine problems for Mike Curoso and Mitch Graham reduced Vikings to four effective riders.

Vikings fans were saddened to learn of the death of former rider Josef Angermuller, who was killed in a track crash in Italy on 24 April. It was a truly tragic few days for speedway as Poole's Kevin Holden was fatally injured three days later.

The Boulevard misery continued as King's Lynn won 40-38 on 27 April, Vikings surrendering an 8-point lead. Tracking only six riders, and lacking a third heat-leader was leaving no margin for error and with Mitch Graham and Frank Auffret having poor spells, Vikings were bound to struggle. This meeting featured a three-heat Junior match against King's Lynn, Phil Kynman top scoring for the young Vikings, who also included Nigel Crabtree, taking his first steps in the sport. The Teesside-based racer bounced back with a 12-point score in an otherwise dismal 24-53 reverse at Sheffield, mechanical problems preventing Joe Owen from troubling the scorers. The smiles returned on 4 May when a sparkling 14-point return from Mike Curoso helped to beat depleted Wimbledon. Colin Richardson, father of current rider Lee, top-scored for the Dons.

Hull Vikings 1977 – Left to right: Phil Kynman, Ian Thomas (co-promoter), Frank Auffret, Graham Drury, Joe Owen, Brian Larner (co-promoter), Mitch Graham, Mike Curoso. On machine – Bobby Beaton.

Vikings then began their defence of the Inter-Divisional Knock-Out Cup with a trip to their 1976 semi-final victims Workington. This hurdle was comfortably negotiated 50-28 although Workington threatened to pull out of the meeting when the referee changed his decision to exclude Frank Auffret in heat 2 for rearing and interfering with Comets' Des Wilson out of the gate. The matter was resolved when the referee reverted to his original decision.

The following night Vikings lost 30-48 on League business at the Shay, and then squeaked home against Leicester courtesy of a heat 13 5-1 from Graham Drury and Bobby Beaton. These two scored 27 of Hull's 41 points. Tom Owen was drafted in the following week against Birmingham as Rider Replacement was cancelled, both teams having riders missing. The Brummies were despatched 51-27 in a meeting where Joe Owen shaved 0.2 seconds off Scott Autrey's three-year-old track record.

On 24 May (a Tuesday to avoid a clash with soccer's European Cup final which featured Liverpool) Hull staged the last in a five-match England v. Rest of the World Test series. Although the Rest of the World had a winning 3-1 lead in the series, a close and exciting match ensued which swung both ways before England ran out winners 55-53. Joe Owen's track record lasted just one week, Dave Jessup setting a new time of 70.8 seconds in heat 2. Current Viking Bobby Beaton scored 4, and former Vikings Barry Briggs and Egon Muller scored 1 and 2 points respectively for the Rest of the World side.

Returning to the League, Vikings were edged out 39-38 at Wolverhampton, former Viking Jim McMillan winning a last-heat decider. A welcome return to form for Mitch

Graham with a 9-point return helped to defeat Halifax 48-30. It was reported that Mitch was concerned about his fitness and had fixed up some training sessions at a local boxing club! Vikings then paid their first visit to Bristol's newly opened Eastville track. A 27-51 defeat ensued, Vikings not even producing a heat winner. Joe Owen showed a liking for the track, though; despite arriving late due to traffic delays he scored 12 points from six races.

Vikings drew Cradley Heath in the K.O. Cup and for the first time in the Boulevard era progressed beyond the first stage. Cradley were without Anders Michanek and Bernie Persson for both matches; this contributed to their 46-32 defeat at the Boulevard. Tom Owen stood in for Mike Curoso who injured his hand at a meeting in Germany and scored 10. Curoso was back for the second leg three days later and helped to restrict Cradley to a 42-36 win. A 42-36 defeat at Reading presaged a stormy Boulevard clash with Ipswich on 15 June. The Witches management complained about the height of the fence and the tapes, the width of the track and the general condition of the circuit. Ipswich then blamed track conditions for Kevin Jolly being excluded in heat 6 for unfair riding. Racing was then delayed for 15 minutes while both

Internationales

Speedway-Rennen

am 2. 7. 1977 in Landshut-Ellermühle

als Vergleichskampf
zwischen
engl. 1. Divisionsmannschaft
Hull
und der Bundesligamannschaft
des AC-Landshut

Veranstalter: Automobil-Club Landshut im ADAC
Genehmigt von der OMK am 31. 5. 1977
unter Reg.-Nr. 247/77 – FIM Reg.-Nr. PT 7 – 1/55

Programme from Vikings' match in Germany.

managements and the referee were involved in a heated mid-track argument. The situation appeared to have been sorted out until the start of the second half when the Ipswich team manager together with two riders started measuring the track. This nearly inflamed the crowd to come over the fence, but fortunately an ugly scene was averted. The 26 points from Drury and Beaton led to a 44-34 Vikings win.

Seven days later White City won a last-heat decider to complete the double over Hull on their way to the title. This meeting also had incident as before heat 9, Graham Drury and Mike Curoso came to blows on track following an argument over gate positions. Both riders were severely reprimanded and were split as a pairing.

In the third of a run of consecutive home matches, Vikings advanced to the semi-final of the Inter-Divisional Knock-Out Cup with a 48-30 defeat of Bristol, 17 points from Bobby Beaton and a paid maximum from Frank Auffret the major contributors. On 2 July Hull ventured abroad for only the second time, taking on German side Landshut. Barry Briggs guested for Vikings who led throughout and ran out winners 42-36. Back home, Reading inflicted the biggest home defeat since Hull joined the top flight with a 47-31 success. Graham Drury suffered a seized motor in his first race, finished last on a borrowed machine second time out and then withdrew from the meeting. The defeat would have been worse but for Joe Owen returning 13 points, his best score of the season so far. Frank Auffret suffered a second-half injury which caused him to miss three matches.

The Yorkshire Cup first leg at Halifax was lost 33-45, Mitch Graham scoring 15 of Hull's points on what would be his home track before the season was out. Two depleted teams met at the Boulevard on 13 July with Hull, missing Frank Auffret and with Mike Curoso on World Championship duty defeating Bristol 42-36, Joe Owen scoring 13 points. Joe also contributed 11 in a 26-52 reverse at King's Lynn.

The fourth YTV Trophy was staged on 20 July, and was won by Ole Olsen with an immaculate 15-point maximum. For the Vikings, Graham Drury scored 8, Bobby Beaton managed 7, Joe Owen 4, Frank Auffret 1 and Mitch Graham failed to score.

An uneasy season-long relationship between the Hull management and Mitch Graham came to a head in early August when the rider did not ride in the league match at Exeter. He stated that he did not have a machine available, the management provided one but he still refused to ride. Hull fined him £100, withdrew a threat to ban him from taking guest bookings, and accepted a transfer request from the rider. Bobby Beaton also missed the Exeter match, which was lost 25-53, breaking down en route.

Mitch Graham was back in the side while on the transfer list, and scored 7 points in Hull's 49-29 defeat of Bristol in their Knock-Out Cup tie, a 15-point maximum from Phil Crump the Bulldogs' best. The lead was not to prove enough, as two days later Bristol took the second leg 52-26. Joe Owen's 11 points again demonstrated his liking for the Eastville circuit but he received little support. A 15-point maximum from Bobby Beaton helped Hull to two points at Birmingham, two comfortable home wins over Wolverhampton and Sheffield followed, and on 22 August Joe Owen returned to Newcastle with the Vikings for a challenge match. A close match fell Vikings' way 41-37, honours being even between Joe and brother Tom with one win over each other. A third visit to Bristol was undertaken on 26 August, this time for league points which

Joe Owen in action.

were lost 31-47. Unsurprisingly, Eastville track specialist Joe Owen topped Vikings' score chart with 11, Graham Drury missing this meeting and the following night's clash at Swindon with an injury. He returned for the Bank Holiday Monday morning match with Poole which was celebrated as the 200th meeting at the Boulevard. Vikings cruised to a 47-31 win with a superb 15-point maximum from Bobby Beaton leading the way.

The return match on the South Coast two days later was lost, as was the next home match against Belle Vue. An act of generosity on the part of the Hull management in allowing the Aces to use rider replacement for Peter Collins despite not having a No. 8 backfired, the seven points earned from the facility deciding the outcome.

The Viking pair of Graham Drury and Bobby Beaton took part in the British League Pairs semi-final at Hackney on September 9 and finished last with 7 points owing to Bobby Beaton sustaining a back injury in his second race, which kept him out for three league matches. Although a heavy defeat ensued at Coventry where Graham Drury retired in his first race and took no further part, the Beaton-less team beat Swindon with a double-figure score from reserve Frank Auffret, and amazingly won at Belle Vue, taking advantage of mechanical problems suffered by the Aces to record their first ever win at Hyde Road.

1977 was Graham Drury's best ever season.

Hull staged their round of the Grand Prix on 21 September which was won by Ole Olsen with Graham Drury and Bobby Beaton taking the other rostrum places. Joe Owen finished with 9 points but was the only rider to defeat Olsen.

Ivan Mauger-led Exeter proved too strong and beat Hull 42-36 on 28 September, Drury and Beaton scoring 26 of Hull's points, and then followed three consecutives matches against Cradley Heath. The teams exchanged home wins in the league before the Heathens spoiled Hull's chance of retaining the Inter-Divisional Knock-Out Cup with a narrow 41-37 win at Dudley Wood. Young Phil Kynman scored 8 points from reserve in this match. By now Mitch Graham had agreed to move to Halifax for 1978, but no longer wished to race for Hull and guested for Halifax on the same night his registered team were riding at Cradley Heath!

A further Cup disappointment came when Halifax (minus the aforementioned Mitch Graham) restricted Vikings to a 43-35 win and thus took the Yorkshire Cup back. The league campaign came to an end with a 44-34 defeat at Ipswich, Foxhall specialist Tom Owen leading the way with 13 points, and the Boulevard curtain was drawn with a 50-28 challenge success over champions White City. The team then took part in a benefit meeting at Glasgow for Tiger and former Viking Grahame Dawson who had suffered career-ending head injuries earlier in the season. Happily, Graham was well enough to be able to attend the meeting.

On the individual front, both Graham Drury and Bobby Beaton reached the World Championship British semi-final at Birmingham scoring 3 and 8 points respectively. Mike Curoso scored 9 in the USA final. Bobby Beaton again rode for Scotand in the World Team Cup recording 4 points in the Reading qualifier, also gaining a Test cap for the Rest of the World at the Boulevard. No Hull rider progressed beyond the qualifying rounds of the Grand Prix.

Graham Drury was Hull's representative at Belle Vue's BLRC, managing 2 points, while nearer to home he was runner up in the Northern Riders' final at Sheffield, with Bobby Beaton claiming third place.

All in all, not the most memorable season in the Vikings' short history. Too often Graham Drury and Bobby Beaton were on their own with insufficient support. For Drury it was to be his best-ever season and the Briggs influence from 1976 was clear. Bobby Beaton put half a point on his average, and Joe Owen found the top flight tough at times. The ongoing problems with Mitch Graham caused his average to plummet, he really should have been the missing heat leader which would have allowed Joe Owen to settle in to the team in a less pressurized situation. Another disappointment was Mike Curoso who failed to live up to his 1976 promise and indicated late in the year that he would like a move for 1978, stating that he would like to be southern-based, and closer to his fellow American riders. Frank Auffret was steady and Tom Owen was a more than able stand-in. Local boy Phil Kynman showed some promise in his few outings. The priority for 1978 was a heat leader, a problem that would be solved in spectacular fashion.

Transfer-listed Mitch Graham had four seasons with Hull.

1977 British League – Final Table

		M	Home W	Home D	Home L	Home F	Home A	Away W	Away D	Away L	Away F	Away A	Pts
1	White City	36	16	0	2	840	558	11	1	6	703	700	55
2	Exeter	36	17	0	1	913	489	8	3	7	712	689	53
3	Reading	36	16	2	0	807	597	9	1	8	675	726	53
4	Ipswich	36	18	0	0	838	564	7	1	10	669	729	51
5	Belle Vue	36	12	2	4	782.5	619.5	7	1	10	691	711	41
6	Kings Lynn	36	14	1	3	789	611	5	1	12	659	739	40
7	Cradley Heath	36	13	0	5	792.5	602.5	7	0	11	645	755	40
8	Coventry	36	16	1	1	837	561	3	0	15	617.5	779.5	39
9	Wimbledon	36	16	1	1	789	612	1	1	16	624	775	36
10	Poole	36	14	1	3	802	595	3	1	14	580	821	36
11	Swindon	36	16	1	1	832.5	569.5	1	0	17	591	810	35
12	Bristol	36	16	0	2	817	583	1	0	17	564	834	34
13	Sheffield	36	15	2	1	805.5	595.5	1	0	17	569	835	34
14	**HULL**	**36**	**13**	**0**	**5**	**776**	**627**	**2**	**0**	**16**	**573.5**	**827.5**	**30**
15	Wolverhampton	36	10	0	8	709	689	4	0	14	625	779	28
16	Hackney	36	13	0	5	733.5	659.5	0	1	17	523	878	27
17	Halifax	36	12	0	6	777	625	0	0	18	511	879	24
18	Birmingham	36	8	0	10	675	725	0	0	18	545	856	16
19	Leicester	36	6	0	12	678	723	0	0	18	528.5	807.5	12

1977 Northern Trophy – Final Table

		M	Home W	Home D	Home L	Home F	Home A	Away W	Away D	Away L	Away F	Away A	Pts
1	Belle Vue	4	1	0	0	52	26	3	0	0	131	103	8
2	Sheffield	5	2	0	1	134	98	1	0	1	73	83	6
3	**HULL**	**5**	**2**	**0**	**1**	**133**	**101**	**0**	**0**	**2**	**50**	**104**	**4**
4	Halifax	6	1	0	2	121	112	0	0	3	83	150	2

The Northern Trophy was won by the team scoring the most race points

As the competition was not completed, Belle Vue were awarded the trophy, as it was decided that they would have ended with the most race points with two home matches left unraced.

Final Averages (League and K.O. Cup matches)

	M	R	1st	2nd	3rd	Unp	Pts	BP	Tot	Avg	Max F	Max P
Graham Drury	38	189	67	71	34	17	377	31	408	8.63	2	2
Bobby Beaton	36	184	58	70	32.5	23.5	346.5	22	368.5	8.01	2	2
Joe Owen	40	190	31	68	52	39	281	33	314	6.61	0	0
Tom Owen	11	44	6	12	19	7	61	5	66	6.00	0	0
Mike Curoso	33	125	14	27	43	41	139	31	170	5.44	0	0
Frank Auffret	38	140	13	24	52	51	139	44	183	5.23	0	0
Mitch Graham	37	132	16	24	34	58	130	26	156	4.73	0	1
Phil Kynman	9	21	0	2	7	12	11	5	16	3.05	0	0
Neil Coddington	1	1	0	0	0	1	0	0	0	0.00	0	0

	M	R	1st	2nd	3rd	Unp	Pts	BP	Tot	Avg	Max F	Max P
Also Rode												
Ian Cartwright	1	6	3	1	0	2	11	0	11	7.33	0	0
Paul Clements	1	3	0	0	1	2	1	0	1	1.33	0	0
Trevor Geer	1	4	0	0	2	2	2	1	3	3.00	0	0
Vic Harding	1	5	0	1	2	2	4	1	5	4.00	0	0
Alan Johns	1	3	0	1	0	2	2	1	3	4.00	0	0
Craig Pendlebury	1	4	0	0	2	2	2	0	2	2.00	0	0

1978 – British League

There were not too many changes in the Vikings' line-up in 1978 from 1977, but what changes there were were about as big as they get. The best New Year present ever came Hull's way when World Champion Ivan Mauger signed on the dotted line for a record £12,000 transfer fee from Exeter.

Less significant at the time was the acquisition of seventeen-year-old Californian Kelly Moran, who was spotted by Ian Thomas racing at Ascot Park. Exciting on-track and charismatic off-track, Vikings fans would come to love Kelly over the next two seasons.

Hull Vikings 1978 – Left to right: Phil Kynman, Bobby Beaton, Joe Owen, Graham Drury, Frank Auffret. On machine – Ivan Mauger. Kneeling – Kelly Moran.

Left: *1978 programme cover.*
Right: *Record signing and all-time great Ivan Mauger.*

From 1977, Bobby Beaton, Joe Owen, Frank Auffret and Graham Drury remained, while local youngster Phil Kynman was given his chance in the reserve berth, a sponsorship from a local store providing him with a brand-new machine. Hull had expected to have Halifax's Henny Kroeze in the line-up, but the deal fell through when the Dutchman was offered the managership of a garage in Holland. On the management side, Ellesmere Port co-promoter Ernie Park joined the Boulevard management team.

The traditional Northern Trophy season opener started with the traditional home defeat. Over 6,000 packed the Boulevard to see Ivan Mauger make a perfect debut with a 15-point maximum, but it was not enough to prevent Halifax holding sway 42-36. Mauger remained unbeaten through a wet 33-45 defeat in the return at the Shay, and did not suffer defeat until his twelfth race for Hull, when Sheffield's Reg Wilson lowered his colours, in a hotly contested derby which produced Vikings' first win. The return at Owlerton was lost, and two days later Hull held Belle Vue to a 40-38 margin, in a match where Kelly Moran started to show the signs of what a performer he would become. The home fixture with the Aces was a big disappointment, astute use of tactical substitutes by team manager Eric Boocock inspiring the Hyde Road side to pull back a 12-point deficit to run out 6-point victors.

Tragedy struck early in the season, when Hull junior Chris Prime, racing at Newcastle, crashed and was fatally injured. The league campaign swung into action in the best way possible with an away win at Hackney, Vikings sneaking home by two points against a Hawks side virtually down to five riders with injuries to Keith White and Bo Petersen. The following Wednesday, Bristol were swept aside 48-30, with a full house for Mauger and Joe Owen and reserve Phil Kynman being paid for the lot.

Normal service in the Knock-Out Cup was resumed against King's Lynn, a 10-point lead being frittered away, the Boulevard leg finishing level, with Ivan Mauger posting an uncharacteristic 6 points and Kelly Moran top-scoring with 7. Although Hull never led in the return in Norfolk, they gave the Stars a scare in the finish, only losing on aggregate by two points.

Winning ways were resumed as champions White City were despatched 47-31, Belle Vue's Alan Wilkinson proving an able deputy for Ivan Mauger who was on long-track duty. Next Vikings travelled to Birmingham and lost narrowly 38-40, two incidents involving Mauger having an influence on the result. In heat 5, he was excluded for breaking the tapes, but when it was discovered that the tapes were not properly elasticated, he was reinstated and won the race. Then in heat 11, he was excluded for delaying the start and after much protest the match resumed and the chance of what could have been a match winning 5-1 from Mauger and Moran was lost. The following night, however, Mauger was back to his maximum best in a 46-32 win over Cradley Heath, for whom Bruce Penhall scored 13 on his Boulevard debut.

Eight days later in a break from league action, the Boulevard staged qualifying rounds for the World Championship and Grand Prix which had been combined into one meeting. Ivan Mauger cruised to victory, after four straight wins he only needed one point from his last ride, and tucked in behind Bobby Beaton for two. Bobby with 13 and Graham Drury with 12 points completed a Vikings 1-2-3 of the rostrum places.

Following a defeat at Belle Vue, Hull took revenge for their Knock-Out Cup defeat by hammering King's Lynn 52-26, Mauger producing the maximum and Kelly Moran producing the thrills. The match proved to be Phil Kynman's last match for the club, the rider stating that he had retired and was considering moving to America. This could not have worked out as late in the year Phil agreed terms with National League Berwick for 1979.

National League Eastbourne hosted Vikings in the first round of the Inter-League Cup. The British League club comfortably won 45-32 despite an uncharacteristic 2-point return from Ivan Mauger, who was troubled with machine problems. Home wins over Reading and Wimbledon followed with a defeat at Ipswich sandwiched in between. Vikings might have pushed the Witches closer had Kelly Moran not broken down on the way to Foxhall Heath. Joe Owen was producing some stunning form both home and away, and returned a full maximum in a 46-32 win over a Barry Briggs Select in a Charity Challenge staged for the benefit of the Variety Club of Great Britain's Sunshine Coaches. The meeting raised over £3,000 for the charity.

Champions-to-be Coventry were demolished 55-22 in a match where Ivan Mauger reduced the track record to 70.4 seconds. Kelly Moran scored a spectacular best-yet 15 points in a defeat at Wimbledon, and the league match at Reading was drawn, but for a mechanically troubled zero return for Bobby Beaton Vikings would have emerged with both points.

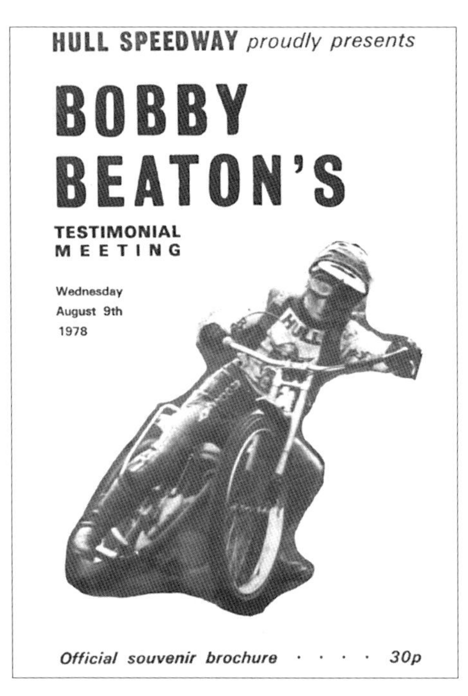

Left: *Programme from Bobby Beaton's testimonial.*
Right: *Long-serving Boulevard favourite Frank Auffret.*

The match with Hackney on 28 June was a routine 52-26 home win, but in the second half Joe Owen crashed heavily and was taken to hospital with multiple injuries, including a punctured lung, a broken arm and a broken nose. Joe was very close to losing his life, and his condition was critical for some days. Happily the threat to his life passed and he started the long road to recovery.

The annual Yorkshire TV Trophy was staged the following week and was surprisingly won by Exeter's Vaclav Verner in a disappointing meeting. The highest-placed Viking was fourth-placed Frank Auffret with 11 points. Ivan Mauger was out of sorts and could only manage a single point. Resuming league action, Vikings drew at Woverhampton after leading the match by 6 points halfway through, and then lost 33-45 at Halifax. Kelly Moran was beginning to emerge as a quality performer, many of his points coming from the back in exciting fashion. Frank Auffret scored what was to be his only full maximum in Hull colours in the win over Leicester, and then, once again Belle Vue brought the rain with them to the Boulevard. Peter Collins pulled out after one ride and left his teammates on the wrong end of a 54-24 thrashing. Hull then won two away matches in a row, at Swindon and White City and squeezed home 41-37 against Halifax, before losing disappointingly at Coventry in a match that was televised in the Midlands.

On 9 August, Hull staged a testimonial meeting for Bobby Beaton, to honour his ten years in the sport. The fourth-year Viking top scored as Vikings beat an All Stars team 48-30. Three days later a solid display ensured victory at King's Lynn, and on 16 August the Boulevard staged the fourth in a five-match England v. Australasia Test series. The

England side was decimated owing to the rescheduling of the postponed British final at Coventry for the same night, and unsurprisingly went down to a heavy 36-70 defeat, the Lions' top-scorer being reserve Tom Owen with 10 points.

At this point, Hull were third in the league, six points behind leaders Belle Vue with a match in hand, certainly it was looking like it would be the best finishing place in club history, but for the second time in the season serious injury hit the team. After Sheffield were sent packing 49-29, Vikings visited Hackney in the Inter-League Cup and a victory looked on the cards until a horrific heat 8 crash cost Hull the services of Kelly Moran for the rest of the season. Kelly's front wheel lifted on the pits bend and Hackney's Bobby McNeill crashed into him, with Viking guest Robbie Gardner unable to avoid the carnage. Kelly's partner Frank Auffret laid his machine down to avoid further problems, Robbie Gardner suffered bruising after being extracted from the centre green flowerbeds, and Bobby McNeill recovered sufficiently to take part in the rerun, but Kelly came off far the worst. He was taken to hospital with a broken arm and leg, hip, shoulder and back injuries and a fractured pelvis. He was to have several weeks in traction as part of the recovery process.

The five-man Vikings did exceptionally well to only lose the match by four points, and unsurprisingly were heavily defeated at Cradley Heath the following night. Poole arrived for their annual August Bank Holiday visit to the Boulevard, this time with an 11am start, both sides tracking only six riders as the Pirates were without Neil Middleditch. Vikings squeezed home 41-37, with Ivan Mauger rattling in another maximum, but another full house from the Kiwi couldn't prevent a 30-48 reverse in the return at Wimborne Road two days later. The 1937 World Champion Jack Milne attended this meeting.

Visits from Ipswich always seemed to be accompanied by controversy, and this time was no exception. The fault lay with the referee who initially credited Bobby Beaton with a win in heat 7, despite the Scot losing his silencer during the race. It was only after Ivan Mauger intervened that the result was corrected, and an Ipswich walkout was averted. Vikings still held third place, which was maintained with a 48-30 success over Wolverhampton, Ivan Mauger maintaining his stunning form with a 15-point maximum, sound back-up coming from Tom Owen who posted a reserve's paid maximum.

A depleted-looking side failed to give Mauger enough back-up to avoid a loss at Bristol, and a similar story at Leicester put paid to any lingering hopes of winning the title. Yet another full house from the New Zealander against his old club Exeter inspired another win, and the league programme approached the end with defeat in a three-man show at Sheffield and a 49-29 win over Swindon which ensured a 100 per cent home league record was achieved for the first time in club history.

Vikings won the Yorkshire Cup for only the second time, defeating Halifax 84-72, comfortably overturning a four-point first-leg deficit with a 12 paid 14 return from Frank Auffret at the Boulevard stealing the show. The final league match at Exeter was lost 22-56 with the Vikings side unrecognisable, five guests being used to stand in for absentees.

Easily the best season resulted in a third-place league finish which but for injuries to Joe Owen and Kelly Moran could have been even better. Ivan Mauger led the side by example, maintaining an average of just under ten, but even he would concede that Kelly Moran was Mr Excitement at the Boulevard in his debut season with his spectacular dashes from the back. Joe Owen was on top form prior to his injury. Graham Drury and Bobby Beaton dropped their averages from 1977 while Frank Auffret's average moved almost a point in the other direction. Phil Kynman had made a steady start before his untimely retirement, and Tom Owen proved a solid stand-in when injuries struck.

Away from team events, in the World Championship Ivan Mauger was unable to retain his World Title with an 8-point return at Wembley. Apart from Bobby Beaton who reached the British semi-final, no other Viking survived the qualifying rounds. A 12-point return from the Kiwi helped his country achieve a runners-up placing in the World Pairs final at Katowice, while he managed fourth place in the World Long Track Championship.

Both Bobby Beaton and Ivan Mauger qualified for the White City-staged Grand Prix final, neither enjoying a distinguished meeting. Ivan represented Vikings in the BLRC at his old track Belle Vue, but it wasn't his night, only scoring five points. Locally, Ivan finished third in the Sheffield-staged Northern Riders Championship.

Typically spectacular action from Kelly Moran.

1978 British League – Final Table

			Home					Away					
		M	W	D	L	F	A	W	D	L	F	A	Pts
1	Coventry	36	18	0	0	840	560	9	0	9	702	697	54
2	Belle Vue	36	16	0	2	809	595	10	0	8	682.5	720.5	52
3	**HULL**	**36**	**18**	**0**	**0**	**867**	**533**	**4**	**2**	**12**	**610**	**792**	**46**
4	Wimbledon	36	16	0	2	826	572	6	1	11	676	728	45
5	Cradley Heath	36	17	0	1	829	573	4	1	13	648	749	43
6	Ipswich	36	17	0	1	816	583	4	1	13	655	747	43
7	Exeter	36	17	0	1	902	501	3	1	14	630	768	41
8	Sheffield	36	17	1	0	793.5	608.5	2	1	15	573	831	40
9	Bristol	36	17	0	1	823	579	2	0	16	609	788	38
10	Poole	36	15	1	2	804	599	2	2	14	622	780	37
11	Leicester	36	15	0	3	781	621	2	0	16	587	813	34
12	Halifax	36	14	1	3	810.5	589.5	0	2	16	561	842	31
13	Kings Lynn	36	12	2	4	786	616	2	0	16	605	796	30
14	Reading	36	11	2	5	739	659	2	1	15	599	803	29
15	White City	36	9	2	7	709	686	3	1	14	610.5	788.5	27
16	Swindon	36	11	2	5	714	688	1	1	16	541	856	27
17	Wolverhampton	36	10	1	7	707	693	1	0	17	605	798	23
18	Birmingham	36	11	1	6	743	660	0	0	18	537	865	23
19	Hackney	36	9	1	8	724	677	1	0	17	540	861	21

1978 Northern Trophy – Final Table

Home					Away								
		M	W	D	L	F	A	W	D	L	F	A	Pts
1	Belle Vue	6	3	0	0	126	107	2	0	1	120	114	10
2	Halifax	6	3	0	0	131	103	1	0	2	110	123	8
3	Sheffield	6	2	0	1	127	106	0	0	3	103	131	4
4	**HULL**	**6**	**1**	**0**	**2**	**114**	**120**	**0**	**0**	**3**	**103**	**131**	**2**

The Northern Trophy was won by the team scoring the most race points

Final Averages (League and K O Cup matches)

											Max	
	M	R	1st	2nd	3rd	Unp	Pts	BP	Tot	Avg	F	P
Ivan Mauger	32	145	89	31	14	11	343	11	354	9.77	8	2
Joe Owen	16	64	19	29	10	6	125	20	145	9.06	0	3
Bobby Beaton	37	157	47	41	37	32	260	25	285	7.26	1	0
Kelly Moran	26	109	23	27	31	28	154	37	191	7.01	0	0
Tom Owen	25	102	16	37	29	20	151	21	172	6.75	0	0
Robbie Blackadder	2	6	1	2	1	2	8	2	10	6.67	0	0
Graham Drury	37	155	24	59	40	32	230	27	257	6.63	0	0
Frank Auffret	38	138	19	30	59	30	176	48	224	6.49	1	0
Phil Kynman	9	27	4	5	7	11	29	5	34	5.04	0	0
Rod Hunter	8	24	0	2	6	16	10	4	14	2.33	0	0

	M	R	1st	2nd	3rd	Unp	Pts	BP	Tot	Avg	Max F	Max P
Also Rode												
Martin Ashby	1	5	1	1	3	0	8	3	11	8.80	0	0
John Barker	1	2	0	0	0	2	0	0	0	0.00	0	0
Mike Bowden	1	3	0	0	0	3	0	0	0	0.00	0	0
Phil Collins	2	9	0	3	4	2	10	4	14	6.22	0	0
Phil Crump	1	5	2	1	1	1	9	1	10	8.00	0	0
Mike Davis	1	4	0	0	1	3	1	0	1	1.00	0	0
Pete Ellams	1	2	0	0	1	1	1	0	1	2.00	0	0
Ian Fletcher	1	3	0	0	0	3	0	0	0	0.00	0	0
Trevor Geer	1	5	1	1	3	0	8	0	8	6.40	0	0
John Jackson	2	7	0	1	2	4	4	2	6	3.43	0	0
Jim McMillan	1	5	0	2	1	2	5	1	6	4.80	0	0
Chris Morton	1	5	2	3	0	0	12	0	12	9.60	0	0
Mike Pither	1	3	0	0	0	3	0	0	0	0.00	0	0
Alan Wilkinson	1	4	2	2	0	0	10	0	10	10.00	0	0

1979 – British League

Following the successful 1978 season, the Vikings team for 1979 was largely unchanged. Happily, Joe Owen and Kelly Moran were pronounced fit and resumed their Boulevard careers. Phil Kynman did not return, opting to race in the National League with Berwick. Vikings continued to look across the Atlantic for talent and signed nineteen-year-old Californian Dennis Sigalos who had spent a season racing in Australia with former Viking Dave Mills. Initially though, Vikings were unable to track their full team in each match because of the 50-point rule and operated a squad system, bringing in a rider from sister track Newcastle as each Hull rider took a turn on the sideline.

Off track, a club sponsorship was secured with locally based Satra Motors, importers of Lada Cars, and the team became the Hull Lada Vikings. A note of sadness was the death after a period of illness of forty-nine-year-old co-promoter Ernie Park. His widow joined the board and became co-promoter.

The season got off to the customary start with a 36-42 Northern Trophy defeat by Halifax on Friday 30 March, after the match was rained off two days earlier. Vikings frittered away an 8-point lead, but Joe Owen and Kelly Moran both made an encouraging return from injury, and Dennis Sigalos scored 3 on his British debut, winning his first race. Graham Drury sat this match out, his stand-in Rod Hunter scoring 1 point. The following night, with Hunter again deputising, this time for Frank Auffret, Vikings pulled off a surprise 40-38 win at Belle Vue. A solid team performance earned the win with only five heat winners out of thirteen. This form was not, however carried over to the following Wednesday against Sheffield. With four heats to go Vikings found themselves 6 points adrift, but a brilliant piece of team riding from Ivan Mauger earned him a 5-1 with Frank Auffret, and two heats later the same pair took a 4-2, paving the way for Vikings to salvage a draw. Gating let Hull down with points having to be earned from the back.

1979 programme cover.

Seven days later Hull put in a much better performance, clinching a Northern Trophy double over Belle Vue helped by a perfect full house from the skipper and an exciting 10-point return from Kelly Moran. The league campaign then got underway with a visit to Eastbourne. With Ivan Mauger missing because of a Continental booking, it was no surprise that Vikings lost, but the 27-50 margin was disappointing. Dennis Sigalos, in reserve, showed a liking for the small American-style Arlington circuit with two heat wins, and the score belied the quality of racing which was excellent.

Next up at the Boulevard were champions Coventry, who were despatched 51-27 by a solid team show, led by yet another Mauger maximum. Especially heartening were the 11 and 8-point returns from Kelly Moran and Joe Owen, getting back into the swing of things returning from serious injury. Nobody could have predicted at this stage the circumstances that would surround the return league match at Brandon.

Vikings wrapped up their Northern Trophy programme with two away defeats, at Sheffield and Halifax. Joe Owen sat out the Owlerton meeting while Kelly Moran was 'rested' at the Shay. Ivan Mauger, never the most popular visitor to the Shay, recorded a duck from three races after being excluded from his first outing for delaying the start. Yet again Hull finished bottom of the Northern Trophy table.

A 10-point return for Ivan Mauger at his former track could not save Vikings from a second successive away defeat in the league, Graham Drury sitting out the 33-45

Hull Vikings 1979 – Back row, left to right: Ian Thomas (co-promoter), Graham Drury, Dennis Sigalos, Joe Owen, Frank Auffret, Brian Larner (co-promoter). Front row, left to right: Bobby Beaton, Ivan Mauger (on machine), Kelly Moran.

County Ground defeat. This was followed by a hard-earned 43-35 win over Wolverhampton, 32 of the points coming from Messrs Mauger, Moran and Owen. In this meeting the Vikings captain equalled his own track record of 70.4 seconds. Seven days later, in a break from team racing the Boulevard staged a qualifyng round of the World Championship/Grand Prix, which as in 1978 were combined into one. The home riders enjoyed a very successful evening with Bobby Beaton, Joe Owen and Kelly Moran scoring 13, 12 and 9 points respectively. None of them got near Ivan Mauger who not only won the meeting with a maximum, but this time broke the track record, setting a new best time of 70.2 seconds.

By the time next week's visitors King's Lynn arrived the Green Sheets had been issued, and Hull were able to field a full-strength side for the first time. In a sign of things to come the Stars were taken apart 56-22 with Michael Lee's 14 points providing the only resistance.

Four-Team Tournaments were very popular at this time and the British League launched a championship for all clubs using this format. Hull's qualifying group contained Halifax, Sheffield and Newcastle, with eight teams progressing from all the groups to semi-finals and a final staged in a 48-heat all-day meeting at Sheffield in June. Vikings' home round was first up and the home side could scarcely have got off to a better start with Michael Lohmann's heat-12 defeat of Bobby Beaton the only race not won by a home rider. Two days later Hull took on National League Glasgow in the Inter-

Divisional Knock-Out Cup and the trip to Blantyre produced a comfortable 50-28 win, with Ivan Mauger unbeaten and home hero Steve Lawson the only Tiger to beat Kelly Moran.

The second leg of the Four-Team Championship at Halifax was won by Sheffield. Hull's 22 points for third place kept them in the lead overall. A brief return to league action saw Vikings overcome Exeter 45-33 at the Boulevard. Falcons' Scott Autrey was the star of the show with a track-record-equalling win over Ivan Mauger in heat 1 on his way to a 15-point maximum. Back on the Four-Team trail at Sheffield, Vikings were again third on a rain-affected track and their overall lead was reduced to three points with only the Newcastle leg to go. After losing a fixture filler challenge at Cradley Heath, Vikings commenced their assault on the Knock-Out Cup with home and away matches with Yorkshire rivals Sheffield. A Wednesday Boulevard rain-off meant that the first leg was at Owlerton and it was a tight struggle with Ivan Mauger-less Hull restricting Sheffield to a 12-point advantage. The Boulevard leg was staged on the Friday, and Vikings, led by the skipper returning to the line-up after a back operation, were rampant and ran in 11 5-1s on the way to a record 81 points in the 18-heat formula being used for this competition.

The next match at the Boulevard was brought forward to Tuesday so that Ivan Mauger and Aces' Peter Collins, who were booked to ride in an international grass-track

The squad that won the Four-Team Championship Trophy. Back row, left to right: Brian Larner, Joe Owen, Graham Drury, Frank Auffret, Ian Thomas. Front row, left to right: Dennis Sigalos, Bobby Beaton.

meeting on the Isle of Man, could ride. Collins took the Boulevard best time down to a straight 70 seconds in defeating Mauger in heat 1, but Hull won the match more easily than the 42-36 scoreline suggests.

The final Four-Team qualifier at Brough Park turned into a comfortable Hull win, former-Diamond Joe Owen top scoring with 11. Vikings won the group with 131 points, 22 clear of second-place Halifax, booking their place in the big day at Sheffield thirteen days later. Before that, Vikings had three league matches, the first of which against Birmingham at the Boulevard was again a Tuesday match as Ivan Mauger, Kelly Moran and Dennis Sigalos had to report for practice on Wednesday for the World Team Cup Inter-Continental final staged in Sweden. A solid display restricted the visitors to 20 points and the action then moved on to the Shay. Two controversial incidents threatened to cost Hull the match. The first one was in heat 11 when Ivan Mauger was excluded for delaying the start. This levelled the scores. A Kelly Moran retirement in heat 12 left Vikings needing a 5-1 to win. Bobby Beaton and Ivan Mauger duly led the vital race when Halifax captain Ian Cartwright fell while trying to pass Ivan Mauger near the end of the third lap. Despite Halifax protests, the referee ruled that when the red lights came on to stop the race the three remaining riders were on the last lap and the race was awarded as a 5-1, thus giving Hull the narrowest of wins.

Vikings then comfortably defeated Reading although Kelly Moran took a tumble and this meant that with Ivan Mauger unavailable, the Four-Team Championships would have to be tackled without the top two riders. This was not as bad a blow as it sounds as several big names did not put in an appearance following the World Pairs final, staged the previous day at Vojens. However, Vikings squeezed through a tight semi-final with Bobby Beaton scoring 10 points and Frank Auffret contributing 5 points from reserve. Hull faced Exeter, Cradley Heath and Hackney in the final and it was the Vikings who showed the most appetite for the fray when the forecasted rain finally arrived. Vikings were never headed with Bobby Beaton and rookie Dennis Sigalos both scoring maximums, Frank Auffret again being astutely used as reserve, contributing 6 points. It was only Vikings second national cup win, following 1976's Inter-Divisional Knock-Out Cup success.

With no time to rest, Hull resumed their title challenge with a visit to Birmingham. In a superb meeting, Vikings, still without Kelly Moran, looked dead and buried 8 points adrift with only three heats to go. A fantastic revival was led by the skipper who rode in all three races. He teamed up with Bobby Beaton for a 5-1, then with Graham Drury for a 4-2 which left Hull, as at Halifax, needing a last-heat 5-1 to win which again together with Bobby Beaton was delivered. Vikings' title challenge was now beginning to be taken seriously. Next up at the Boulevard were Hackney. Three Vikings ran unbeaten, including Kelly Moran, returning early from injury against doctor's orders as the Hawks were swept aside 56-22.

The good run came to an end with a 33-42 defeat at Ipswich in a match Hull led until halfway. Vikings' management were not happy about the state of the Foxhall circuit, although it must be recorded that John Louis equalled the track record in heat 10. The fourth of July saw the staging of the annual Yorkshire TV Trophy, although the nearest to an American Independence Day triumph was Kelly Moran's superb third place. Ivan

Mauger's 15-point maximum saw him become the first rider to win the trophy twice and to add to his triumph he was the first man under 70 seconds at the Boulevard, recording 69.8 seconds in heat 8 and then equalling the new best time four heats later.

Seven days later, despite missing Ivan Mauger, who was suffering a recurrence of his back trouble, Eastbourne were defeated 50-28, Kelly Moran returning a full maximum, and then Vikings returned to K.O. Cup action. The quarter-final draw had paired them with chief title rivals Coventry. In what was described as the best meeting of the season so far at Brandon, Vikings repeated their Owlerton result of the previous round, although a Coventry reporter observed that the margin should have been about six instead of twelve. Before the Boulevard leg took place, Hull visited Reading on league business. At this stage Hull were six points behind Coventry with four matches in hand, but a chance to close the gap further was wasted at Smallmead, as firstly Ivan Mauger arrived late and missed his first ride, and then with Vikings only two points down with two heats to go, both Kelly Moran and Joe Owen suffered engine failures, the resultant 5-0 clinching the match for the Racers.

On to the second-leg cup tie and Coventry, missing Mitch Shirra and Alan Molyneux were really up against it. Vikings only took five heats to pull back the deficit and from then on there was only one outcome. Ivan Mauger was yet again unbeaten and Bobby Beaton's paid maximum included a memorable win over Ole Olsen. The stunning form carried over to the league, Vikings first demolishing Belle Vue 49-29 at Hyde Road with a solid down the line team show and then taking bottom club Leicester apart 60-18. The

An excellent first season for Dennis Sigalos.

following night's league match at Wimbledon was in retrospect thought by many to be decisive. Vikings arrived at Plough Lane without Bobby Beaton, Frank Auffret and Graham Drury, all of whom broke down en route. Locally based Graeme Stapleton was drafted in, and courtesy of a paid-15 show from reserve Dennis Sigalos, Hull were level after heat 8. Heat 9 was crucial. Hull only tracked Kelly Moran, and when he was excluded after falling, the resultant Dons 5-0, together with Dennis Sigalos running out of rides proved the end of Hull's challenge. There was no doubt that two points were thrown away at Wimbledon.

Two days later, everybody managed to arrive at Cradley Heath and Vikings led up to heat 10, but the Heathens came strong at the end and squeezed a 41-37 win. All in all a costly three days for the Vikings.

The following Wednesday, Ipswich were in the wrong place at the wrong time and took it from both barrels as Vikings stormed to a 57-21 win, Dennis Sigalos maintaining his recent improvement with a paid maximum. Before the next home match, many Vikings fans travelled to White City for the Inter-Continental final and were delighted to see both Ivan Mauger and Kelly Moran qualify for the World Final to be staged at Katowice on 2 September. Swindon then went the same way as Ipswich, although they were far from happy about the state of the rain-affected Boulevard track and threatened to walk out at one stage. This win left Hull six points behind Coventry with four matches in hand going into the last third of the season.

The next port of call was Eastbourne in the quarter-final of the Inter-Divisional Knock-Out Cup, something of a forgotten competition as the previous round was staged back in May! Vikings borrowed Poole's Ron Preston to cover for Ivan Mauger who was taking part in the World Long Track semi-final, and were never behind in the match which ended up 41-37. The rain again intervened at the Boulevard on 15 August bringing the league match against Sheffield to a halt after seven heats with Vikings comfortably in front. The following week Wimbledon put up a better fight than their 27 points suggested, although Hull had the trump card in Dennis Sigalos at reserve. His 13 points covered for Kelly Moran who fell in his first race and took no further part in the meeting.

The breakdown bogey struck again as Joe Owen failed to arrive at Swindon. Although Dennis Sigalos covered two of his races on the way to a magnificent 15-point maximum, Vikings were held to a draw, and the feeling was of another point tossed away. Records were in the air as Hull staged a Bank Holiday Monday match with fellow Wednesday nighters Poole. The 62-16 scoreline totally belied what was a great meeting with Vikings winning most of their points from the back. Two days later at Wimborne Road, Vikings had victory taken away from them after the meeting when the referee inspected Ivan Mauger's machine and found a faulty silencer. His heat-13 win was adjusted to an exclusion, and a four-point Vikings win became a draw.

The following Sunday all eyes were on Poland and it was double joy for Hull Speedway as Ivan Mauger clinched his record-breaking sixth World title, dropping his only point to Michael Lee, while Kelly Moran finished fourth after a run-off, a wonderful achievement for a rider in only his second year in British speedway.

The next Wednesday at the Boulevard, after all the celebrations, Vikings were very nearly brought down to earth by a Halifax side who provided Hull with a tremendous

The top four from Poland when Ivan Mauger won his record-breaking sixth World Title.

match, and it was largely due to maximum-man Joe Owen and Dennis Sigalos that Hull pulled through for a 43-34 win. Twenty-four hours later, Hull not only achieved that most satisfying result of winning on a local rival's track, but did it by a 20-point margin. Sheffield were the victims and everybody chipped in with some points, and Kelly Moran got back on song with a paid maximum after a duck against Halifax. Hull completed the league double over the Tigers the following Wednesday in the restaged fixture from 15 August by a 57-21 score with no less than four Vikings being unbeaten, including Dennis Sigalos's first full maximum at the Boulevard. After this match the league positions were: Coventry Matches 30 Points 44, Hull Matches 28 Points 42.

The show moved on to King's Lynn and a gripping match with never more than four points between the teams. Vikings led by four with two to go, but a Dennis Sigalos retirement and a fine Pete Smith win over Kelly Moran made it all square with just heat 13 left. Michael Lee made the gate on Ivan Mauger and Richard Hellsen kept Bobby Beaton at the back, thus the Vikings were shaded out by two points. Next day at White City, Ivan Mauger led New Zealand to victory in the World Team Cup final but sustained an injury which kept him out for two matches, the first of which was the first leg of the K.O. Cup semi-final at Exeter. Hull borrowed two juniors from Exeter but they both failed to score. However the six-man team dug in and for the third time in a row went into the second leg with a 12-point deficit. The 9 and 7-point returns from Frank Auffret and Graham Drury particularly deserve mention. Hull moved on to Leicester for a

Programme from the title decider at Coventry.

crucial must-win league match and a cracker ensued with the lead changing hands several times. Predictably the teams went into the last heat all square, and the luck went Vikings' way with Ila Teromaa retiring with engine trouble and a Joe Owen-Bobby Beaton 4-2 saw Vikings home by 2.

The third match in three days was the K.O. Cup semi-final second leg at the Boulevard. It took Hull precisely four heats to pull the aggregate scores level and after that the outcome was inevitable. Only Scott Autrey put up any serious resistance and Vikings were in the final against opponents as yet undecided.

Going into the following week's final home league clash with Cradley Heath, who still had an outside chance of the title, the league position was: Coventry M 32 Pts 46, Hull M 30 Pts 44, Cradley M 26 Pts 38. A tense match ensued where Hull held a slight advantage throughout but could never relax. Heathens' Bruce Penhall posted a 12-point maximum but Hull squeaked home 41-37, and kept the pressure on Coventry. It was already clear that Coventry v. Hull on October 13 was probably going to be the decider.

Vikings were now left with three away matches which would decide the league championship. The first of these was at Hackney on 28 September. The scores were level after heat 8, but Vikings then pulled away for a slightly flattering 45-33 win which turned the top of the league tension up another notch. It didn't seem to matter when a weakened Hull side lost 27-50 at Cradley Heath in the Inter-Divisional K.O. Cup semi-final, nor when Vikings took the Yorkshire Cup with a 53-25 win over Halifax. The last away match before Coventry was at Wolverhampton on 5 October and although Vikings were never in danger of not winning, and even posted their record away win, Kelly Moran crashed in the second half and broke his collarbone, almost certainly ruling himself out of the decider.

It was surprising that a challenge match against a Reg Wilson Select was raced the following Wednesday on a quagmire track, but it is notable as the British debut of 'David East', later revealed to be Kelly Moran's brother Shawn, who was trying out, prior to 1980, without the appropriate authorisation, hence the false name!

Then it was to Coventry for the winner-takes-all decider. A draw would give Hull the title, but Coventry had home advantage and Hull were without Kelly Moran. Vikings drafted in Graeme Stapleton, but got off to a bad start and were 6 points down after heat 2 and Stapleton had been stretchered off after a heat-2 crash. Only Ivan Mauger and Bobby Beaton looked likely Hull race winners, and although there were only two points in it after heat 7, it always looked like Coventry had something in reserve, and so it proved, the Bees running out winners 42-36 and taking the title. Hull looked unbalanced without Kelly Moran, and didn't get the significant contribution from Dennis Sigalos that might have made the difference.

No time for drowning sorrows as it was up the road to Cradley Heath two days later for the first leg of the Cup final. When Graham Drury crashed in the opening heat and had to pull out of the match (and the season as it turned out) it seemed as though Hull would be on the wrong end of a big score, but determined displays from Ivan Mauger and Bobby Beaton restricted the Heathens to a 16-point lead and left Vikings not without a chance of winning on aggregate. The second leg two days later was a controversial affair. Rain had begun to fall at the start of the match and had made the track extremely difficult. Cradley Heath had started the meeting well and by heat 7 had increased their aggregate lead by four points over an injury-weakened Hull side. Hull then protested about the state of the track and after an inspection and much discussion, the referee abandoned the meeting. Cradley were furious as they felt they had one hand on the Cup but Hull were pleased as a rerun gave them the opportunity to get maybe one of their injured riders fit.

The replayed Cup final was scheduled for 31 October, and in the meantime, Vikings were involved in three four-team tournaments. Hull won the first of these at the Boulevard on 24 October, in a meeting where 'David East' rode again. Although no official statement of the mystery man's identity had been made, many Vikings fans had correctly guessed who they were watching, and were already surmising as to what line-up they would be seeing in 1980. Hull were third of four at Halifax, and won by some distance at Newcastle, and then the stage was set for the last match of the season, the Cup final. Once again Hull got off to a poor start and after five heats, Cradley had added six points to their lead. Kelly Moran had made a brave return to the side and was to contribute eight points as Vikings fought back and, after heat 11, led on the night by eight. Home fans were thinking a miracle might actually happen, but the Heathens bounced back to take the match 58-50 and the final 120-96, leaving Vikings runners-up in both Cup and League, a disappointing end to a season that promised so much.

Many Vikings fans felt that the league title was thrown away by fielding below strength teams at Wimbledon and Swindon, and it can only be guessed whether the Coventry match would have been won if Kelly Moran had not been injured in a second-half crash eight days earlier. However, none of this disappointment should detract from Hull's most successful season ever; the club had risen from also-rans to challengers in a few short years. Rider-wise, Ivan Mauger had a tremendous season, posting 11 full or paid maximums in Vikings colours and also led New Zealand to the World Team Cup, apart from the small matter of a record-breaking sixth World title. Both Joe Owen and Kelly Moran, returning from serious injury had excellent seasons, Kelly's World No. 4 status being a wonderful achievement. Graham Drury never recaptured the heady heights of 1977 but together with steady and ever-popular Frank Auffret were solid second strings/reserves. Bobby Beaton, almost unnoticed, increased his average by a point and a half and particularly in difficult away matches in the Cup run produced good scores when they were most needed. Dennis Sigalos had an unbelievable first season, despite taking a little time to settle, he was often a match winner from reserve and displayed the potential to be a top rider.

1979 British League – Final Table

			Home					Away					
		M	**W**	**D**	**L**	**F**	**A**	**W**	**D**	**L**	**F**	**A**	**Pts**
1	Coventry	34	17	0	0	780	545	9	0	8	638	686	52
2	**HULL**	**34**	**17**	**0**	**0**	**878**	**447**	**7**	**2**	**8**	**668**	**652**	**50**
3	Cradley Heath	34	17	0	0	849	473	7	0	10	651	673	48
4	Kings Lynn	34	16	0	1	783	543	6	1	10	613	713	45
5	Exeter	34	16	0	1	800	523	5	0	12	613	707	42
6	Halifax	34	15	0	2	768.5	556.5	3	0	14	568	755	36
7	Reading	34	14	0	3	738	586	3	0	14	607	719	34
8	Swindon	34	12	1	4	738	585	3	2	12	612	714	33
9	Wimbledon	34	14	0	3	750	573	2	1	14	577	747	33
10	Belle Vue	34	10	4	3	700	625	4	0	13	623	701	32
11	Wolverhampton	34	12	0	5	703	620	3	1	13	603	722	31
12	Poole	34	13	2	2	745	579	1	1	15	552	773	31
13	Sheffield	34	13	1	3	716	608	1	1	15	512	812	30
14	Birmingham	34	10	0	7	689	635	3	2	12	568	757	28
15	Ipswich	34	10	1	6	689	631	2	1	14	575	750	26
16	Eastbourne	34	8	2	7	700	623	2	0	15	542	783	22
17	Leicester	34	9	0	8	648	677	1	0	16	502.5	820.5	20
18	Hackney	34	9	1	7	655	670	0	0	17	475	845	19

1979 Northern Trophy – Final Table

			Home					Away					
		M	**W**	**D**	**L**	**F**	**A**	**W**	**D**	**L**	**F**	**A**	**Pts**
1	Sheffield	6	3	0	0	132	100	1	1	1	119	115	9
2	Halifax	6	2	0	1	124	110	1	0	2	114	119	6
3	Belle Vue	6	2	0	1	121	112	0	0	3	103	131	4
4	**HULL**	**6**	**1**	**1**	**1**	**121**	**113**	**1**	**0**	**2**	**99**	**133**	**5**

The Northern Trophy was won by the team scoring the most race points

Final Averages (League and K O Cup matches)

	M	R	1st	2nd	3rd	Unp	Pts	BP	Tot	Avg	Max F	Max P
Ivan Mauger	36	148	100	33	6	9	372	12	384	10.38	9	2
Bobby Beaton	41	173	47	67	46	13	321	52	373	8.62	0	7
Kelly Moran	39	153	55	57	16	25	295	29	324	8.47	2	7
Joe Owen	41	170	52	59	45	14	319	38	357	8.40	4	2
Tom Owen	6	28	4	13	5	6	43	10	53	7.57	0	0
Dennis Sigalos	40	163	60	27	37	39	271	33	304	7.46	2	0
Graham Drury	38	138	22	38	54	24	196	37	233	6.75	0	1
Frank Auffret	40	147	20	35	47	45	177	44	221	6.01	0	0
Neil Coddington	2	5	0	0	3	2	3	1	4	3.20	0	0
Rod Hunter	2	5	0	0	1	4	1	0	1	0.80	0	0
Graeme Stapleton	2	6	0	0	1	5	1	0	1	0.67	0	0
Also Rode												
Mike Bowden	1	2	0	0	0	2	0	0	0	0.00	0	0
Louis Carr	2	7	1	2	0	4	7	1	8	4.57	0	0
Graham Clifton	1	2	0	0	0	2	0	0	0	0.00	0	0
Nigel Close	2	11	0	1	3	7	5	1	6	2.18	0	0
Brian Havelock	1	6	0	0	0	6	0	0	0	0.00	0	0
Benny Rourke	1	3	0	0	0	3	0	0	0	0.00	0	0
John Williams	1	4	0	0	0	4	0	0	0	0.00	0	0

1980 – British League

After finishing third in 1978 and second in 1979 there was much talk of Vikings making that final leap to the title in 1980. The events of the 1979-80 winter were to make that a very difficult mountain to climb. World Champion Ivan Mauger was entering his third season as a Viking, but during the close season it emerged he was suffering from a mystery blood disease which had confined him to a wheelchair. He did recover to race in 1980, but Vikings fans saw a less-than-100%-fit rider. The Hull management were also unable to agree terms with Kelly Moran who initially stayed home but turned up in Birmingham's colours after a £12,000 transfer mid-season. Graham Drury also decided to take a break from British racing, and opted for a season in the German league. To fill the gaps, Kelly Moran's brother Shawn was drafted in, (this time under his real name!) and another promising rider off the Californian production line, John Cook, was recruited. Another new face was John McNeill who had bought his contract from his previous track Leicester. The remaining members of the 1979 side, Bobby Beaton, Joe Owen and Frank Auffret all returned for yet another campaign.

All this activity gave Hull an eight-man squad, which was necessary, as Hull's best seven averages still exceeded the 50-points limit, so as in 1979 they were forced to rotate the team for the first part of the season.

The customary Northern Trophy season opener produced the customary result as Halifax took the victory. With Ivan Mauger still not fit to race, and three debutants in the team, Vikings fought hard, but could only muster five heat winners, Frank Auffret topping the score chart with 8. Dukes' young star Kenny Carter posted a full maximum,

1980 programme cover.

while Shawn Moran and John Cook scored 6 and 3 respectively on their debuts. Still without the skipper, Vikings lost at home again seven days later to Sheffield, with the newcomers struggling for points, without Frank Auffret's splendid 10 points the defeat would have been by more than two. Dennis Sigalos was gradually recovering his 1979 form, and he top scored in a much better display in a 10-point defeat at Belle Vue, although Joe Owen suffered back injuries in a heat 12 crash and would, as a result, miss two matches.

Hull opened their league programme at Cradley Heath, and without Mauger and Owen a 12-point loss was no disgrace against a strong Heathens team. Dennis Sigalos top-scored with 14, and Frank Auffret maintained his fine early season form with a 9-point return. Vikings posted their first victory of the season against Belle Vue in the Northern Trophy, Ivan Mauger celebrating his return with a full maximum. Newcomer Shawn Moran, from reserve, had his best meeting so far with a paid 11 score. Hull led the Trophy clash at the Shay by 8 points after six heats, but the Dukes rallied and the Mauger-less Vikings went down by 2 points. Mauger was back in the line-up for the first home league match against Eastbourne, and inspired the best team performance of the season so far. With Bobby Beaton standing down, 6 and 8 points respectively from reserves Shawn Moran and John McNeill backed another Mauger maximum giving a 46-32 win. Emergency action had to be taken by the Vikings medical staff when Eagles' Kai Niemi crashed in the second half and severed an artery. He was taken to hospital and underwent a three hour emergency operation.

Next up was a league trip to Birmingham, and a below-par 6-point return from Ivan Mauger and a patchy team performance saw Vikings go down 34-44. Two days later, with Dennis Sigalos standing on the centre green, Hull slipped to their first home league defeat since September 1977 when unfancied Hackney took the points with a 40-38 win. John Cook, who was struggling to settle in British speedway, could only manage 1 point and a rare 2-point return from Bobby Beaton left Vikings vulnerable although Shawn Moran gave a glimpse of what was to come in his career with a 13-point score from reserve. To add to that, Hawks' Bo Petersen equalled Ivan Mauger's track record of 69.8 second. In an unusual Monday meeting at Sheffield, Hull managed a 40-37 win against a weakened Tigers team in the final Northern Trophy match. A final Trophy finishing place of third was only the second time Vikings had avoided the wooden spoon.

Two days later, Vikings squeezed home against Wolves. With Bobby Beaton stepping down again, a tight match was decided by a fine piece of team riding by Ivan Mauger and Joe Owen in heat 12. The following week in a break from league racing, the Boulevard staged the third of a five match Test series between England and the USA. England fought bravely but had no answer to the American trio of Penhall, Autrey and Dennis Sigalos who scored 43 of the USA's 61 points.

The Inter-Divisional K.O. Cup was still taking place and Hull paid their first (and only to date) visit to Mildenhall's West Row circuit. The small track suited Hull's American contingent and they scored heavily, as did John McNeill, returning to his old track. A

Shawn Moran had less than a season with the Vikings.

50-28 win eased Vikings into Round Two. Next visitors to the Boulevard were Halifax, and once again Dennis Sigalos could only watch as Vikings slumped to a 32-46 defeat, a result that put paid to any hopes of bettering 1979's league position. The match started with controversy when Kenny Carter chopped across Ivan Mauger as the tapes went up for heat 1, forcing the Vikings skipper on to the centre green. When the referee did not stop the race, Ian Thomas ran on to the track waving a red flag to stop the race. The referee was summoned to the track, and after allegedly changing his decision several times finally excluded Mauger. It was not to be Hull's night!

Joe Owen was the absentee when Vikings raced at Swindon, the Robins' solid team work getting the better of a Hull side with a long tail, Bobby Beaton's 2-point score continuing his run of up and down form. Back at the Boulevard the following Wednesday, Vikings edged past Leicester 42-36 despite losing Ivan Mauger who pulled out at the last minute on doctor's orders. Certainly a case where Vikings' squad system came in handy. Leicester were pretty much a one-man team with Les Collins scoring 16 points, at one stage taking four rides on the trot! The Leicester fixture turned out to be John McNeill's last match for the club. As the owner of his own contract, he chose to move on to Poole. Champions-to-be Reading showed up next in East Yorkshire, Vikings left Joe Owen out and in a tight match with the lead changing hands numerous times, Hull just made it by two points, a Sigalos-Moran 5-1 in heat 11 regaining the lead which Vikings never relinquished. Kenny Carter guested for the Racers, replacing Jan Andersson, and bearing in mind the events of two weeks previously, his clashes with Ivan Mauger were eagerly awaited. However, honours were even, with each beating the other once.

The 18-heat format was retained for the Knock-Out Cup, and Vikings gained revenge for the recent league defeat by knocking out Hackney. Both legs were won, although in the first leg at Waterden Road, Hull overcame a 6-point deficit after 7 heats to win comfortably 63-45 with Dennis Sigalos (15) and Shawn Moran (13) leading the way. The second leg was something of a formality and Hull cruised to a 67-41 win, but the track record was rewritten. First, in heat 1, Bo Petersen reduced his own jointly held best time to 69.6 seconds. The following heat saw Bobby Beaton equal the new fastest time, and three heats later, Dennis Sigalos shaved a further 0.2 off the record, which was reduced to 69.4 seconds.

Vikings' next league fixture was at Reading and as new Green Sheets had been issued, Vikings were entitled to field their best line-up for the first time in a League match. However, Dennis Sigalos was required back in the USA for a compulsory visit, and his guest replacement Les Collins could only manage two points as Vikings slid to a 35-43 defeat in an exciting match which they had managed to lead 10-2 after two races. Two days later, Birmingham were on league duty at the Boulevard and lining up for the Brummies was none other than Kelly Moran! Kelly had a disappointing night, winning only one race, and the Boulevard crowd went wild when John Cook beat the former Vikings favourite in heat 11.The match was a comfortable 51-27 win for Vikings.

The Four-Team Championship was given another run out in 1980, and Vikings began the defence of their trophy at Sheffield in a group also containing Halifax and National League Berwick. Vikings comfortably won the Owlerton leg, finishing 12 points clear of second-place Halifax with a solid display, top scorer being Ivan Mauger with 11 and lowest scorer Joe Owen with 8. The lead was increased by 4 after the Berwick leg on 15 June, all four Vikings contributing good points, and then a place on Finals Day, this year at Wolverhampton, was guaranteed after the Boulevard leg, in which Hull riders only dropped four points, all four home riders posting double-figure scores.

Hull continued their league programme at Leicester. In wet conditions Ivan Mauger seemed to be not keen on racing and recorded only 4 points with reserve John Cook topping the score chart with only 7 in a 35-43 defeat. The following night, 1979's chief contenders produced a Boulevard thriller in which the lead changed hands several times and perhaps fittingly ended all square. Ivan Mauger retrieved his best form seven days later when a perfect 15-point maximum enabled him to retain the Yorkshire TV Trophy. Michael Lee was runner up for the third time in a row while Dennis Sigalos demonstrated his emerging stardom with third place. Rookie Shawn Moran scored 10 entertaining points, mostly from the back.

The Knock-Out Cup quarter-final saw Vikings paired with Belle Vue and Vikings dominated the Boulevard leg, running out 66-42 winners. Chris Morton put on a one-man show for the Aces with 18 points in the absence of injured Peter Collins and Michael Lohmann. A visit to Yorkshire rivals Sheffield on league business resulted in a 35-43 defeat, Dennis Sigalos's 13 points apart in an average performance. Then, an away point was won at Wolverhampton. Ivan Mauger fell in his first race and injured his leg, pulling out after his next heat. This was cancelled out when Jim McMillan retired from the match injured with only 3 points to his name. The teams were all square going into heat 13, the final race having to be started four times before Bobby Beaton came home in front to secure the draw.

The Cup second leg at Belle Vue was abandoned after four heats due to rain. This seemed like a stroke of luck for Hull as the Aces had already pulled back half of Vikings' first-leg advantage. Hull's next home match, against Cradley Heath, was marred by a horrific heat 5 crash in which Bobby Beaton broke a collarbone and a wrist after clipping Ila Teromaa's rear wheel and being catapulted into the fence where he also collected a flying bike. He also swallowed his tongue and had to be given emergency on-track treatment before being transferred to hospital. Hull scrambled home against a weakened Heathens side for whom Bruce Penhall and reserve Derek Harrison scored 27 of the Heathens' 36 points. Saturday next, Vikings tumbled out of the Inter-Divisional Knock-Out Cup at King's Lynn. Dennis Sigalos and Shawn Moran were away in Germany riding in the European Junior Championship final. Guest replacement Reg Wilson scored 10, but Vikings fought a two-man battle, Ivan Mauger returning 9.

A vastly under-strength Hull side tamely surrendered their Four-Team title at Wolverhampton finishing stone last in their semi-final. Cradley Heath became the new holders in what was to be the last year the tournament was staged. Things livened up somewhat on 23 July when Ipswich came to town. A thriller of a match looked to be slipping from Vikings' grasp when Dennis Sigalos and Joe Owen snatched a dramatic last heat 5-1 to earn Vikings a draw. Sigalos crowned a great night by racing to a maximum and shattering the Boulevard track record, setting a new best time of 68.6 seconds. Six days later the same pair were at it again, rescuing a 2-point deficit and

A tough debut season for John Cook.

ensuring another draw, this time against Poole. It must have set some kind of a record when, twenty-four hours later in the return match at Poole the result was ... a draw. Yet again a heat-13 rescue act saved Vikings when Ivan Mauger and Shawn Moran, with his only point of the match, got the 4-2 needed to share the points.

Ivan Mauger was still battling ill health and missed the league match at Wimbledon on 31 July, the sequence of draws ended by a 47-31 defeat. Joe Owen had taken a knock at Poole and did well to score 7 on a track he normally would do much better on. Ivan Mauger failed to qualify for the World Final for the first time since 1965 when he was eliminated in the Inter-Continental final at White City.

The league match against Swindon scheduled for 6 August was rained off and then Vikings recorded what was to be their only away win in the league at Eastbourne, and they did it without Ivan Mauger. A full maximum from Dennis Sigalos plus an 8-point score from Newcastle stand-in Rod Hunter tipped the scales Hull's way. The Boulevard then staged its first ever triangular tournament as the home side took on Sheffield and Newcastle in an 18-heat match. Vikings ran out comfortable winners courtesy of maximums from Dennis Sigalos and Joe Owen, Ivan Mauger pulling out after two rides suffering from chest pains and breathing difficulties.

The league visit to Coventry was in direct contrast to the 1979 match up, both sides tracking guests for absent heat leaders, Vikings going down 26-52. Good news from two days earlier though as Dennis Sigalos won his first major tournament when he took the Grand Prix title after the final at Wimbledon. An exciting encounter at the Boulevard against Belle Vue saw the home side slip to a 38-40 defeat. The continued absence of Ivan Mauger was the telling factor together with a significant 7-point score from Aces' reserve Louis Carr. A 35-43 defeat at Ipswich was two days later followed by the restaged second leg of the K.O. Cup at Belle Vue. It was a titanic struggle with the Aces gradually whittling away Hull's 24-point lead. Despite 13 and 9 from Dennis Sigalos and Frank Auffret, the Beaton and Mauger-less Vikings bowed out of the cup by 4 points on aggregate.

The following Wednesday, 27 August, Vikings entertained Sheffield and were overwhelming winners by 60 18. Both Ivan Mauger and Bobby Beaton returned, Ivan with a full maximum, while Dennis Sigalos also returned a full score with Joe Owen and Shawn Moran returning paid full houses. It was to be Shawn's last match in Hull colours as he was transferred to Sheffield after a discussion over what terms he would be looking for in 1981 followed a newspaper article in which Shawn indicated he was unhappy with the accommodation and transport provided by Hull. Seven days later, Hull, covering Shawn's absence with a guest (who failed to score) edged past Swindon with another full house from Ivan Mauger.

A quick return to Belle Vue for the league fixture produced an 8-point defeat which was a good performance after a disastrous first race in which Frank Auffret fell and Ivan Mauger hit the fence to avoid colliding with his team mate. Ivan sustained two broken ribs for his trouble. Vikings rallied round and led the match after heat 5, but the superiority of Aces heat leaders Chris Morton and Peter Collins pulled the home side through. Use of rider replacement for Ivan Mauger and guest Kenny Carter helped Hull past Wimbledon, and then the skipper returned for the challenge win over Leicester. Vikings rounded off their home league programme with a narrow 41-37 win against King's Lynn, who suffered from an uncharacteristic 5 points from Michael Lee, no doubt still celebrating his recent crowning as World Champion.

The league programme was completed with three away matches in three days. Up first was a trip to title-chasing Hackney. Ivan Mauger could only manage 3 and Joe Owen injured his ankle in a heat 10 fall. With Joe injured and Ivan away racing in the Czech Golden Helmet, Vikings went down 30-48 at Halifax and were then roundly hammered 56-22 at King's Lynn, with 12 points from Dennis Sigalos the only serious resistance. The annual Yorkshire Cup clash with Halifax saw the first leg go Hull's way 42-36, but before the second leg, Vikings trounced Birmingham 54-24, Joe Owen returning with a paid maximum and ex-Viking Kelly Moran failing to win a race with 8 points. The Yorkshire Cup slipped away at Halifax with Ivan Mauger missing and again Dennis Sigalos something of a one-man band. Vikings then raced a challenge against their Lincolnshire neighbours Scunthorpe, winning 43-34. John Cook had one of his best matches in Hull colours with 13, Joe Owen backing up with 12.

The curtain was brought down on the season with a challenge victory over Cradley Heath and three four-team tournaments, while Dennis Sigalos was disappointed with his 6-point score in the British League Riders' Championship at Belle Vue.

After the excitement of 1979, the 1980 season was a disappointment. With Ivan Mauger spending the entire season battling illness and injury, the difficulties of the 50-point rule meant that Hull lost two home league matches before they could field a full side, and any hope of a title challenge was gone. The final blow was the transfer of Shawn Moran to Sheffield which left Vikings fans hoping for better things in 1981.

1980 British League – Final Table

			Home					Away					
		M	W	D	L	F	A	W	D	L	F	A	Pts
1	Reading	32	15	0	1	767	481	9	1	6	667	581	49
2	Hackney	32	15	0	1	719	526	8	0	8	581	662	46
3	Belle Vue	32	16	0	0	711	534	5	1	10	587	659	43
4	Coventry	32	15	0	1	724.5	523.5	5	2	9	601.5	646.5	42
5	Cradley Heath	32	16	0	0	732.5	514.5	4	0	12	569.5	674.5	40
6	Kings Lynn	32	15	0	1	759	487	2	0	14	594	654	34
7	Ipswich	32	14	0	2	739	506	2	2	12	559	688	34
8	Swindon	32	11	2	3	686	562	5	0	11	578	669	34
9	Poole	32	13	1	2	699	545	2	1	13	555	692	32
10	Halifax	32	13	1	2	697	550	2	0	14	522	721	31
11	Leicester	32	12	0	4	676	572	2	0	14	577	669	28
12	**HULL**	**32**	**10**	**3**	**3**	**674**	**572**	**1**	**2**	**13**	**533**	**714**	**27**
13	Wimbledon	32	12	1	3	682	562	0	1	15	513	732	26
14	Birmingham	32	9	0	7	627	621	2	1	13	531	717	23
15	Wolverhampton	32	7	2	7	643	602	2	0	14	549	695	20
16	Eastbourne	32	8	1	7	615	630	1	0	15	478	769	19
17	Sheffield	32	8	0	8	618	628	0	0	16	421	826	16

1980 Northern Trophy – Final Table

			Home					Away					
		M	W	D	L	F	A	W	D	L	F	A	Pts
1	Halifax	6	3	0	0	128	105	2	0	1	120	113	10
2	Belle Vue	6	3	0	0	127	105	1	0	2	108	124	8
3	**HULL**	**6**	**1**	**0**	**2**	**120**	**114**	**1**	**0**	**2**	**112**	**121**	**4**
4	Sheffield	6	0	0	3	109	123	1	0	2	107	126	2

The Northern Trophy was won by the team scoring the most race points

Final Averages (League and K.O. Cup matches)

											Max	
	M	R	1st	2nd	3rd	Unp	Pts	BP	Tot	Avg	F	P
Dennis Sigalos	31	142	81	35	10	16	323	8	331	9.32	3	0
Ivan Mauger	25	96	54	18	12	12	210	6	216	9.00	5	0
Joe Owen	29	121	21	53	35	12	204	25	229	7.57	1	1
Bobby Beaton	25	103	25	22	34	22	153	19	172	6.68	0	0
Shawn Moran	29	128	28	33	29	38	179	28	207	6.47	0	1
Frank Auffret	35	140	10	37	50	43	154	30	184	5.26	0	1
John McNeill	6	19	2	4	5	8	19	4	23	4.84	0	0
David Bargh	9	24	0	6	10	8	22	6	28	4.67	0	0
Rod Hunter	10	37	5	4	14	14	37	6	43	4.65	0	0
John Cook	35	116	11	14	44	47	105	15	120	4.14	0	0
Tom Owen	1	3	0	0	2	1	2	1	3	4.00	0	0
Robbie Blackadder	3	7	0	1	2	4	4	1	5	2.86	0	0
Nigel Crabtree	3	7	0	0	3	4	3	1	4	2.29	0	0
Also Rode												
Carl Baldwin	1	2	0	0	0	2	0	0	0	0.00	0	0
Peter Carr	1	3	0	1	1	1	3	1	4	5.33	0	0
Kenny Carter	1	5	3	2	0	0	13	1	14	11.20	0	0

	M	R	1st	2nd	3rd	Unp	Pts	BP	Tot	Avg	Max F	Max P
Les Collins	1	4	0	1	0	3	2	1	3	3.00	0	0
Pete Ellams	1	2	0	0	1	1	1	0	1	2.00	0	0
Paul Embley	1	1	0	0	0	1	0	0	0	0.00	0	0
Mick Fullerton	1	2	0	0	1	1	1	0	1	2.00	0	0
Ian Gledhill	1	5	1	1	0	3	5	0	5	4.00	0	0
Robert Henry	1	2	0	0	2	0	2	0	2	4.00	0	0
Denzil Kent	1	3	0	0	0	3	0	0	0	0.00	0	0
Jim McMillan	1	3	0	0	1	2	1	0	1	1.33	0	0
Craig Pendlebury	1	2	0	0	0	2	0	0	0	0.00	0	0

1981 – British League

The winter of 1980-81 saw several changes in the Vikings line-up, the most significant one being the transfer of 1980's No. 1 Dennis Sigalos to Ipswich. Dennis had failed to agree terms with Hull and moved to East Anglia along with fellow American John Cook who had struggled to establish himself at the Boulevard. In return, Hull got Billy Sanders from Ipswich together with a cash adjustment. Vikings also welcomed back Graham Drury after his season in Germany, and signed promising young Dane John Eskildsen on loan from Birmingham. Ivan Mauger decided to soldier on for another season, and long-term favourites Bobby Beaton, Joe Owen and Frank Auffret once again were back for another campaign.

The traditional Northern Trophy season opener had given way to the League Cup, a new tournament occupying the first couple of months of the season in which the British League teams were divided into two sections on geographical lines and the section winners would meet in a two-leg final. Vikings were placed in the section with the Northern and Midland teams. League Cup matches were to be raced to a different, 16-heat formula.

The season got underway as usual with a visit to Halifax, which yielded the usual result: newcomer Billy Sanders shone with 14 points but Ivan Mauger scored only 3, being plagued with engine problems. The first meeting at the Boulevard was the 300th meeting since 1971 and the visitors were Belle Vue. Vikings came out on top 50-46 with Ivan back on song with a paid maximum. The unbeaten home record only stayed intact for a week as Coventry were 10-point winners on 8 April. Billy Sanders was making an excellent start to his Hull career, but Graham Drury was struggling for points and Paul McHale from Newcastle, who filled the No. 7 slot for the first three matches found the British League too tough. For the visit to Sheffield, John Eskildsen made his first appearance and an exciting meeting saw Vikings lead early on with Tigers finally squeezing home with the required second place in a last-heat decider.

Hull won their next home match, against Birmingham, but the match will be remembered for a spectacular heat-4 crash involving Ivan Mauger and Hans Nielsen. Mauger crashed heavily into the fence and was taken to hospital with bad bruising and concussion while Nielsen followed him with suspected back injuries. Vikings coped the

Billy Sanders, No. 1 in the last season at the Boulevard.

better without their No. 1 and solid scoring from Bobby Beaton and Joe Owen plus a full maximum from Billy Sanders saw them home. The return at Perry Barr two days later was close but the Brummies led all the way, Hans Nielsen shaking off his Wednesday night injury to record a maximum, while Billy Sanders (16) and Joe Owen (13) were best for a Hull side using rider replacement for Ivan Mauger.

The following night at Belle Vue, Vikings led up to heat 8 but the continued absence of the skipper told and the Aces ran out 51-45 winners. Again Billy Sanders was outstanding with 19 points, backed up by Joe Owen with 12. Back to winning ways at home to Sheffield with Ivan Mauger back in the team and then seven days later Leicester, without their No. 1 Les Collins, were trounced 68-28 with everyone scoring well.

With the demise of the Inter-Divisional Knock-Out Cup, National League teams were admitted to the Speedway Star Cup. The first round saw Hull drawn at Boston and although Vikings led up to heat 14, a Steve Regeling/Michael Holding 5-1 in heat 15 left Vikings needing a 5-1 in the final heat to avoid being victims of a giant-killing. A controversial first bend saw Billy Sanders and Bobby Beaton emerge in front to secure the 5-1 needed but Boston fans were very unhappy about the tactics used. Vikings were unable to hold a strong Cradley Heath team at the Boulevard and fell to a 44-52 defeat.

Ivan Mauger did not ride in this match, nor the Boston match as he had received a fourteen-day suspension for failing to ride at Boston. Ivan had a long-standing engagement in West Germany scheduled for that date, and was told that he did not have permission to fulfil this engagement as the Boston match, the date of which was arranged later, took precedence. Ivan was so angry with this that he retired and then when he cooled down he rescinded this, only to be told that his 'retirement' was extended to fourteen days. Hull therefore raced three matches without Mauger's services. The Cradley match saw Vikings tracking Alan Emerson in Mauger's place, while David Bargh replaced John Eskildsen who broke a bone in his foot at Boston. Bruce Penhall was majestic for the Heathens. League Cup business at Coventry with the same seven riders saw Hull put up a creditable display going down by 10 points, Billy Sanders best with 16.

Vikings won the final match of Mauger's suspension with a remarkable recovery from being 10 points down after heat 4 against Halifax, a 15-point score from Billy Sanders the inspiration. The league programme got underway with a visit from Eastbourne with former-Viking Kelly Moran in their team. Moran and Gordon Kennett were a two-man team for the Eagles as Vikings won 46-32. The American produced his best Boulevard performance as a visitor with 12 points and denied Ivan Mauger a maximum in an exciting heat-12 battle.

The scheduled league match with Reading on 27 May fell victim to the weather and Vikings next took to the track at Leicester on 2 June in the League Cup. Ivan Mauger was absent in Los Angeles, involved in preparations for the American final at Los Angeles, the venue due to host the 1982 World Final. Vikings were also without Graham Drury and fell to a 59-37 defeat. An Inter-League challenge victory over sister track Newcastle preceded the final League Cup match at Cradley Heath. Bruce Penhall was absent for the Heathens, Ivan Mauger and Billy Sanders were missing for Hull, all three on World Pairs duty. Only Bobby Beaton with 16 points put up any serious resistance as Vikings were soundly beaten 63-33.

Home and away league matches with Poole followed with Hull winning the Boulevard clash 45-33, Ivan Mauger back in maximum mood, while the result was exactly reversed at Wimborne Road one day later. Vikings then, as in 1980, were drawn against Belle Vue in the next round of the Knock-Out Cup, and the first leg at Hyde Road produced a good Hull performance. A 10-point defeat gave Vikings a good hope of further progress. Two days later, Vikings went down to a 31-47 defeat at Reading in the last match without Graham Drury who had missed several meetings because of an ankle injury sustained in Germany. The next visitors to the Boulevard were Hackney who fell behind by 16 points after heat 7 and staged a mini-revival largely courtesy of a 14-point return from Bo Petersen, restricting Hull to a 45-33 win.

A 10-point Yorkshire Cup first-leg loss at Halifax preceded the Cup second leg against Belle Vue. A tense, thrilling battle ensued with Hull falling 6 further points behind before getting to grips with the situation and gradually whittling away the Aces' lead with the teams level on aggregate going into the final heat thanks to a tremendous heat 15 win by Frank Auffret over Chris Morton and Jim McMillan. Billy Sanders beat Larry Ross and Joe Owen kept Chris Morton at the back to clinch a place in the next round.

Foxhall Heath, never a track Hull got much joy on, produced another defeat, 26-52 in a match that was better than the score indicated. In a break from team racing, the Yorkshire TV Trophy was won with an imperious 15-point maximum from Bruce Penhall. The best Viking performance was third-equal from Billy Sanders with 11 points. Ivan Mauger only completed two rides for 4 points because of mechanical problems.

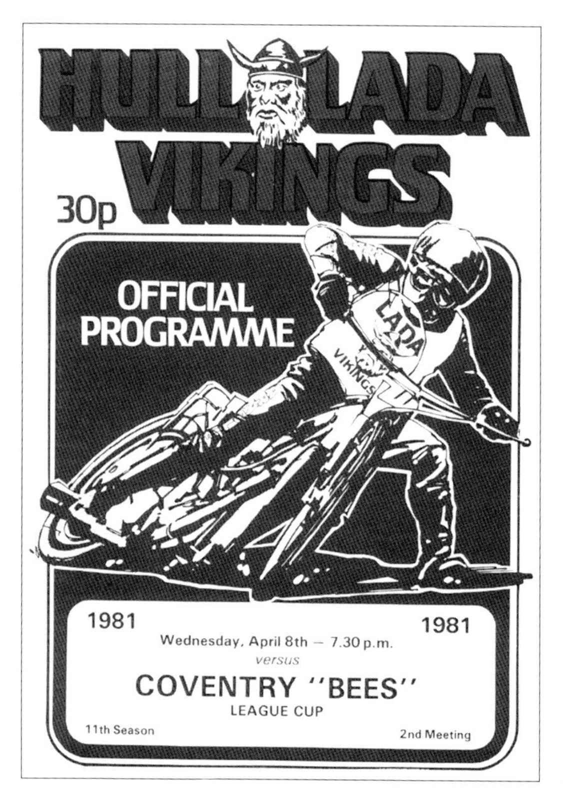

1981 programme cover.

Back to league business Vikings swept Sheffield aside 47-30 in a match that nearly was not completed as torrential rain fell late in the match and a referee's inspection was needed after heat 10. A solid team performance made up for an uncharacteristic 2-point return from Billy Sanders. Controversy reigned at King's Lynn as Ivan Mauger did not race, producing a doctor's certificate for damaged ribs. The Stars' management felt that Ivan should not have been allowed to ride in the following day's Overseas final. Without the captain, Hull fell to a 29-49 defeat, and Ivan scored 8 points at White City, failing to qualify for the World Final.

Vikings' first home defeat in the league was suffered on 15 July, with a strong Cradley Heath side plundering the points, Ivan Mauger and Billy Sanders being restricted to 5 and 3 points respectively, while Bruce Penhall was unbeaten for his third consecutive Boulevard appearance. Next up was Round Three of the Knock-Out Cup and Hull fancied their chances of progress against Birmingham, but inspired by double-figure scores from Hans Nielsen and Andy Grahame the Brummies did a great job restricting Vikings to a 2-point advantage. Two days later, in the return leg, Vikings put up a tremendous scrap, only falling behind on aggregate after heat 9, and a last heat 4-2 would have earned a replay. However, in a thrilling final race, Andy Grahame and Ari Koponen came from behind to get the deciding 5-1, taking the Perry Barr side into the semi-finals. Former-Viking Shawn Moran guested for Ivan Mauger who was in Denmark for the Inter-Continental final and was paid for 10 points.

Once again conceding a last-heat 5-1 cost Vikings points as Wimbledon, who had only led once in the match celebrated Royal Wedding day with a point at the Boulevard, Malcolm Simmons and Anders Eriksson edging out Joe Owen and Billy Sanders in the final heat. The teams met again twenty-four hours later and the Plough Lane fixture was close with a crucial heat-12 engine failure for Ivan Mauger when in as a tactical substitute finally tipping the balance the Dons way.

Into August, the league match at Leicester saw Vikings battle back from an 8-point deficit to force a last-heat decider, but Lions' Rolf Gramstad and Les Collins held Bobby Beaton at bay to give the home side a 4-point win. The next day, Swindon turned up at the Boulevard with six men, Steve Gresham being ill. Without a medical certificate Robins could not use a guest or rider replacement. The lead changed hands several times before Swindon, making light of being a man short and inspired by a 13-point score from reserve Mike Ferreira, earned a deserved draw. A disappointing performance at Eastbourne resulted in a 30-48 reverse, with Ivan Mauger only managing 6 and Bobby Beaton failing to trouble the scorers. Kelly Moran rattled up a full house against his former club and for good measure set up a new Arlington track record of 58.2 seconds in heat 4.

Halifax, the next visitors to the Boulevard, usually provided a close match and this one could not have been closer as the third consecutive home match ended in a draw. The Dukes, with Kenny Carter in maximum form, came back from 10 points down to take a point with Billy Sanders suffering a tapes exclusion in the crucial heat 13. On the road to Cradley Heath and unsurprisingly Hull were well beaten by the champions-to-be, Heathens providing all thirteen heat winners.

The draw sequence at home was finally broken with a 47-31 win over Leicester in a wet meeting. Much-improved performances from Ivan Mauger and Bobby Beaton together with the steady improvement of John Eskildsen at reserve were the key to this win. The following Saturday, 22 August, Hull fell to a 32-46 defeat at Halifax, only providing three heat winners. The score would have been closer but for Graham Drury sustaining an ankle injury in his first race when his engine seized solid. Even a 15-point maximum for Michael Lee could not prevent defeat for King's Lynn, the next Boulevard visitors. Seven points each from reserves Frank Auffret and John Eskildsen laid the foundations for the win, while 1976 YTV Trophy winner Dave Jessup could only manage 2 for the visitors.

The pleasure at this victory was short lived; two days to be precise, as Vikings were hammered 55-23 at Hackney in a poor display. More seriously though, Billy Sanders broke his scaphoid in a crash and was out for the season. Unsurprisingly, Hull were beaten on Bank Holiday Monday at Coventry. Rider Replacement operated for Billy Sanders and Joe Owen was absent as his wife was in hospital. The Bees were 36-12 up after heat 8 but three heat wins from Ivan Mauger ensured that Coventry did not extend their lead further. The team rallied to defeat Reading on 2 September with a 10-point contribution from reserve Frank Auffret, and followed up seven days later with a win over Belle Vue, although fortune favoured Vikings in heat 12 when, with the scores level, Aces' Chris Morton and Jim McMillan both had engine trouble allowing Hull a 5-1 which turned the final score Hull's way.

John Eskildsen in action.

The following week, speedway moved to Tuesday and Vikings hosted Ipswich and it was a tremendous return to the Boulevard for Dennis Sigalos and John Cook who brought the Witches back from 12 points down to earn a draw. Frank Auffret was Vikings' top-scorer with 9 while the two former Vikings scored 25 of Ipswich's points.

Ivan Mauger raced in the World Long Track final in Yugoslavia and was involved in a high-speed crash, sustaining a badly broken ankle, ending his season. Vikings used Shawn Moran as a guest for the following Wednesday's match against Coventry, and he responded with 10 points as the match was won 43-35. Two away matches in the league then followed with, unsurprisingly, two defeats. Dave Morton guested at Birmingham where Hull kept the match close for the first half of the match, before falling away to a 47-30 loss. Graham Drury rode in this match despite being injured against Coventry, but he was unable to ride at Swindon where, in terrible conditions, Vikings were suffering a good hammering 40-14 when the referee called a halt, the result being allowed to stand.

The final home league match on 30 September against Birmingham was won 42-36, with Phil Collins scoring 11 as guest for Ivan Mauger. Hans Nielsen was only denied a full 15-point maximum by a heat 13 engine failure. The last two away league matches at Sheffield and Belle Vue ended in defeats and the Boulevard season ended with Vikings taking the Yorkshire Cup with a 46-32 defeat of Halifax, although there was no trophy to present as no one knew where it was!

However, the real drama occurred off track, after the season had finished. Hull FC, Vikings' Boulevard landlords terminated speedway's licence, alleging breaches of contract. Although these allegations were strongly refuted by Vikings' management, it had been rumoured that the rugby club, who were enjoying an extremely successful period, no longer wished to accommodate speedway in their stadium. The end result was that the eleven-year tenure of speedway at the Boulevard was over. Most speedway fans thought that the sport would not return as there was no alternative venue available at the time as Hull KR were still at their original Craven Park ground and the stadium in which the Vikings now race had not been built.

1981 British League – Final Table

			Home					**Away**					
		M	**W**	**D**	**L**	**F**	**A**	**W**	**D**	**L**	**F**	**A**	**Pts**
1	Cradley Heath	30	15	0	0	710	445	11	1	3	629	538	53
2	Ipswich	30	14	1	0	683	483	7	3	5	567	602	46
3	Swindon	30	12	1	2	641	503	7	2	6	581	586	41
4	Belle Vue	30	13	0	2	671	498	6	1	8	568	588	39
5	Coventry	30	13	0	2	659	510	5	0	10	573	593	36
6	Birmingham	30	12	1	2	654	515	1	0	14	509	659	27
7	Halifax	30	13	0	2	658	509	0	1	14	491	679	27
8	Hackney	30	10	0	5	639	530	2	2	11	543	627	26
9	Poole	30	9	1	5	616.5	551.5	3	1	11	512	657	26
10	Sheffield	30	11	0	4	656	513	2	0	13	464	701	26
11	Reading	30	7	4	4	601	568	2	3	10	528	640	25
12	**HULL**	**30**	**10**	**4**	**1**	**634**	**535**	**0**	**0**	**15**	**434**	**710**	**24**
13	Eastbourne	30	9	2	4	627	542	1	1	13	467	702	23
14	Kings Lynn	30	7	1	7	622	548	3	1	11	560	610	22
15	Leicester	30	9	0	6	602	568	2	0	13	515.5	653.5	22
16	Wimbledon	30	6	2	7	578	587	1	1	13	464	706	17

1981 League Cup Section A – Final Table

			Home					**Away**					
		M	**W**	**D**	**L**	**F**	**A**	**W**	**D**	**L**	**F**	**A**	**Pts**
1	Coventry	14	7	0	0	408	263	5	0	2	347	325	24
2	Cradley Heath	14	7	0	0	405	267	4	0	3	342	330	22
3	Belle Vue	14	5	0	2	350.5	320.5	2	0	5	298	373	14
4	Sheffield	14	6	0	1	356	316	1	0	6	285.5	386.5	14
5	Birmingham	14	5	0	2	362	310	1	0	6	304	367	12
6	**HULL**	**14**	**5**	**0**	**2**	**367**	**305**	**0**	**0**	**7**	**286**	**386**	**10**
7	Leicester	14	4	0	3	358	314	0	0	7	294	376	8
8	Halifax	14	4	0	3	341	328	0	0	7	267	404	8

Final Averages (League and K O Cup matches)

	M	R	1st	2nd	3rd	Unp	Pts	BP	Tot	Avg	Max F	Max P
Billy Sanders	25	107	43	39	15	10	222	10	232	8.67	2	0
Ivan Mauger	26	116	55	28	22	11	243	8	251	8.66	2	1
Joe Owen	33	143	24	59	47	13	237	17	254	7.10	0	0
Rod Hunter	3	11	1	4	2	4	13	2	15	5.45	0	0
Frank Auffret	31	108	16	24	28	40	124	23	147	5.44	0	0
Bobby Beaton	35	148	11	46	43	48	168	30	198	5.35	0	0
Graham Drury	28	111	4	23	50	34	108	29	137	4.94	0	0
John Eskildsen	32	112	9	23	36	44	109	29	138	4.93	0	0
David Bargh	7	24	2	3	9	10	21	6	27	4.50	0	0
Barry Simpson	2	7	0	1	0	6	2	0	2	1.14	0	0
Alan Emerson	1	2	0	0	0	2	0	0	0	0.00	0	0
Paul McHale	0	0	0	0	0	0	0	0	0	0.00	0	0
Also Rode												
Ian Cartwright	1	5	0	1	3	1	5	2	7	5.60	0	0
Mark Collins	1	3	0	0	0	3	0	0	0	0.00	0	0
Phil Collins	1	5	3	0	2	0	11	2	13	10.40	0	0
Andy Elliott	1	2	0	0	0	2	0	0	0	0.00	0	0
Andy Grahame	1	6	3	1	2	0	13	0	13	8.67	0	0
Shawn Moran	2	11	3	2	5	1	18	3	21	7.64	0	0
Dave Morton	1	5	1	2	1	1	8	1	9	7.20	0	0
Mark Reeve	1	2	0	0	0	2	0	0	0	0.00	0	0
Mike Spink	1	2	0	0	0	2	0	0	0	0.00	0	0
Finn Thomsen	1	4	0	1	2	1	4	0	4	4.00	0	0

3
HULL SPEEDWAY RIDERS 1948-1981

The statistics provided for each rider record his achievements with Hull Speedway

Kazimierz ADAMCZAK (1976)

Born – 4 March 1954, Leszno, Poland. Died October 1994

Made his debut for Unia Leszno in 1973 and won a round of the Polish Silver Helmet in 1974. Was one of a few young Poles allowed to race in the British League in 1976 to gain experience and he was allocated to Hull. He failed to make an impression and was released after one league match and linked with Exeter and then Newport where he made some improvement but he did not return to British speedway in 1977. Kaz died in 1994.

M	R	1st	2nd	3rd	Unpl	Pts	BP	Tot	Avge	FM	PM
1	2	0	0	0	2	0	0	0	0.00	0	0

Ken ALLICK (1949)

Born – 22 February 1922, Middlesbrough

Ken raced for Wombwell in 1947 and 1948 and when the Colliers closed decided to try his luck at Hull in 1949. He did not score many points as an Angel, and when Hedon closed its doors to speedway, he raced a few meetings for Newcastle, but was not seen in the sport afterwards.

M	R	1st	2nd	3rd	Unpl	Pts	BP	Tot	Avge	FM	PM
11	26	0	2	11	13	15	1	16	2.46	0	0

Al ALLISON (1948)
Born – 14 December 1918, Selby, Yorkshire

After five years of Army service, Al joined Bradford. He was loaned to Hull in 1948, making his debut with a 12-point score from reserve at Cradley Heath in a National Trophy fixture. Al made significant progress, averaging just under 7 in Angels' colours before being recalled to Odsal in September. He was transferred to Halifax for the 1949 season and spent three seasons at the Shay before reverting to Bradford in 1952 where he remained until 1957; then, after a brief spell with Leicester, he retired.

M	R	1st	2nd	3rd	Unpl	Pts	BP	Tot	Avge	FM	PM
23	65	17	20	12	16	103	9	112	6.89	0	0

Nicky ALLOTT (1972)
Born – 15 December 1954, Buxton, Derbyshire

Member of a famous speedway family spanning the history of the sport (Uncle Tommy and father Guy both rode and son Adam is a current rider), Nicky made his debut in second-half racing in 1971, and made his first team appearance for Hull in 1972. He raced two matches for the Vikings and then missed the 1973 season because of a serious car crash. He then spent two years with Ellesmere Port before moving to Scunthorpe where he achieved heat-leader status. Two Division One seasons at Sheffield were followed by a return to Scunthorpe in 1981. The next two years at Long Eaton produced a decline in form, and he retired in 1984 after a further short spell at Scunthorpe.

M	R	1st	2nd	3rd	Unpl	Pts	BP	Tot	Avge	FM	PM
2	6	0	0	2	4	2	0	2	1.33	0	0

Kym AMUNDSON (1975)
Born – 20 April 1952, Adelaide, South Australia

Brother of fellow Viking Robin, Kym sampled cycle speedway before starting the sport proper at Adelaide in 1969. He came to the UK with Robin in 1971, and linked with Workington where he made steady progress for three seasons. Like Robin, he missed 1974, but returned to Derwent Park in 1975 and raced half the season before being snapped up by under-strength Division One Hull. Kym showed promise at the higher level, but an injury in August led him to return to Australia. He never returned to British speedway.

M	R	1st	2nd	3rd	Unpl	Pts	BP	Tot	Avge	FM	PM
13	40	6	7	11	17	43	8	51	5.10	0	0

Robin AMUNDSON (1971-73, 1975)
Born – 24 June 1948, Adelaide, South Australia

Robin's first steps in speedway were at Adelaide's Rowley Park in 1967-68. He intended to come to the UK in 1969 but he was called up for National Service. His medical was deferred as he was serving an apprenticeship as a motor mechanic. He eventually failed the medical, but it was too late to come to the UK for 1969. He saved up during 1970 and arrived in the UK for the 1971 season with brother Kym, joining the new Hull team. He was a Boulevard favourite and progressed steadily to heat-leader status by 1973, but a dispute with the Hull promotion led him to return home mid-season. He returned to join the now-Division One Hull team in 1975, but he struggled to adjust to the higher level, and in a repeat of two years previously, he quit the club mid-season. This time he never returned to British speedway.

M	R	1st	2nd	3rd	Unpl	Pts	BP	Tot	Avge	FM	PM
92	342	58	106	89	85	475	73	548	6.41	0	1

Josef ANGERMULLER (1974)
Born – 6 November 1949, Wolznach, Germany. Died 24 April 1977

An established performer on the continental long-track circuit, 'Seppi' had a brief spell with Reading in 1971. He joined newly promoted Hull in 1974, and rode well in the 20 matches he had in Vikings colours, although he found it difficult to fit British speedway in with all his European commitments. He broke a leg early in 1975 which ruled him out for that season. He was killed in a track crash in Italy in April 1977.

M	R	1st	2nd	3rd	Unpl	Pts	BP	Tot	Avge	FM	PM
20	72	7	19	16	30	75	17	92	5.11	0	1

Eddie ARGALL (1973)
Born – 22 October 1950, Melbourne, Victoria

Son of former rider Ted, Eddie had his first rides at Toowoomba, Queensland in 1972. He arrived in the UK in 1973, and joined Hull as a stop-gap late in the season, showing some promise. For 1974 and 1975, Eddie raced at both Bradford and Coatbridge, improving to second-string level, a status he retained at Berwick in 1976. After a few matches in 1977, he suffered a broken leg which ended his season and led to his retirement.

M	R	1st	2nd	3rd	Unpl	Pts	BP	Tot	Avge	FM	PM
9	33	1	3	7	22	16	0	16	1.94	0	0

Tony ARMSTRONG (1971)
Born – 25 December 1945, Wordsley, West Midlands

Tony raced three seasons at Crayford from 1968 – 70, and when the Highwaymen closed raced one meeting for Hull in 1971 before retiring.

M	R	1st	2nd	3rd	Unpl	Pts	BP	Tot	Avge	FM	PM
1	2	0	0	0	2	0	0	0	0.00	0	0

Frank AUFFRET (1976-81)
Born – 23 December 1950, Middlesbrough

Middlesbrough-born Frank, who was Tyneside Cycle Speedway champion in 1967, moved to the motorised version of the sport, having second-half rides at Teesside from 1969 and graduated to the team in 1971, progressing well before moving to British League sister track Leicester in 1974. Frank was a member of an English Test side that toured Poland in 1975. He was snapped up by Vikings in the run up to the 1976 season, and his cheery personality made him an instant favourite both with the fans and in the pits where he was always encouraging his teammates. Although Frank was capable of the occasional top score, he was a steady second string/reserve who stayed the distance until 1981. He briefly rode for Middlesbrough in 1982 before retiring. He later worked for the local authority and also as a self-employed conference organiser.

M	R	1st	2nd	3rd	Unpl	Pts	BP	Tot	Avge	FM	PM
219	818	95	183.5	293.5	261	945.5	237	1182.5	5.78	1	1

Roger AUSTIN (1973)
Born – 21 May 1950, Canterbury, Kent

Roger was one of New Zealand's leading motocross riders before trying the shale sport at Christchurch in 1972. He came to Britain in 1973 to progress his career, and had spells with Ellesmere Port and injury-hit Hull, where he did not prove to be the answer to Vikings' problems, followed by Bradford and Division One Newport in 1974. He was not able to command a regular place with a British club, and after three matches with Mildenhall in 1975, he retired from British speedway.

M	R	1st	2nd	3rd	Unpl	Pts	BP	Tot	Avge	FM	PM
10	30	2	2	9	17	19	2	21	2.80	0	0

Bob BAKER (1948-49)
Born – 14 September 1922, London

Bob started racing at Rye House in 1947, and gave up his bricklaying job when New Cross signed him. Hull took him on loan for 1948, and he remained with the Angels until they closed, making excellent progress, holding the Hedon track record for a time and forming a twin spearhead with Mick Mitchell, particularly in the troubled 1949 season. From September 1949, Bob returned to New Cross where he raced for two years before transferring to Yarmouth. After spending three seasons with the Bloaters, Bob moved on again, this time to Oxford where he spent the rest of his career, finally retiring during the 1956 season.

M	R	1st	2nd	3rd	Unpl	Pts	BP	Tot	Avge	FM	PM
74	288	82	81	79	46	487	56	543	7.54	5	5

Peter BALDOCK (1971)
Born – Adelaide, South Australia

Peter first came to the UK in 1968 to join Wimbledon, but never actually raced for the Dons after breaking a leg in a car crash. He returned to British speedway in 1970 and joined Glasgow. The Tigers loaned him out to Division Two Berwick to gain experience, but a broken wrist after seven matches ended his season. Keen to pursue his career he linked up with the newly opened Hull team but found points hard to come by, the Vikings releasing him in mid-1971. He never appeared again in British speedway.

M	R	1st	2nd	3rd	Unpl	Pts	BP	Tot	Avge	FM	PM
12	34	1	3	11	19	20	8	28	3.29	0	0

David BARGH (1980-81)

Born – 14 March 1952, Martinborough, New Zealand

Dave began racing in his native New Zealand in 1976 and joined Newcastle in 1978 on the recommendation of Ivan Mauger. He made a handful of appearances for the Diamonds in 1978, but was banned from the Australasian final because of his age. This did not prevent him making good progress with Newcastle and he reached heat-leader status in 1980. He had a few outings at sister track Hull and was contemplating a British League career with the Vikings, but the Boulevard closed and Dave began his top-flight career with Sheffield. He adjusted well to the higher level of racing, staying at Owlerton for two seasons before returning to Newcastle in 1984 for their ill-fated season in the British League. He then moved to Coventry for three seasons as a steady performer. Dave missed a couple of British seasons before completing the circle with three final years at Newcastle.

M	R	1st	2nd	3rd	Unpl	Pts	BP	Tot	Avge	FM	PM
16	48	2	9	19	18	43	12	55	4.58	0	0

Bobby BEATON (1974-81)

Born – 14 May 1952, Blantyre, Scotland

Bobby started his speedway career after the meeting at Glasgow White City in 1968 and gained a regular place in the Tigers' team for 1969. He remained with Glasgow until 1973, racing at Hampden Park and Coatbridge before moving to Hull in 1974 with the licence. He helped the Vikings establish themselves in Division One and was a steady 7 or 8-point man, staying with the Vikings until closure in 1981, enjoying a testimonial meeting in 1978. In 1982 he moved into the National League with Newcastle for two seasons, with a further two at Edinburgh, finishing his career in 1987 at Glasgow. A member of a speedway family, his father promoted at Glasgow and brothers Jim and George rode. The family connection with the sport continues as nephew Gary has now started riding. Bobby has for many years been involved in the family coach business.

M	R	1st	2nd	3rd	Unpl	Pts	BP	Tot	Avge	FM	PM
279	1209	306	393	308.5	202.5	2012.5	216	2228.5	7.37	7	10

George BEATON (1971)
Born – 4 January 1951, Blantyre, Scotland. Died October 1972.

Brother of Bobby, George rode nine meetings for Berwick in 1971, also standing in once for Hull. He continued his career at Berwick in 1972 before being tragically killed in a car crash late in that year.

M	R	1st	2nd	3rd	Unpl	Pts	BP	Tot	Avge	FM	PM
1	4	0	0	0	4	0	0	0	0.00	0	0

Robbie BLACKADDER (1978, 1980)
Born – 7 December 1955, Cessnock, near Newcastle, NSW, Australia

Started racing at Newcastle, NSW in 1973, and joined new National League Newcastle in 1975. He progressed to a 9-point average by 1978 and retained heat-leader status for the rest of his career all of which was spent at Brough Park. He was used by sister track Hull as an injury stand-in on several occasions and acquitted himself well. A twice-broken arm in 1983 ended his season and led him to end his British career.

M	R	1st	2nd	3rd	Unpl	Pts	BP	Tot	Avge	FM	PM
5	13	1	3	3	6	12	3	15	4.62	0	0

Chris BLYTHE (1973)
Born – Liverpool

Aussie Chris had his first outings in King's Lynn's Division Two side in 1969. He then moved to Workington for 1970 and made some progress at Derwent Park before joining Ellesmere Port in 1972. He added some strength to the lower order of the Gunners team but did not build on it in 1973. Six meetings for injury-hit Hull were not particularly successful, and Chris drifted out of the sport.

M	R	1st	2nd	3rd	Unpl	Pts	BP	Tot	Avge	FM	PM
6	14	0	0	4	12	4	1	5	1.43	0	0

Peter BOSTON (1971-73)
Born – 10 May 1949, Hayling Island, England

Although he was born in England, Pete's family emigrated to Australia at an early age, settling in Perth. A draughtsman by trade, he came back to Britain in 1971 to try to break into speedway, and found a place at Hull, which was to be his only British club. One of the tallest riders in the sport, Pete unusually for a while lived in a van. He had some good matches for Vikings but was inconsistent and never sure of a regular place. He retired from the sport in mid-1973.

M	R	1st	2nd	3rd	Unpl	Pts	BP	Tot	Avge	FM	PM
62	207	24	33	67	83	205	43	248	4.79	0	0

Ian BOTTOMLEY (1971-72)
Born – 30 April 1948, Bradford, West Yorkshire

A Halifax second-halfer, Ian raced a few matches for Reading in 1968 before joining newly opened Crewe in 1969. He was happy on the large Earle Street bowl, but his scores suffered firstly when he suffered chest injuries in 1970, and secondly when the Crewe circuit was redesigned in 1971, and in mid-season he joined Hull. He fared little better at the Boulevard and was dropped after a few meetings in 1972, retiring from the sport.

M	R	1st	2nd	3rd	Unpl	Pts	BP	Tot	Avge	FM	PM
21	71	7	14	16	32	65	13	78	4.39	0	0

Harold BOTTOMS (1949)
Born – 26 July 1921, Birmingham.

Harold began racing at Fleetwood in 1948, and tried to break into the Hull team in 1949. He failed to make an impact at Hedon, and drifted out of the sport.

M	R	1st	2nd	3rd	Unpl	Pts	BP	Tot	Avge	FM	PM
1	2	0	0	0	2	0	0	0	0.00	0	0

Alan BRADLEY (1971-72)

A local grass-tracker, Alan lined up for the Vikings in their first ever match at Bradford in March 1971, but was injured in that match and never raced again until the following season, when he again turned out in one match, but he never seemed likely to make the grade on shale, preferring to concentrate on grass-track racing.

M	R	1st	2nd	3rd	Unpl	Pts	BP	Tot	Avge	FM	PM

Alan never rode a League or K.O. Cup match for Hull.

Barry BRIGGS (1976)

Born – 30 December 1934, Christchurch, New Zealand

In 1951, Barry first rode speedway in his native Christchurch. He came to the UK in 1952 and joined Wimbledon, staying with the Dons until 1959 by which time he had developed into one of the greatest riders with two world titles in 1957 and 1958 together with five league titles with Wimbledon. Spells with New Cross and Southampton followed before he joined Swindon in 1964, remaining with the Robins until 1972 by which time he had won two further world titles and the first six British League Riders' Championships. Barry was awarded the MBE in 1973 and returned to Wimbledon in 1974, spending two seasons before being persuaded to end his career with a season at Hull, where he had been extremely popular as an opponent. He led Vikings to their best British League season to date. Barry was involved in the promotion of the 1982 Los Angeles World Final.

M	R	1st	2nd	3rd	Unpl	Pts	BP	Tot	Avge	FM	PM
34	136	58	51	17	10	293	11	304	8.94	1	1

Bandy BURNETT (1971)

A second-halfer seeking a place in Hull's team when the Boulevard opened its doors to speedway in 1971, Bandy made the odd appearance at the start of the season as a stand-in but never made the grade and drifted out of the sport.

M	R	1st	2nd	3rd	Unpl	Pts	BP	Tot	Avge	FM	PM

Bandy never raced a League or K.O. Cup match for Hull

Tony CHILDS (1971-74)
Born – 16 January 1942, Felmingham, Norfolk

Bought his first bike in 1959 and practised in the Norwich car park at the Firs. He made his debut the same year in a match race against Cyril Crane. He raced for Yarmouth in 1960 but then did not appear in the sport until 1966 at Wimbledon. Tony linked with Crayford when Division Two started in 1968 and when the Highwaymen closed in 1970 he moved to Hull and as Vikings skipper he enjoyed great popularity at the Boulevard, becoming involved in more than his fair share of controversial incidents. It was only in 1973 that an ankle injury robbed Tony of the record of never missing a single Division Two fixture since 1968. He moved up to Division One with Hull in 1974 but found the going tough, reverting to Division Two with Scunthorpe, but he was in and out of the sport until his retirement in 1981. As a veteran, Tony made a few appearances in the second half in the early years at Craven Park.

M	R	1st	2nd	3rd	Unpl	Pts	BP	Tot	Avge	FM	PM
95	441	181	158	68	34	927	51	978	8.87	8	3

Neil CODDINGTON (1977, 1979)
Born – 22 May 1953, Brisbane, Queensland, Australia

Neil took up speedway after a career racing boats. Came to the UK in 1977, joining Newcastle. He made steady progress before breaking his collarbone and ankle in 1979 crashes which ended his season. He stood in for short-handed sister track Hull on three occasions. Neil never returned to race in the UK after 1979.

M	R	1st	2nd	3rd	Unpl	Pts	BP	Tot	Avge	FM	PM
3	6	0	0	3	3	3	1	4	2.67	0	0

Tom COGGINS (1948)

A second-halfer at Hedon, Tom made one appearance for Angels as a stand-in, but was not able to gain a place in the Angels side and retired from the sport.

M	R	1st	2nd	3rd	Unpl	Pts	BP	Tot	Avge	FM	PM
1	2	0	0	0	2	0	0	0	0.00	0	0

John COOK (1980)
Born – 18 December 1958, Van Nuys, California, USA

Initially a scrambler, John took up speedway, heading for Southern California to further his career. Following third and seventh places in the USA long-track and speedway finals in 1979, John followed in the footsteps of Kelly Moran and Dennis Sigalos and joined Hull in 1980, but found the going tough in his first season. As part of the deal that took Billy Sanders to Hull, John and Dennis Sigalos moved to Ipswich in 1981. He made great strides at Foxhall Heath, but his six years in East Anglia were a roller-coaster ride with disputes, walkouts on one side and on the other some great speedway, with a USA championship and World Final qualification in 1985 (he scored 9 points). He had become something of a cult figure among Witches fans. John had a few meetings for King's Lynn in 1987 and then did not appear in British speedway until 1993 with Poole. He reappeared in King's Lynn's colours for a few matches in 2000, also turning out for the USA at test level. John also represented his country in the 2001 World Cup.

M	R	1st	2nd	3rd	Unpl	Pts	BP	Tot	Avge	FM	PM
35	116	11	14	44	47	105	15	120	4.14	0	0

Alan COWLAND (1973, 1975)
Born – 17 March 1944, St Austell, Cornwall

Alan was a toolmaker by trade, and also has multi-lingual skills. He first started speedway at Rye House in 1962, linking with Exeter where he became a solid team member. He then had spells at Wolverhampton, Wimbledon, back at Exeter and Leicester before joining Hull's short-handed Division Two side in 1973. Hull's promotion saw Alan move to Workington before returning to the Boulevard in 1975 for another try in the top flight. Alan struggled at this level and retired after spells at Peterborough and Mildenhall. During his career Alan raced in many countries including in 1973 when he combined his Boulevard commitments with a season in the German league with Bopfingen.

M	R	1st	2nd	3rd	Unpl	Pts	BP	Tot	Avge	FM	PM
58	218	42	48	49	79	271	31	302	5.54	0	1

George CRAIG (1948-49)

Born – 6 January 1915, Bristol

George became interested in speedway after spectating at New Cross. He joined Dagenham in 1938, and impressed sufficiently to be signed by New Cross for 1939, who loaned him to Bristol. The war intervened and George served as a despatch rider in the Royal Corps of Signals, and was wounded in Italy. After the war, George returned to Bristol, before being signed by Hull for £90 in early 1948. George was a leading performer at Hedon although his scores dropped off a little in 1949. He moved to Swindon when the Angels closed, remaining at Blunsdon until his retirement after the 1950 season. George is still active in his senior years and lives in Australia.

M	R	1st	2nd	3rd	Unpl	Pts	BP	Tot	Avge	FM	PM
82	332	75	94	70	93	483	48	531	6.40	3	1

Mike CUROSO (1976-1977)

Born – 15 April 1954, Huntingdon Beach, California, USA

After some success on the Californian scene, Mike decided to try his luck in British speedway, signing for Hull in 1976 on the recommendation of Barry Briggs. He found it difficult to adjust at first, but improved machinery helped him to a debut 6-point average. He was not able to improve on this in 1977, being a rider who relied heavily on his gating skills. He moved to Poole in 1978, and after one season in Dorset retired from British speedway.

M	R	1st	2nd	3rd	Unpl	Pts	BP	Tot	Avge	FM	PM
66	241	28	50	91	72	275	72	347	5.76	0	0

Phil DARGUE (1948)

Phil raced in the second half at Hedon and made an appearance for a short-handed Angels side but never progressed further and dropped out of the sport.

M	R	1st	2nd	3rd	Unpl	Pts	BP	Tot	Avge	FM	PM
1	2	0	0	1	1	1	0	1	2.00	0	0

Graeme DAWSON (1973)
Born – 2 February 1953, Colne, Lancashire

Graeme had his first rides at Nelson in 1968, then left the sport to concentrate on his job as an upholsterer and carpet fitter. He was tempted back to the sport, racing at Belle Vue in 1971 before signing for Hull in late 1973. He gained a regular place at Coatbridge, and achieved heat-leader status by 1976. Serious head injuries sustained at Barrow ended his career in 1977 and Hull sent a team to race in a benefit meeting for Graeme at Glasgow in October 1977.

M	R	1st	2nd	3rd	Unpl	Pts	BP	Tot	Avge	FM	PM
14	53	4	3	18	28	36	6	42	3.17	0	0

George DEVONPORT (1971-1972)
Born – 31 December 1945, Netherton

George, a bricklayer by trade, made his debut at Doncaster in 1969, moving to Crayford in 1970. His all-action style caused him to have a few spills and this did not change when he signed for Hull in 1971. He raced half the season before sustaining a serious back injury which ruled him out of the sport until 1972 when he made a brief and unsuccessful comeback. He raced a few matches for newly opened Chesterton in 1973 before retiring.

M	R	1st	2nd	3rd	Unpl	Pts	BP	Tot	Avge	FM	PM
11	26	6	2	7	11	29	1	30	4.62	1	0

Peter DODDS (1948)
Born – 1925, London

Peter rode several matches for the Angels when they were establishing themselves at Hedon, not securing a regular team place as the team was strengthened. He appears not to have pursued his career further.

M	R	1st	2nd	3rd	Unpl	Pts	BP	Tot	Avge	FM	PM
5	10	0	0	2	8	2	0	2	0.80	0	0

Graham DRURY (1976-1979, 1981)
Born – 13 February 1952, Chester

Graham started out on the grass, enjoying great success in the Cheshire area. His first rides on shale were at the Belle Vue training school in 1971, and then he linked with Rochdale. He followed the licence to Ellesmere Port in 1972 and by 1973 had achieved a 9-point average. Graham maintained his form at Crewe in 1975, and a couple of guest appearances for Hull late that year persuaded the Vikings to sign him for 1976. He made good progress at the top level under the influence of Barry Briggs and this was reflected in 1977 when Graham was Hull's No. 1 rider. Unfortunately the form was not maintained and he became a solid second string up until Vikings' closure in 1981 apart from 1980 when he spent the year racing in the German league. After 1981, Graham reverted to the National League with two-year spells at both Oxford and Long Eaton, winning a championship medal with the Invaders in 1984. Retiring from racing, Graham became involved in the promotion of the annual ice meeting at Telford with his former Hull boss Ian Thomas. He also became the promoter at Long Eaton in 1995 until Station Road closed, and is currently the promoter at Conference League Mildenhall.

M	R	1st	2nd	3rd	Unpl	Pts	BP	Tot	Avge	FM	PM
178	727	129	226	226	146	1065	167	1232	6.78	2	4

Alan EMERSON (1981)
Born – 29 May 1957, Haltwhistle, Northumberland

Alan made his debut for Teesside in 1973. Three years at Cleveland Park saw him progress to heat-leader status and in the next two seasons he had outings in the British League with Leicester and Birmingham while remaining at Teesside. He then moved to Workington in 1979 followed by Glasgow in 1980 where he had his best season while also racing at Birmingham. Joining Newcastle, he spent the last three years of his career at Brough Park, and appeared for sister track Hull once in 1981.

M	R	1st	2nd	3rd	Unpl	Pts	BP	Tot	Avge	FM	PM
1	2	0	0	0	2	0	0	0	0.00	0	0

John ESKILDSEN (1981)

Born – 21 November 1960, Febjerg, Denmark

John, who raced for Uldjydene in Denmark, came to Britain in 1980 trying to break into Birmingham's team but only managed a few outings. As Danish junior champion, he was loaned to Hull in 1981 and had an extended run in the Vikings team in the last year at the Boulevard, making steady progress. He continued to improve back at Perry Barr in 1982, and moving on to Eastbourne, he achieved heat-leader status in two seasons. On the move again, he was back in the Midlands at Wolverhampton, where he enjoyed two good seasons. Just after the start of 1987, when he seemed to be in the best form of his career, he decided to return to Denmark, and never raced again in the UK.

M	R	1st	2nd	3rd	Unpl	Pts	BP	Tot	Avge	FM	PM
32	112	9	23	36	44	109	29	138	4.93	0	0

Clark FACEY (1972-73)

Born – 8 March 1952, Taunton, Somerset

Clark made his senior debut with Plymouth in 1969, but only had one match in 1970, spending his time second-halfing at several tracks before having five matches for both Swindon and Romford in 1971. Several matches for Exeter in 1972 led him to sign for Hull mid-season. He showed promise at the Boulevard but the travelling involved made it difficult for him to get time off work. He remained at the Boulevard, racing a handful of matches in 1973 before ending his career with a spell at Weymouth in 1974.

M	R	1st	2nd	3rd	Unpl	Pts	BP	Tot	Avge	FM	PM
21	80	14	11	15	40	79	8	87	4.35	0	0

Glyn FACEY (1973)

Born – 27 January 1955, Taunton, Somerset

A tyre fitter by trade, Glyn first rode in public at Exeter in 1971 after attending the 1970-1971 Weymouth training school. He signed for Hull in 1973 following brother Clark to the Boulevard. He raced a few North Eastern Trophy matches at the start of the season before an injury cost him his team place. The following year, Glyn had a spell at Weymouth before drifting out of the sport.

M	R	1st	2nd	3rd	Unpl	Pts	BP	Tot	Avge	FM	PM

Glyn never rode a League or K.O. Cup match for Hull.

Robbie GARDNER (1974-75)

Born – 20 March 1953, Bury, Lancashire

Robbie's first rides were at the 1970 Belle Vue training school and he joined Rochdale and then Ellesmere Port where he graduated to a second-string berth. He made the surprise move into Division One with Hull in 1974 where he had a promising season but at the start of 1975 he unexpectedly quit the club to return to the National League with Workington. He moved back to Ellesmere Port in 1976, and then on to Newcastle. He was injured at the start of the 1979 season without racing an official fixture and subsequently retired from the sport.

M	R	1st	2nd	3rd	Unpl	Pts	BP	Tot	Avge	FM	PM
35	119	16	23	27	53	121	28	149	5.01	0	1

Dennis GAVROS (1972-73)

Born – 17 June 1943, Adelaide, South Australia

Twenty-one-year-old Dennis came to the UK, joining Halifax in 1965. He was at the Shay for five years, making steady improvement to second-string status. He then took a break from the sport, and now being resident in West Yorkshire, set up a garage business. He looked set to return to Halifax in 1972 but Hull stepped in for his signature. He was immediately the centre of a controversy as it was felt he should have been offered to another Division One club, and he rode for Hull in a K.O. Cup tie with Teesside which Hull won. Teesside protested about his eligibility and Dennis's points were deducted, reversing the outcome of the tie. Hull were allowed to keep Dennis, and he proved to be a steady middle-order man at the Boulevard being appointed captain in 1973. He did not move up to Division One with Hull in 1974, and after a handful of matches for Sunderland, he retired.

M	R	1st	2nd	3rd	Unpl	Pts	BP	Tot	Avge	FM	PM
47	188	41	30	58	59	241	22	263	5.60	0	0

Dave GIFFORD (1974)
Born – 18 April 1944, Herne Bay, Kent

Dave, whose family emigrated to New Zealand, first rode at New Plymouth in 1960. He came to Britain in 1965 and had six seasons with Newcastle before moving to Wolverhampton and then Coatbridge. In 1974, he doubled up with the Tigers and Hull, racing half the season at the Boulevard before being sensationally sacked after joining Belle Vue in their walkout on 31 July. Reverting to the National League, he completed the 1974 season at Coatbridge before moving to Berwick where he spent the last four seasons of his career.

M	R	1st	2nd	3rd	Unpl	Pts	BP	Tot	Avge	FM	PM
19	57	4	11	15	27	49	10	59	4.14	0	0

Derek GLOVER (1948-49)
Born – 2 February 1930, Wigan, Lancashire

A Wigan-based farmer, Derek was always interested in motorcycles and took up speedway at Wigan in 1947, having some meetings at reserve. He joined Hull in 1948, and after a steady first season made considerable improvement in 1949, achieving a just-under-7-point average. He moved to Swindon on Hull's closure, and linked with Liverpool for 1950, but when the Chads moved up into Division Two in 1951, Derek retired and resumed farming.

M	R	1st	2nd	3rd	Unpl	Pts	BP	Tot	Avge	FM	PM
78	274	52	57	85	80	355	54	409	5.97	2	0

Mick GLOVER (1971)
Born – 23 August 1950, Sheffield

Mick is the cousin of Carl and Les Glover, the famous Sheffield-based speedway brothers. He was friendly with Tigers rider Bengt Larsson and had his first rides on a trip to Sweden with Bengt. He rode in the second half at Sheffield and Halifax, but made his only two league appearances at the Boulevard, once as a stand-in for Hull, and then against Hull, filling in for a short-handed Romford team. He never progressed further in the sport and retired in the early seventies.

M	R	1st	2nd	3rd	Unpl	Pts	BP	Tot	Avge	FM	PM
1	2	0	0	0	2	0	0	0	0.00	0	0

Les GODWIN (1949)
Born – 1949, London

Les was a novice at Rye House and joined Hull for the 1949 season. He had a few matches in Angels' colours but failed to secure a regular team place, after which he retired from the sport.

M	R	1st	2nd	3rd	Unpl	Pts	BP	Tot	Avge	FM	PM
1	2	0	0	1	1	1	0	1	2.00	0	0

Brian GORMAN (1948)
Born – 1 June 1924, Sheffield

An apprentice fitter, Brian saved for a machine, and joined Bluey Wilkinson's training school at Sheffield. He served as a Royal Marine during the war, and afterwards set up a taxi-hire business in Sheffield. He had a trial at Harold Stephenson's training school, and was signed by Stoke. In 1948 he transferred to Hull, but did not achieve a regular team place. He signed for his home-town track in 1949 and stayed at Owlerton for 1950, before retiring.

M	R	1st	2nd	3rd	Unpl	Pts	BP	Tot	Avge	FM	PM
12	35	2	4	13	16	27	2	29	3.31	0	0

Mitch GRAHAM (1974-77)
Born – 16 December 1948, Great Broughton, Cumbria

Mitch rode scrambles before joining his local club Workington and progressed to heat leader by 1974 by which time he was doubling up with Division One Hull. A rider whose temperament often cost him points, he stayed at Hull until 1977 when a turbulent relationship with Hull promoter Ian Thomas led him to ask for a transfer and he moved to Halifax in 1978. He had a good season at the Shay before moving on to National League Stoke, but after a few meetings in 1979, Mitch retired. When Workington reopened in 1999, Mitch was appointed Commercial Manager, a position he still holds.

M	R	1st	2nd	3rd	Unpl	Pts	BP	Tot	Avge	FM	PM
134	522	111.5	141.5	120	149	737.5	75	812.5	6.23	3	1

Johnny GREEN (1949)
Born – 25 July 1927, Burnley, Lancashire

Johnny raced for Hull Angels in their final season, but was not really the answer to the team's lack of strength. He then moved to Sheffield, and in 1951 signed for Newcastle moving again to Edinburgh in August of that year. He remained at Meadowbank for two seasons, again moving mid-season in 1952, this time to Motherwell. He was never a star rider but he stayed with the Eagles until 1955 when after a spell with Leicester he retired. He was briefly tempted out of retirement by Newcastle in 1961, but notoriety came Johnny's way in 1983 when he received a jail sentence for his part in a drugs ring.

M	R	1st	2nd	3rd	Unpl	Pts	BP	Tot	Avge	FM	PM
17	47	4	11	12	20	46	8	54	4.60	0	0

Steve GRESHAM (1974)
Born – 18 August 1954, Santa Monica, California, USA

Steve was a scrambler who also did motocross before first trying speedway in 1969. He appeared at Costa Mesa in 1970 and raced for Irwindale Eagles in 1972. In the wake of Scott Autrey's success in Britain, Steve decided to try his luck, signing for Hull in 1974. He found it difficult to establish a regular team place and he quit mid-season. He returned in 1975 with Newport and progressed to heat leader, continuing his improvement with Bristol in 1977 and 1978 Steve then moved to Swindon where, apart from 1982 at Reading, he spent the rest of his British career.

M	R	1st	2nd	3rd	Unpl	Pts	BP	Tot	Avge	FM	PM
6	23	0	6	7	10	19	5	24	4.17	0	0

Brian HAVELOCK (1975–1976, Team Manager 1995)
Born – 9 May 1942, Yarm, North Yorkshire

An accomplished scrambler and grass-track performer, Brian turned to speedway and a second-half appearance at Teesside in 1971 led to a few appearances for the Teessiders in 1972. He moved to Sunderland in 1973 and improved to heat-leader standard in his two years on Wearside. An abbreviated season at Berwick in 1974 preceded him joining Newcastle who had reopened in 1975. He spent two seasons at Brough Park while putting in some appearances for sister track Hull. Brian then enjoyed his most successful three seasons at Workington before spells with

Middlesbrough (again) and Stoke led to his retirement in 1983. Father of 1992 World Champion Gary, Brian was team manager for a spell during 1995 at Craven Park when Vikings reopened.

M	R	1st	2nd	3rd	Unpl	Pts	BP	Tot	Avge	FM	PM
11	37	6	8	6	17	40	10	50	5.41	0	0

Shane HEARTY (1972)
Born – 27 July 1945, Kingston upon Thames, Surrey

Shane was a keen second-halfer who had one league match with Hull in 1972. He ran a motorcycle clothing and accessories business before riding for several new National League teams in 1975 without appearing in an official fixture. He never managed to secure a regular team place and subsequently retired.

M	R	1st	2nd	3rd	Unpl	Pts	BP	Tot	Avge	FM	PM
1	1	0	0	0	1	0	0	0	0.00	0	0

Jurgen HEHLERT (1974)
Born – 15 April 1941, Meissen, Germany

East German who defected to the West in 1972. He signed for Hull in 1974 and rode one Northern Trophy match before being released. He never rode for another British club, preferring to concentrate on the continental circuit.

M	R	1st	2nd	3rd	Unpl	Pts	BP	Tot	Avge	FM	PM

Jurgen never raced a League or K.O. Cup match for Hull.

Ron HENDERSON (1975-1976)
Born – 27 February 1957, Brisbane, Queensland, Australia

Ron's start in speedway was at the age of 16 in Brisbane. He raced for Queensland in 1974-1975 before coming to Britain in 1975 to join Newcastle. He achieved heat-leader status in his brief three-year British career. Ron had a few matches as a stand-in for injury-hit sister track Hull. He gave up speedway during 1977 to become a social worker in Newcastle before returning to Australia in early 1978.

M	R	1st	2nd	3rd	Unpl	Pts	BP

TotAvge	FM	PM									
3	13	0	2	1	10	5	1	6	1.85	0	0

Bernie HORNBY (1972)
Born – 15 September 1947, Manchester

Bernie had his first rides at Long Eaton in 1968 and raced several meetings for the Rangers in 1969. Missing 1970, he linked with Workington in 1971 racing ten matches for the Cumbrian club. He had eight matches for Hull in 1972, after signing on loan for injury-hit Vikings. He returned to Derwent Park in 1973, and made some improvement in the next two seasons, before moving to Berwick in 1975, where ironically he achieved his highest average of 4.69 before retiring at the end of that season.

M	R	1st	2nd	3rd	Unpl	Pts	BP	Tot	Avge	FM	PM
8	23	0	1	7	15	9	1	10	1.74	0	0

Rod HUNTER (1978-1981)
Born – 25 April 1956, Melbourne, Victoria, Australia

A former junior scrambles champion and 1978 Australian long-track champion, Rod signed for Newcastle. Initially he was loaned to Glasgow but he returned to Brough Park, making a satisfactory debut season. Rod progressed to heat leader in the following seasons, and he remained with the Diamonds until 1984. He stood in at Hull when Vikings were short handed. He raced in the senior league with Newcastle in 1994, and when Brough Park closed, moved to Halifax for 1985. After three years away he returned to Newcastle in 1989, and his last year in British speedway was spent at Middlesbrough in 1990 when he helped the Bears to the runners-up spot in both league and cup.

M	R	1st	2nd	3rd	Unpl	Pts	BP	Tot	Avge	FM	PM
23	77	6	10	23	38	61	12	73	3.79	0	0

Tommy JOHANSSON (1975)
Born – 21 October 1950, Tveta, Småland, Sweden

Tommy first rode at the age of seven on a 100cc machine, making his first public appearance when eleven years old. When he reached the age for senior speedway he rode in the Swedish league, eventually deciding to come to the UK in 1971, joining Newport. He then raced for Ipswich in 1972 and briefly in 1973 before missing out in 1974 because of the ban on Swedes riding in British speedway, although it did not prevent him reaching the World Final in Gothenburg where he scored 8 points. In 1975 he was signed by Hull and was a valuable middle-order rider although because of other riding commitments he missed many Vikings matches. He never returned to British speedway after 1975.

M	R	1st	2nd	3rd	Unpl	Pts	BP	Tot	Avge	FM	PM
11	44	5	16	14	9	61	12	73	6.64	0	0

Norman JOHNSON (1948-1949)

Born – 16 June 1919, Newcastle upon Tyne

Norman served as a Home Guard despatch rider, and later an engineer during the war, after which he started riding at Newcastle in 1947, appearing in second halves. He was a founder member of the newly formed Hull Angels in 1948, occupying a second-string role for all of the Angels' existence, his scores being much stronger at Hedon than on away tracks. Norman moved to Ashfield in September 1949, and spent two seasons in Glasgow, and then one season at Newcastle before retiring.

M	R	1st	2nd	3rd	Unpl	Pts	BP	Tot	Avge	FM	PM
80	301	34	71	73	123	317	41	358	4.76	0	0

Phil KYNMAN (1976-1978)

Born – 21 August 1956, Hull

Phil first rode at Scunthorpe in 1976, moving to Newcastle on loan from parent club Hull in 1977. He had improved considerably and opted for a full-time British League career with Hull in 1978. Despite a reasonable start, Phil retired at the end of May, but resumed his career at Berwick in 1979. Once again he retired, resurfacing at Scunthorpe in 1981. A further two-year break saw Phil back at Berwick for two seasons, and then after two matches in 1987 he finally retired, although when Craven Park opened in 1995, he had a few second-half rides.

M	R	1st	2nd	3rd	Unpl	Pts	BP	Tot	Avge	FM	PM
18	48	4	7	14	23	40	10	50	4.17	0	0

Bryan LOAKES (1972)
Born – Brisbane, Queensland, Australia

Bryan, a big name in Queensland speedway, followed a well-trodden path taken by many Aussies wanting to make their speedway name and came to the UK. He had some second halves at Halifax in 1972 before signing on loan for Hull. He became popular at the Boulevard with his all-action style and outgoing personality. He was a middle-order man, but did not return to the UK until 1995, once again signing for a Hull side trying to establish themselves in the top flight. It did not work out as Bryan was injured racing for Australia against Poland in Brisbane and although he travelled to Britain he never took to the track and returned home, never to ride again in the UK.

M	R	1st	2nd	3rd	Unpl	Pts	BP	Tot	Avge	FM	PM
22	94	14	16	34	30	108	19	127	5.40	0	0

George McGOVERN (1948)

George had trials at Norwich, moving to Hull in 1948. He raced one challenge match, and failed to keep his team place. George was unable to obtain a team place elsewhere and drifted out of the sport.

M	R	1st	2nd	3rd	Unpl	Pts	BP	Tot	Avge	FM	PM

George never raced a League or K.O. Cup match for Hull.

Paul McHALE (1981)
Born – 3 October 1964, Wallsend, Tyne and Wear

Paul had second-half rides at Newcastle in 1980, and had a few outings for the Diamonds in 1981. Paul stood in at Hull for a few League Cup matches in 1981. He appeared again at Newcastle in 1983 before riding for Edinburgh the following season. He had two seasons at Berwick before retiring in 1987. Paul achieved fifteen minutes of TV fame when he did a wall of death ride on Noel Edmonds' Late Late Breakfast Show.

M	R	1st	2nd	3rd	Unpl	Pts	BP	Tot	Avge	FM	PM

Paul never rode a League or K.O. Cup match for Hull

Jim McMILLAN (1974-1975)
Born – 3 December 1945, Glasgow, Scotland

Jim first rode at a training school at Cowdenbeath in January 1966, winning a place in Glasgow's team for 1967.

By 1969 he had become the Tigers' No. 1 with a 10-point average. He was reserve for the 1972 World Final and moved to Hull with Coatbridge's Division One licence. He spent two years as Vikings captain, holding together an under-strength side. He moved to Wolverhampton in 1976 as part of the deal that was supposed to send Ole Olsen to Hull. He spent five years at Monmore Green followed by two at Belle Vue. He was beginning to find the pace in the top division too hot and moved into the National League back at Glasgow, then finishing his career with three seasons at Berwick. He was team manager for a spell at Berrington Lough. Jim was a regular choice for Scotland and Great Britain teams, and can nowadays be found assisting in the pits at Coventry home matches.

M	R	1st	2nd	3rd	Unpl	Pts	BP	Tot	Avge	FM	PM
69	315	158	118	26	13	736	28	764	9.70	5	3

John McNEILL (1980)

Born – 4 August 1955, Footscray, Melbourne, Victoria, Australia

John started in 1972 at Melbourne and came to Britain in 1975. He had second halves at Exeter and Newport before joining first-year new National League Mildenhall. He moved to Scunthorpe in 1977 and progressed to heat leader. John decided to try his luck with Division One Leicester, and had two seasons at Blackbird Road before buying his contract and linking with Hull in 1980. He only raced a few matches for the Lada Vikings, moving on to Poole. Spells with Cradley Heath and National League Weymouth preceded his retirement at the end of the 1982 season.

M	R	1st	2nd	3rd	Unpl	Pts	BP	Tot	Avge	FM	PM
6	19	2	4	5	8	19	4	23	4.84	0	0

Eric MASON (1949)

Born – Herefordshire

Trying to break into a league side, Eric raced eight matches for Angels just prior to the shutters coming down at Hedon, and re-emerged in 1951 at Long Eaton. He appeared for both the Archers and Edinburgh in 1952 before retiring.

M	R	1st	2nd	3rd	Unpl	Pts	BP	Tot	Avge	FM	PM
8	17	1	3	5	8	14	6	20	4.71	0	0

Ivan MAUGER (1978-81)

Born – 4 October 1939, Christchurch, New Zealand

Arguably the greatest rider in the history of the sport, Ivan's start in speedway was not easy. He joined Wimbledon in 1957 but returned home in 1958, not having established himself. He returned for another try in 1963, joining Provincial League Newcastle. He made an immediate impact and was clearly determined to go to the very top. He stayed at Newcastle before moving to Belle Vue in 1969 as the league's No. 1 rider, and became the first rider to win three consecutive World Finals in Katowice in 1970. By 1972 he had won his fourth title and had maintained an 11-point average for five years in a row, helping Belle Vue to the championship from 1970-1972. Ivan joined Exeter in 1974, and immediately led them to the title, remaining with the Devon club until 1977, by which time he had been honoured with an MBE in 1976. 1977 saw Ivan equal Ove Fundin's record five World Titles. He signed for Hull in January 1978 for a record £12,000 fee and transformed the Vikings into title contenders in 1978 and 1979. The record-breaking sixth World title came in 1979 at Katowice, and in the same year he captained New Zealand to the World Team Cup. A blood disorder and back injuries reduced his scoring in 1980, but he remained at the Boulevard until its final closure in 1981. He was involved in promoting the 1982 World Final in Los Angeles and was persuaded to have a final season of home matches only for Exeter in 1984 before retiring.

M	R	1st	2nd	3rd	Unpl	Pts	BP	Tot	Avge	FM	PM
119	505	298	110	54	43	1168	37	1205	9.54	24	5

Phil MICHELIDES (1976)

Born – 6 August 1952, Perth, Western Australia

Phil's first speedway experiences were at Adelaide's Rowley Park. He then had after the meeting rides at Bunbury, Western Australia before debuting at Claremont in 1972-1973. He joined the Australian contingent at Brough Park in 1975 and was a steady middle-order man, standing in at the Boulevard when Hull were short-handed. He quit and returned to Australia during 1977 after mechanical and psychological problems.

M	R	1st	2nd	3rd	Unpl	Pts	BP	Tot	Avge	FM	PM
2	7	0	2	2	3	6	0	6	3.43	0	0

Dave MILLS (1972-1973)
Born – 12 October 1948, Ashfield, Australia

After racing at Liverpool, NSW, Dave made the trip to the UK in 1972 and was an immediate success at Hull where he replaced Reg Wilson in the Vikings line-up. His all-action style and cheerful personality made him a massive Boulevard favourite, and he raced two years for Hull before business and personal reasons led to his retirement. Dave has maintained his links with the sport, as he is now the chief of referees in Australia. His daughter Wendy has spent 2003 in the UK assisting fellow Australians Craig Watson and Frank Smart at Newport.

M	R	1st	2nd	3rd	Unpl	Pts	BP	Tot	Avge	FM	PM
63	288	130	88	43	27	609	37	646	8.97	9	4

Mick MITCHELL (1948-1949)
Born – 19 December 1914, London

A diminutive character of only 5ft 2ins, Mick had appeared for Crystal Palace, New Cross, Edinburgh, Newcastle and Glasgow, but only made progress when loaned to Birmingham in 1947. New Cross released him to sign for Hull in 1948, and his spectacular leg-trailing style made him a great Hedon favourite. When Alf Webster was injured, Mick took over the captaincy which he never relinquished. He finished 1948 as the Hedon track-record holder and the Division Three Match Race Champion. He remained at Hedon until closure, moving to Swindon with the licence. During 1950 he transferred to St Austell, remaining in Cornwall until his retirement in 1952. As a link with the past, Mick was the guest of honour for the first meeting at the Boulevard in 1971.

M	R	1st	2nd	3rd	Unpl	Pts	BP	Tot	Avge	FM	PM
81	326	157	90	37	42	688	31	719	8.82	12	8

Kelly MORAN (1978-1979)

Born – 21 September 1960, Huntingdon Beach, California, USA

Kelly, together with brother Shawn, had raced motor cycles from an early age, and made rapid progress through the grades in California. He was spotted by Hull promoter Ian Thomas, and lured by Ivan Mauger, who had signed for the Vikings, agreed to come to Hull in 1978. He made a steady start, but soon the ability to come from the back, learned from handicap racing on small tracks began to show, and Kelly was soon a massive Boulevard favourite, his outgoing personality adding to his charisma. He was beginning to turn in some big scores when he received multiple injuries in a crash at Hackney. He returned to Hull the following season and he confirmed his star status as Vikings challenged for the league title, although he missed the title decider because of a broken collarbone sustained at Wolverhampton. The icing on the cake for Kelly was a sensational fourth place in his debut World Final in Poland. Hull could not agree terms with Kelly for 1980 and he sat out the start of the season, joining Birmingham midway through. The following year he joined Eastbourne and had two happy years at Arlington which included another World Final fourth place, this time at Los Angeles. He spent the next three years racing at home although he was again fourth in the Gothenburg World Final of 1984. Kelly returned to the British League in 1986, spending three seasons at Sheffield with brother Shawn a teammate. He then moved on to Belle Vue where he remained until 1992, when after a few matches for the Aces he went on loan to Swindon, but the magic had faded and it was his last season in Britain. In a wonderful career, Kelly was capped many times for the USA, and was a member of the World Team Cup winning side in 1982 and 1990. To those who saw him race, Kelly would be in most fans' top ten most exciting riders to watch, and it was probably his fun-loving approach to life that denied him even greater honours. At the age of forty-two, Kelly has started riding again in Canada.

M	R	1st	2nd	3rd	Unpl	Pts	BP	Tot	Avge	FM	PM
65	262	78	84	47	53	449	66	515	7.86	2	7

Shawn MORAN (1979-1980)

Born – 19 November 1961, Lakewood, California, USA

Shawn had grown up on the same circuit as brother Kelly, and it was almost inevitable that he would follow his brother to the UK. He raced a couple of meetings at the end of 1979 under the pseudonym of David East, before signing for Hull in 1980. He raced until August at the Boulevard but was unhappy and signed for Sheffield for £8,000. He was a stunning success at Owlerton and was Tigers' No. 1 right through to 1988. He

won the World Long Track Championship in 1983 and finished eighth and fifth in the 1984 and 1985 World Finals. He was a member of the 1982 World Team Cup winning side. From 1986 to 1988 he rode in the same Sheffield side as Kelly. Following Sheffield's closure, Shawn moved to Belle Vue where he remained until 1993. While with the Aces, he lost a run-off for the 1990 world title at Bradford, and also was again a member of the USA team championship victors in the same year. In 1989, Shawn won the British League Riders Championship. He returned to Sheffield in 1994 but after a few matches admitted he had lost his nerve and retired. Like brother Kelly he was an exciting rider to watch and is regarded by many Sheffield fans as the club's greatest rider, although his charismatic personality made him loved by fans everywhere.

M	R	1st	2nd	3rd	Unpl	Pts	BP	Tot	Avge	FM	PM
29	128	28	33	29	38	179	28	207	6.47	0	1

Ray MUIR (1948)

Born – 29 May 1913, Newcastle upon Tyne

Ray made several appearances for the fledgling Angels without earning a regular place in the Angels side. He is not thought to have raced after 1948.

M	R	1st	2nd	3rd	Unpl	Pts	BP	Tot	Avge	FM	PM
7	18	2	2	6	8	16	1	17	3.78	0	0

Kelvin MULLARKEY (1973)

Born – 29 March 1951, Chelmsford, Essex

Kelvin started riding at King's Lynn in 1970 at the training school and raced two matches for the Stars in 1971. Unable to find a team place in 1972, he linked with Hull in the latter part of 1973, showing considerable promise. A season at Weymouth saw Kelvin achieve heat-leader status, before he linked with Rye House. He was eight seasons as a Rocket, and was a top rider at Hoddesdon, also having matches for British League Poole in 1978. Kelvin spent the 1983 season at Canterbury and then returned to Rye House, although by now his scores were declining, and after a seven-match spell at Mildenhall in 1976, he retired.

M	R	1st	2nd	3rd	Unpl	Pts	BP	Tot	Avge	FM	PM
10	39	4	6	13	16	37	5	42	4.31	0	0

Egon MULLER (1976)
Born – 26 November 1948, Kiel, Germany

An accomplished Continental circuit long-track performer much sought after by British clubs, Egon rode two matches for Coatbridge in 1973. He was persuaded to join Hull in mid-1976 to prepare for the 1976 World Final, and rode eight matches for the Vikings creating a tremendous impact with his charismatic personality and exciting racing style before sensationally quitting the club. He never again rode in British speedway, but enjoyed his finest hour winning the 1983 World Final at Norden to add to his three Long Track titles.

M	R	1st	2nd	3rd	Unpl	Pts	BP	Tot	Avge	FM	PM
8	32	14	11	2	6	66	4	70	8.75	0	0

Bob NEWELL (1949)

Second-halfer Bob made a single appearance in Angels colours but did not establish himself in the sport.

M	R	1st	2nd	3rd	Unpl	Pts	BP	Tot	Avge	FM	PM
1	2	0	0	0	2	0	0	0	0.00	0	0

Alan NICHOLSON (1948)
Born – 29 August 1924, Newcastle upon Tyne

Alan was discharged from the Navy with shell shock, and riding speedway allowed him to recover his confidence, curing himself of the problem. He signed for Hull in 1948 and made a good start before an injury at Wombwell sidelined him for several months. He never regained his team place at Hedon and subsequently retired from the sport.

M	R	1st	2nd	3rd	Unpl	Pts	BP	Tot	Avge	FM	PM
3	12	3	5	2	2	21	3	24	8.00	0	0

Dave O'CONNOR (1973)

Born – 13 July 1947, Melbourne, Victoria, Australia

Dave had raced successfully in Australia, and came to Britain in 1970, joining Newport. He struggled to make an impact, but persisted with the Wasps in 1971, only managing a 2.11 average. He tried his luck again in 1973, racing only one match for Hull, before having two outings for Crewe. Dave then decided enough was enough and retired from the sport.

M	R	1st	2nd	3rd	Unpl	Pts	BP	Tot	Avge	FM	PM
1	2	0	0	0	0	0	0	0	0.00	0	0

Joe OWEN (1975-1981)

Born – 13 September 1956, Ormskirk, Lancashire

Joe started at Barrow with after-the-meeting rides in 1972 and earned a team place at Holker Street in 1973 when he made an instant impact, being marked out as a star of the future. On Barrow's closure, Joe moved to Newcastle where he remained for four years, becoming the National League's outstanding rider. He also rode for sister track Hull as No. 8 and confirmed his potential at the Boulevard. He joined the Vikings full time in 1977 and adapted slowly to life in the higher league. However, in 1978 Joe was showing sparkling form when he suffered near-fatal injuries in a second-half crash at the Boulevard. Bravely he returned to the saddle in 1979 and was not far off recovering his full form. He remained at Hull until closure in 1981 and then reverted to Newcastle, assuming again the mantle of the National League's No. 1 rider, staying with the club for their ill-fated 1984 season in the British League. Joe joined National League Ellesmere Port for 1985, helping the Gunners to the league title in their final season. Joe crashed in the Gunners' final league match of the season at Birmingham and suffered serious back injuries which have seen him confined permanently to a wheelchair.

M	R	1st	2nd	3rd	Unpl	Pts	BP	Tot	Avge	FM	PM
182	792	179	300	215	98	1352	153	1505	7.60	7	6

Tom OWEN (1974, 1976-1980)
Born – 19 June 1951, Ormskirk, Lancashire

Brother of Joe, Tom was accomplished on grass before turning to speedway. He attended the 1971 Belle Vue winter training school and joined Barrow in 1972, reaching heat-leader status by the time the Bombers closed in 1974, having already doubled up for Division One Hull and acquitting himself very well. He accompanied Joe to Newcastle and became his brother's rival as the National League's No. 1 rider. His 1975 British League experience came at Newport, where he became a track specialist. Tom was then an able stand-in at the Boulevard until 1979 while remaining a star performer for Newcastle. Injuries ravaged his seasons in 1980 and 1981 and his form began to decline although he remained a heat leader through four seasons at Stoke, finishing his career with one last campaign at Newcastle.

M	R	1st	2nd	3rd	Unpl	Pts	BP	Tot	Avge	FM	PM
65	253	32	81	83	57	341	53	394	6.23	0	0

Stein PEDERSEN (1974)
Born – 6 January 1955, Sandnes, Norway

Stein had come to the UK for an Ole Olsen training school and was given one Northern Trophy match for the Vikings, who had just moved into Division One. He did not impress and was not given any further outings. Stein returned to Norway and retired from speedway.

R	1st	2nd	3rd	Unpl	Pts	BP	Tot	Avge	FM	PM

Stein never raced a League or K.O. Cup match for Hull.

Stan PENNELL (1948)
Born –

Stan raced in Hull Angels' first ever fixture at Hanley but made no further appearances, and does not appear to have raced elsewhere.

R	1st	2nd	3rd	Unpl	Pts	BP	Tot	Avge	FM	PM

Stan never raced a League or K.O. Cup match for Hull.

Tommy ROPER (1974)

Born – 6 July 1940, Bradford, West Yorkshire

Tommy started out with his home-town track in the Provincial League, then moving to Sheffield before joining Halifax at the start of the British League. He then had a four-year spell with Belle Vue which was followed by brief spells at Oxford and back at Halifax in 1972. Throughout his career Tommy was a dependable rather than a star rider, always valuable to have around. He retired after 1972 but was lured back after a spin at Sheffield, but the Tigers were too strong so he was snapped up by Hull, seeking to strengthen in their debut Division One season. Tommy acquitted himself well with the Vikings, posting some fine scores at the Boulevard. He finally hung up his leathers at the end of the 1974 season.

M	R	1st	2nd	3rd	Unpl	Pts	BP	Tot	Avge	FM	PM
32	121	26	23	32	40	156	11	167	5.52	1	1

Billy SANDERS (1981)

Born – 9 September 1955, Sydney, New South Wales, Australia. Died 23 April 1985

Billy's first rides were at Liverpool, Sydney in 1970-1971. He rode for Australia v. USA in 1971-1972 before joining newly promoted Ipswich in 1972. After a settling-in season Billy advanced to heat-leader status, and became an adopted son of Suffolk. He was a member of the 1975 and 1976 Ipswich championship sides. Billy left Foxhall Heath in 1979 for Birmingham but returned to Suffolk in September of that year before joining Hull in 1981 in the deal that took Dennis Sigalos and John Cook to Ipswich. Injury curtailed Billy's season in Hull's final term at the Boulevard, and he raced for King's Lynn in 1982, returning to Ipswich for 1983 and 1984. Tragically in April 1985 personal problems led to Billy taking his own life.

M	R	1st	2nd	3rd	Unpl	Pts	BP	Tot	Avge	FM	PM
25	107	43	39	15	10	222	10	232	8.67	2	0

Lou SANSOM (1975)
Born – 29 December 1946, Adelaide, South Australia

Starting out at Murray Bridge, South Australia in 1969, Lou first rode in public at Rowley Park, Adelaide. He joined new Division Two club Workington in 1970, quickly becoming a star at Derwent Park, and by 1973 had achieved a 10.5 average. He missed 1974, returning to Cumbria in 1975, also having a few matches for Hull at the start of the season, but did not choose a Division One career at the time, remaining with the Comets until the end of 1976 when he moved into the top flight with Birmingham. A 5.5-point average at Perry Barr was not enough to persuade Lou to return to the UK for 1978.

M	R	1st	2nd	3rd	Unpl	Pts	BP	Tot	Avge	FM	PM
9	36	5	6	11	14	38	9	47	5.22	0	0

Dick SHEPHERD (1948)
Born –21 February 1920, Leicester

Dick watched the sport at Leicester, and tempted to try racing, he learned the rudiments at Harold Stephenson's 1946-47 winter training school. He had a trial at Wembley and then went on loan to Plymouth, but opportunities were scarce at Pennycross and he signed for Hull in 1948. He was nearly unbeatable at Hedon but struggled on away tracks. He was transferred to Walthamstow for 1949 for a £150 fee, but suffered head injuries and missed most of the season. He returned to the sport in 1951 at New Cross and then had two seasons at Ipswich before leaving the sport. During the winter Dick performed for Kirby's Flying Ballet Pantomime and when speedway ran at the Boulevard, he was booked for a similar show.

M	R	1st	2nd	3rd	Unpl	Pts	BP	Tot	Avge	FM	PM
41	165	51	39	38	37	269	27	296	7.18	4	2

Dennis SIGALOS (1979-1980)
Born – 16 August 1959, Garden Grove, California, USA

Dennis started riding in Orange County at the age of thirteen and became the leading junior rider in California. He spent a season racing in Australia with former Viking Dave Mills, and then followed in Kelly Moran's footsteps, signing for Hull in 1979. His potential was obvious from the start and he had a successful first season, which he built on in 1980, edging Ivan Mauger out as Vikings' No. 1, and winning the VW Grand Prix. Dennis has the distinction of being the final track-record holder at the Boulevard. He

was not able to agree terms for 1981 and moved to Ipswich where he was made captain and continued his progress, becoming one of the world's leading riders. He broke an ankle in 1982 but that did not prevent him finishing 3rd in the Los Angeles World Final. Dennis moved on in 1984, joining Wolverhampton, but he suffered another broken ankle in June which ended his season. He made a brief return in late 1985 with Ipswich but was far from fit and retired from the sport. In a superb but too-brief career, Dennis was half of the USA team that won the World Pairs final in 1992.

M	R	1st	2nd	3rd	Unpl	Pts	BP	Tot	Avge	FM	PM
71	305	141	62	47	55	594	41	635	8.33	5	0

Barry SIMPSON (1981)
Born – 15 June 1959, Carlton in Cleveland

Barry won the East Yorkshire Under-21 grass-track championship in 1976, before taking up speedway at Middlesbrough in 1978. He sat out 1979 but returned to the sport the following year with rides at the Felton training track. He rode second halves at Newcastle and then in 1981 he rode twice for short-handed Hull before retiring during the season. Barry was later the timekeeper at Middlesbrough's Cleveland Park and now works in Darlington.

M	R	1st	2nd	3rd	Unpl	Pts	BP	Tot	Avge	FM	PM
2	7	0	1	0	6	2	0	2	1.14	0	0

Graeme STAPLETON (1979)
Born – 1 February 1946, Christchurch, New Zealand

Graeme was scrambles champion of New Zealand before taking up speedway at his local track in 1970. He came to Britain in 1971, racing for Canterbury and Division One Wimbledon. He went full time at Plough Lane in 1972, spending three years with the Dons, reaching second-string level. He missed the 1975 and 1976 seasons for business reasons. He returned to Wimbledon in 1977 but broke a wrist in August. In 1978, he joined Newcastle on loan and remained at Brough Park for 1979. He was injured while standing in for Hull in the 1979 title decider at Coventry and never raced again in British speedway. Graeme was regularly capped by New Zealand and was a member of the Kiwi side that won the World Team Cup in 1979.

M	R	1st	2nd	3rd	Unpl	Pts	BP	Tot	Avge	FM	PM
2	6	0	0	1	5	1	0	1	0.67	0	0

Stan STEVENS (1972)
Born – 26 April 1934, Ilford, Essex

Former cycle speedway star who turned to the motorised version of the sport at a Rye House training school. Stan rode for Rayleigh, Cradley Heath, New Cross, Southampton and West Ham before joining Oxford in the first year of the British League. Stan had levelled out as a second string, spending a season at King's Lynn before reverting to West Ham where he remained until 1970. A move to Division Two Romford followed in 1971, and that track's closure led him to West Ham and then Barrow in 1972. Injury-hit Hull snapped him up in mid-1972 and he helped steady the ship at the Boulevard. He largely missed 1973, racing for Rye House and then helping Mildenhall to establish themselves as a National League club before retiring in 1976 to concentrate on his trade as a printer.

M	R	1st	2nd	3rd	Unpl	Pts	BP	Tot	Avge	FM	PM
11	45	12	10	11	12	67	9	76	6.76	0	0

Ron STRINGER (1949)

Ron raced for Odsal in 1949 while also appearing twice for the Angels. He does not appear to have raced after 1949.

M	R	1st	2nd	3rd	Unpl	Pts	BP	Tot	Avge	FM	PM
2	3	0	0	0	3	0	0	0	0.00	0	0

Peter THOMPSON (1973)
Born – 12 June 1947, Bunbury, Australia

Peter came to Britain in 1973 and had a few matches for Hull and Crewe without gaining a regular team place. He had a good 1973-1974 season in Australia, but was not able to carry this form into 1974 as spells with Peterborough and Exeter failed to earn him a team place and he subsequently did not return to the UK.

M	R	1st	2nd	3rd	Unpl	Pts	BP	Tot	Avge	FM	PM
2	5	1	0	0	4	3	0	3	2.40	0	0

Colin TUCKER (1971-72, Team Manager and Track Curator 1972-1973)
Born – 8 January 1945, Auckland, New Zealand

A qualified carpenter, Colin's first British club was Rayleigh in 1968. He moved to newly opened Crewe in 1969, being responsible for building the track. He fell out with the Kings in 1970 and after a few meetings for Long Eaton, moved to Hull in 1971, also being involved in the construction of the Boulevard track. Colin was a solid middle-order rider, and was popular with the fans. He retired from racing in mid-1972, taking on the team manager's role as well as continuing as track curator. He decided to retire from the sport completely at the end of 1973 and return to his native New Zealand. Such was his Boulevard popularity that a Colin Tucker Farewell meeting was staged.

M	R	1st	2nd	3rd	Unpl	Pts	BP	Tot	Avge	FM	PM
41	149	19	36	47	47	176	41	217	5.83	0	0

Doug UNDERWOOD (1972)
Born – 28 May 1949, Perth, Western Australia

Originally a scrambler, Doug started his speedway career at Claremont Park, Perth in 1971-1972. He came to Britain for the 1972 season and had one match for Hull before joining Scunthorpe. He progressed to second-string status at Quibell Park and moved to Teesside in 1975 where he became a heat leader. He had raced a few matches for sister track Leicester, and he joined the Lions full time in 1976. Doug was a second string during a season and a half at Blackbird Road, joining Reading in mid-1977 in an exchange deal that took Boleslaw Proch to Leicester. He dropped into the National League with Weymouth in 1979 and retired at the end of that season.

M	R	1st	2nd	3rd	Unpl	Pts	BP	Tot	Avge	FM	PM
1	2	0	0	0	2	0	0	0	0.00	0	0

Mike VERNAM (1973)
Born – 5 June 1944, Winchester, Hampshire

A Poole junior, Mike was loaned to Weymouth in 1968 to obtain experience. He achieved an 8-point average at Radipole Lane, before moving to Reading where in two seasons he improved further. He was not able to translate this form into Division One in the handful of outings he had with his parent club, and his form dipped in 1972 when at Canterbury. He improved a little the following season at Eastbourne but was released and joined injury-hit Hull. He raced two matches for Vikings, before admitting that he was not riding well enough to justify the journey. He then retired from the sport.

M	R	1st	2nd	3rd	Unpl	Pts	BP	Tot	Avge	FM	PM
2	8	1	0	1	6	4	1	5	2.50	0	0

Dennis WASDEN (1971-1973)
Born – 23 August 1948, Sheffield. Died – 1989

Dennis started his speedway career at his local track, second halfing without winning a team place. He tried his luck with Ipswich's Division Two team in 1969 before joining Doncaster in 1970. When the South Yorkshire club closed, he moved to Hull where he became a regular second string/reserve. He retired during 1973 and sadly passed away in 1989.

M	R	1st	2nd	3rd	Unpl	Pts	BP	Tot	Avge	FM	PM
82	293	24	61	101	107	295	55	350	4.78	0	0

Jack WATTS (1949)
Born – 13 November 1920, Middlesbrough

Jack first saw speedway before the war, but hostilities had commenced before he was old enough to ride. After serving in the Merchant Marine, he acted as mechanic for Kid Curtis at Middlesbrough, and started racing after borrowing a bike. He broke a wrist and then had a few races at Cleveland Park before joining Hull in 1949. He was a regular in the Hedon side, achieving a 4.5-point average. In 1950 he appeared at Leicester before drifting out of the sport.

M	R	1st	2nd	3rd	Unpl	Pts	BP	Tot	Avge	FM	PM
34	92	4	24	29	35	89	16	105	4.57	0	0

Alf WEBSTER (1948-1949)
Born – 29 August 1925, Manchester

Alf saw speedway at Belle Vue, and assisted Eric Chitty of West Ham, where he won the mechanics race in 1947. Division Three in 1948 gave Alf his chance at Hull. He was the first track-record holder at Hedon and Angels' skipper until injury. Alf made good progress at Hedon and moved with the licence to Swindon. The Robins released him for 1950 and he signed for Liverpool where he had three seasons before moving to St Austell in 1952. Alf finished his career with two seasons at Exeter, retiring when the Falcons closed.

M	R	1st	2nd	3rd	Unpl	Pts	BP	Tot	Avge	FM	PM
57	196	33	46	67	50	258	48	306	6.24	0	3

Johnny WHITE (1948)
Born – 11 October 1916, London

Developed an interest in the sport when watching Crystal Palace in 1929. He was a regular at Rye House practices from 1939 to 1941 and also gained much experience at the wartime Belle Vue meetings. He had a trial for West Ham in 1946, then racing for New Cross and Bradford in 1947, before transferring to Hull in 1948. Johnny adapted well to the unusual Hedon track, developing a reputation for snaking through narrow gaps to pass riders. He transferred to Yarmouth in 1949 for a £50 fee and spent the last three years of his career with the Bloaters.

M	R	1st	2nd	3rd	Unpl	Pts	BP	Tot	Avge	FM	PM
45	171	45	29	47	50	240	27	267	6.25	2	2

Don WILKINSON (1949)
Born – 13 November 1920, Morpeth, Northumberland

Don second-halfed at Newcastle before joining Hull in 1949. On the closure of Hedon, he switched to Newcastle where he spent two seasons, showing an improvement in form in 1951. He then moved to Glasgow White City where he spent two seasons as a middle-order rider, retiring when the Scottish side folded. The advent of the Provincial League tempted Don out of retirement and in 1961 he raced the first part of the season at Middlesbrough before moving to Newcastle in May. He started the 1962 season at Brough Park but his season and indeed his career was ended by a shoulder injury.

M	R	1st	2nd	3rd	Unpl	Pts	BP	Tot	Avge	FM	PM
5	13	0	0	5	8	5	2	7	2.15	0	0

Reg WILSON (1971)
Born – 26 January 1948, Sheffield

Reg started in speedway at the 1968 Sunday afternoon training school at Sheffield. He made his debut the following year, racing a few matches with Doncaster and Sheffield before linking with Workington in 1970. Establishing himself as a top second string at Derwent Park, he moved to Hull the following year when the Boulevard club opened. He made great strides and was Hull's No. 1 before being recalled by parent club Sheffield in 1972 to race in Division One. Obviously destined for a great future, Reg had achieved a 10-point average when he suffered a broken leg. He resumed at Owlerton in 1976, although he never quite achieved his previous average. He spent part of 1984 at Newcastle before sampling the National League with Birmingham in 1985 and 1986 prior to retirement. Reg has for several years been the Sheffield team manager.

M	R	1st	2nd	3rd	Unpl	Pts	BP	Tot	Avge	FM	PM
33	163	88	55	13	7	387	8	395	9.69	5	1

Mike WOOD (1949)
Born – 16 December 1923, London

Mike had a few races as a novice at Exeter in 1948, before signing for Hull in 1949. He had a few matches for the Angels but did not earn a regular team place, and when the Hedon circuit closed its doors, Mike retired.

M	R	1st	2nd	3rd	Unpl	Pts	BP	Tot	Avge	FM	PM
8	19	0	2	3	14	7	1	8	1.68	0	0

Bill WORGAN (1948)

Hedon junior who stood in when Angels were short handed. He never secured a regular place and was not seen in the sport after 1948.

M	R	1st	2nd	3rd	Unpl	Pts	BP	Tot	Avge	FM	PM
2	4	0	0	2	2	2	0	2	2.00	0	0

Fred YATES (1948)
Born – 1 May 1916, London

A Tamworth schoolteacher who served in all three services during the war, Fred had trials at Belle Vue and was a mechanic at Hyde Road before signing for Tamworth in 1947. He was plagued by injury in that season. Fred had had one match for Hull in 1948, but ended up signing for Coventry before racing at Ashfield and Fleetwood in 1949. Fred was one of the few riders of his era who rode wearing contact lenses.

M	R	1st	2nd	3rd	Unpl	Pts	BP	Tot	Avge	FM	PM

Fred never raced a League or K.O. Cup match for Hull.

4
HEAD-TO-HEAD RESULTS 1948-1981

Venues for Hull home matches are 1948-1949 Hedon Stadium; 1971-1981 The Boulevard. Venues for Hull away matches are shown with the record for each opponent.

Abbreviations: A – Abandoned, D – Drawn, L – Lost, W – Won.

Domestic Competitions

Hull v. Barrow

Barrow home matches all staged at Holker Street

Year	*Date*	*Type*	*Home*	*Away*
1972	23 Aug	League	W48-30	–
1973	3 Jul	Challenge	–	L35-43
1973	22 Aug	League	D39-39	–
1973	11 Sep	League	–	L20-57
1973	10 Oct	Challenge	W40-37	–

(Barrow took over West Ham's fixtures in mid-1972 when Hull had already raced at West Ham in the league. See West Ham.)

Hull v. Belle Vue

Belle Vue home matches staged (1974-1981) Hyde Road

Year	*Date*	*Type*	*Home*	*Away*
1974	17 Apr	Northern Trophy	L37-41	–
1974	20 Apr	Northern Trophy	–	L25-53
1974	29 Jun	League	–	L26-52
1974	31 Jul	League	W60-9*	–
1975	5 Apr	Northern Trophy	–	L33-45
1975	9 Apr	Northern Trophy	L37-41	–
1975	7 May	League	D39-39	–

Year	*Date*	*Type*	*Home*	*Away*
1975	23 Aug	League	–	L32-46
1975	10 Sep	Challenge	W46-30	–
1976	3 Apr	Northern Trophy	–	L30-48
1976	30 Jun	League	L36-42	–
1976	30 Jun	Northern Trophy	L36-42	–
1976	9 Oct	League	–	L37-41
1976	27 Oct	Challenge	W51-26	–
1977	20 Apr	Northern Trophy	L36-42	–
1977	7 Sep	League	L36-42	–
1977	17 Sep	League	–	W39-38
1978	8 Apr	Northern Trophy	–	L38-40
1978	12 Apr	Northern Trophy	L36-42	–
1978	20 May	League	–	L31-47
1978	19 Jul	League	W54-24	–
1979	31 Mar	Northern Trophy	–	W40-38
1979	11 Apr	Northern Trophy	W46-32	–
1979	5 Jun	League	W42-36	–
1979	21 Jul	League	–	W49-29
1980	4 Apr	Northern Trophy	–	L34-44
1980	9 Apr	Northern Trophy	W45-33	–
1980	9 Jul	Knock-Out Cup	W66-42	–
1980	*12 Jul*	*Knock-Out Cup*	–	*A6-18*
1980	20 Aug	League	L38-40	–
1980	23 Aug	Knock-Out Cup	–	L40-68
1980	6 Sep	League	–	L35-43
1981	1 Apr	League Cup	W50-46	–
1981	18 Apr	League Cup	–	L45-51
1981	13 Jun	Knock-Out Cup	–	L43-53
1981	24 Jun	Knock-Out Cup	W54-42	–
1981	9 Sep	League	W42-36	–
1981	3 Oct	League	–	L33-44

* Belle Vue walked out after 4 heats in protest at track conditions. Hull completed the match uncontested. The result stood.

The 1976 match at Hull dated 30 June counted for both League and Northern Trophy points.

The 1977 Northern Trophy match at Belle Vue was rained off and never restaged.

Hull v. Berwick

Berwick home matches all staged at Shielfield Park

Year	*Date*	*Type*	*Home*	*Away*
1971	26 May	League	W42-36	–
1971	25 Sep	League	–	L33-45

Year	*Date*	*Type*	*Home*	*Away*
1972	5 Apr	North-Eastern Trophy	L33-44	–
1972	8 Apr	North-Eastern Trophy	–	L30-48
1972	28 Jun	League	W50-28	–
1972	29 Jul	League	–	L38-40
1973	4 Apr	North-Eastern Trophy	W46-32	–
1973	7 Apr	North-Eastern Trophy	–	L35-43
1973	23 Jun	League	–	W41-37
1973	27 Jun	League	W60-18	–
1976	3 Jul	Inter-Divisional Knock-Out Cup	–	W43-35

Hull v. Birmingham

Birmingham home matches all staged at Perry Barr Stadium

Year	*Date*	*Type*	*Home*	*Away*
1971	26 Jul	League	–	L37-41
1971	29 Sep	League	D39-39	–
1972	3 May	League	W43-35	–
1972	21 Aug	League	–	L34-44
1973	23 May	League	L38-40	–
1973	25 Jul	Challenge	W46-32	–
1973	1 Oct	League	–	L23-55
1976	28 Jun	League	–	W44-34
1976	28 Jul	League	W52-26	–
1977	18 May	League	W51-27	–
1977	8 Aug	League	–	W40-38
1978	8 May	League	–	L38-40
1978	2 Aug	League	W57-21	–
1979	12 Jun	League	W58-20	–
1979	25 Jun	League	–	W40-38
1980	21 Apr	League	–	L34-44
1980	11 Jun	League	W51-27	–
1980	8 Oct	Challenge	W54-24	–
1981	15 Apr	League Cup	W55-41	–
1981	17 Apr	League Cup	–	L45-51
1981	22 Jul	Knock-Out Cup	W49-47	–
1981	24 Jul	Knock-Out Cup	–	L44-52
1981	25 Sep	League	–	L30-47
1981	30 Sep	League	W42-36	–

Hull v. Boston

Boston home matches all staged at New Hammond Beck Road

Year	*Date*	*Type*	*Home*	*Away*
1971	28 Jul	League	L35-43	–
1971	5 Sep	League	–	L36-42
1971	6 Oct	Challenge	W41-36	–
1971	10 Oct	Challenge	–	L38-40
1972	9 Apr	Challenge	–	L18-60
1972	12 Apr	Challenge	W42-36	–
1972	19 Jul	League	L29-49	–
1972	23 Jul	League	–	L33-45
1972	25 Oct	Challenge	W40-38	–
1973	8 Apr	Challenge	–	L32-45
1973	18 Jul	League	W43-34	–
1973	22 Jul	League	–	L33-45
1973	24 Oct	Challenge	W45-33	–
1981	3 May	Knock-Out Cup	–	W48-47

Hull v. Bradford

Bradford home matches all staged at Odsal Stadium

Year	*Date*	*Type*	*Home*	*Away*
1971	31 Mar	Challenge	–	L25-52
1971	31 May	League	D39-39	–
1971	30 Aug	Challenge	W42-36	–
1971	1 Sep	League	–	L37-41
1971	13 Oct	Challenge	W42-35	–
1972	22 Mar	Challenge	–	L35-42
1972	29 May	League	L36-42	–
1972	31 May	League	–	L34-44
1972	28 Aug	Challenge	W53-24	–
1973	27 Aug	League	W42-35	–
1973	*29 Aug*	*League*	–	*A17-31*
1973	19 Oct	League	–	L25-53

Hull v. Bristol

Bristol home matches all staged at Eastville Stadium

Year	*Date*	*Type*	*Home*	*Away*
1977	3 Jun	Challenge	–	L27-51
1977	29 Jun	Inter-Divisional Knock-Out Cup	W48-30	–
1977	13 Jul	League	W42-36	–
1977	3 Aug	Knock-Out Cup	W49-29	–
1977	5 Aug	Knock-Out Cup	–	L26-52
1977	26 Aug	League	–	L31-47
1978	19 Apr	League	W48-30	–
1978	15 Sep	League	–	L34-44

Hull v. Canterbury

Canterbury home matches all staged at Kingsmead Stadium

Year	*Date*	*Type*	*Home*	*Away*
1971	16 Jun	League	W45-33	–
1971	18 Sep	League	–	W42-35
1972	2 Sep	League	–	W43-35
1972	6 Sep	League	W41-37	–
1973	1 Sep	League	–	L28-50
1973	5 Sep	League	D39-39	–

Hull v. Coventry

Coventry home matches all staged at Brandon Stadium

Year	*Date*	*Type*	*Home*	*Away*
1948	22 May	League	W44-39	–
1948	24 Jul	League	W56-28	–
1948	25 Sep	League	–	L29-55
1948	30 Oct	League	–	L36-48
1974	7 Aug	League	W58-20	–
1974	14 Sep	League	–	L30-48
1975	23 Apr	League	W42-36	–
1975	10 May	League	–	D39-39
1976	31 Jul	League	–	L37-41
1976	22 Sep	League	W51-27	–
1977	13 Apr	League	W44-33	–
1977	10 Sep	League	–	L20-58
1978	21 Jun	League	W55-22	–
1978	29 Jul	League	–	L30-48

Year	*Date*	*Type*	*Home*	*Away*
1979	18 Apr	League	W51-27	–
1979	14 Jul	Knock-Out Cup	–	L48-60
1979	18 Jul	Knock-Out Cup	W75-33	–
1979	13 Oct	League	–	L36-42
1980	25 Jun	League	D39-39	–
1980	16 Aug	League	–	L26-52
1981	8 Apr	League Cup	L43-53	–
1981	9 May	League Cup	–	L43-53
1981	31 Aug	League	–	L27-51
1981	23 Sep	League	W43-35	–

Hull v. Cradley Heath

Cradley Heath home matches staged between 1948-1981 at Dudley Wood Stadium
Cradley Heath rode under the name 'Cradley United' seasons 1973-1976 inclusive

Year	*Date*	*Type*	*Home*	*Away*
1948	1 May	Knock-Out Cup	L42-66	–
1948	7 May	Knock-Out Cup	–	L29-78
1948	5 Jun	League	L36-48	–
1948	11 Jun	League	–	L30-54
1948	27 Aug	League	–	L31-53
1948	18 Sep	League	W54-30	–
1974	24 Apr	League	L37-41	–
1974	17 Aug	League	–	L36-42
1975	16 Jul	Challenge	W47-31	–
1975	2 Aug	League	–	L27-51
1975	20 Aug	League	W47-31	–
1976	17 Jul	League	–	L38-39
1976	18 Aug	League	L37-41	–
1977	8 Jun	Knock-Out Cup	W46-32	–
1977	11 Jun	Knock-Out Cup	–	L36-42
1977	1 Oct	League	–	L33-44
1977	5 Oct	League	W44-34	–
1977	8 Oct	Inter-Divisional Knock-Out Cup	–	L37-41
1978	9 May	League	W46-32	–
1978	26 Aug	League	–	L25-53
1979	28 May	Challenge	–	L23-55
1979	28 Jul	League	–	L37-41
1979	26 Sep	League	W41-37	–
1979	1 Oct	Inter-Divisional Knock-Out Cup	–	L27-50
1979	15 Oct	Knock-Out Cup	–	L46-62
1979	*17 Oct*	*Knock-Out Cup*	*A19-23*	–

Year	*Date*	*Type*	*Home*	*Away*
1979	31 Oct	Knock-Out Cup	L50-58	–
1980	7 Apr	League	–	L33-45
1980	16 Jul	League	W42-36	–
1980	15 Oct	Challenge	W44-34	–
1981	6 May	League Cup	L44-52	–
1981	6 Jun	League Cup	–	L33-63
1981	15 Jul	League	L34-44	–
1981	15 Aug	League	–	L26-52

Hull v. Crewe

Crewe home matches all staged at Earle Street

Year	*Date*	*Type*	*Home*	*Away*
1971	21 Apr	Challenge	W46-32	–
1971	14 Jun	League	–	L32-46
1971	21 Jul	League	W47-31	–
1972	12 Jul	League	W41-36	–
1972	18 Sep	League	–	L27-51
1972	11 Oct	Challenge	L38-40	–
1973	11 Jul	League	W48-30	–
1973	17 Sep	League	–	L30-48

Hull v. Eastbourne

Eastbourne home matches all staged at Arlington Stadium

Year	*Date*	*Type*	*Home*	*Away*
1971	14 Jul	League	W41-37	–
1971	3 Oct	League	–	L32-46
1972	3 Sep	League	–	L24-53
1972	20 Sep	League	W40-38	–
1973	2 Sep	League	–	L26-52
1973	19 Sep	League	D39-39	–
1978	26 May	Inter-Divisional Knock-Out Cup	–	W45-32
1979	13 Apr	League	–	L27-50
1979	11 Jul	League	W50-28	–
1979	12 Aug	Inter-Divisional Knock-Out Cup	–	W41-37
1980	16 Apr	League	W46-32	–
1980	10 Aug	League	–	W41-37
1981	20 May	League	W46-32	–
1981	9 Aug	League	–	L30-48

Hull v. Ellesmere Port

Ellesmere Port home matches all staged at Thornton Road

Year	Date	Type	Home	Away
1972	11 Apr	Challenge	–	L22-56
1972	2 Aug	League	W44-34	–
1972	15 Aug	League	–	W40-38
1972	18 Oct	Challenge	W47-31	–
1973	2 May	League	W41-37	–
1973	8 May	League	–	W42-36
1973	1 Aug	Challenge	W44-34	–

Hull v. Exeter

Exeter home matches all staged at The County Ground

Year	Date	Type	Home	Away
1948	26 Apr	League	–	L23-60
1948	17 Jul	League	W63-21	–
1948	16 Oct	League	W50-34	–
1948	25 Oct	League	–	L22-62
1949	20 Jun	League	–	L36-48
1949	23 Jul	League	L40-44	–
1974	22 May	League	L34-44	–
1974	29 Jul	League	–	L24-51
1974	18 Sep	Challenge	L38-40	–
1975	2 Jul	League	L36-42	–
1975	18 Aug	League	–	L27-51
1976	19 May	League	W45-33	–
1976	23 Aug	League	–	L35-43
1977	1 Aug	League	–	L25-53
1977	28 Sep	League	L36-42	–
1978	27 Sep	League	W44-33	–
1978	23 Oct	League	–	L22-56
1979	23 Apr	League	–	L33-45
1979	23 May	League	W45-33	–
1979	17 Sep	Knock-Out Cup	–	L48-60
1979	19 Sep	Knock-Out Cup	W70-38	–

Hull v. Glasgow

Glasgow home matches staged between 1977-1979 at Blantyre Stadium

Year	*Date*	*Type*	*Home*	*Away*
1977	23 Oct	Challenge	–	W40-38
1979	18 May	Inter-Divisional Knock-Out Cup	–	W50-28

Hull v. Hackney

Hackney home matches all staged at Waterden Road

Year	*Date*	*Type*	*Home*	*Away*
1974	24 May	League	–	L30-48
1974	3 Jul	League	W44-34	–
1975	30 Apr	League	W42-36	–
1975	15 Aug	League	–	L37-41
1976	14 May	League	–	L35-42
1976	16 Jun	League	W46-32	–
1977	27 Jul	League	W48-30	–
1977	23 Sep	League	–	L36-42
1978	14 Apr	League	–	W40-38
1978	28 Jun	League	W52-26	–
1978	25 Aug	Inter-Divisional Knock-Out Cup	–	L37-41
1979	27 Jun	League	W56-22	–
1979	28 Sep	League	–	W45-33
1980	23 Apr	League	L38-40	–
1980	30 May	Knock-Out Cup	–	W63-45
1980	3 Jun	Knock-Out Cup	W67-41	–
1980	26 Sep	League	–	L31-46
1981	17 Jun	League	W45-33	–
1981	28 Aug	League	–	L23-55

Hull v. Halifax

Halifax home matches all staged at The Shay

Year	*Date*	*Type*	*Home*	*Away*
1949	25 May	League	–	L26-57
1949	18 Jun	League	L37-46	–
1949	13 Jul	Challenge	–	L33-51
1949	30 Jul	League	L39-45	–
1949	31 Aug	League	–	L22-62
1974	3 Apr	Northern Trophy	D39-39	–
1974	6 Apr	Northern Trophy	–	L25-52

Year	Date	Type	Home	Away
1974	15 Jun	League	–	L36-42
1974	11 Sep	League	W49-29	–
1974	28 Sep	Yorkshire Cup	–	L33-44
1974	16 Oct	Yorkshire Cup	L37-41	–
1975	22 Mar	Northern Trophy	–	L30-48
1975	2 Apr	Northern Trophy	L37-40	–
1975	31 May	League	–	D39-39
1975	25 Jun	League	D39-39	–
1975	13 Sep	Yorkshire Cup	–	L33-45
1975	17 Sep	Yorkshire Cup	D39-39	–
1976	20 Mar	Northern Trophy	–	L38-40
1976	31 Mar	Northern Trophy	D39-39	–
1976	9 Jun	Knock-Out Cup	W44.5-33.5	–
1976	27 Jun	Knock-Out Cup	–	L32-46
1976	7 Aug	League	–	L38-40
1976	8 Sep	League	W45-33	–
1976	13 Oct	Yorkshire Cup	W45-33	–
1976	17 Oct	Yorkshire Cup	–	W43-35
1977	26 Mar	Northern Trophy	–	L26-51
1977	30 Mar	Northern Trophy	W51-27	–
1977	7 May	League	–	L30-48
1977	1 Jun	League	W48-30	–
1977	9 Jul	Yorkshire Cup	–	L33-45
1977	12 Oct	Yorkshire Cup	W43-35	–
1978	29 Mar	Northern Trophy	L36-42	–
1978	1 Apr	Northern Trophy	–	L33-45
1978	8 Jul	League	–	L33-45
1978	26 Jul	League	W41-37	–
1978	7 Oct	Yorkshire Cup	–	L37-41
1978	11 Oct	Yorkshire Cup	W47-31	–
1979	30 Mar	Northern Trophy	L36-42	–
1979	21 Apr	Northern Trophy	–	L31-47
1979	16 Jun	League	–	W40-38
1979	5 Sep	League	W43-34	–
1979	3 Oct	Yorkshire Cup	W53-25	–
1980	26 Mar	Northern Trophy	L37-41	–
1980	12 Apr	Northern Trophy	–	L38-40
1980	13 May	League	L32-46	–
1980	27 Sep	League	–	L30-48
1980	1 Oct	Yorkshire Cup	W42-36	–
1980	11 Oct	Yorkshire Cup	–	L30-48
1981	28 Mar	League Cup	–	L36-60
1981	13 May	League Cup	W54-42	–

Year	Date	Type	Home	Away
1981	20 Jun	Yorkshire Cup	–	L34-44
1981	12 Aug	League	D39-39	–
1981	22 Aug	League	–	L32-46
1981	7 Oct	Yorkshire Cup	W46-32*	–

* The final meeting at The Boulevard.

Hull v. Hanley

Hanley home matches all staged at Sun Street

Year	Date	Type	Home	Away
1948	25 Mar	Challenge	–	L16-64
1948	27 Mar	Challenge	L30-52*	–
1948	17 Apr	League	L37-47	–
1948	26 Jun	League	L38-44	–
1948	28 Aug	Challenge	L35-49	–
1948	2 Sep	League	–	L25-59
1948	28 Oct	League	–	L21-62
1949	2 Apr	League	L40-43	–
1949	7 Apr	League	–	L20-63
1949	1 Aug	League	W47-37	–

* The first meeting at Hedon Stadium.

Hull v. Hastings

Hastings home matches all staged at Pilot Field

Year	Date	Type	Home	Away
1948	8 May	League	W45-39	–
1948	25 Aug	League	–	L40-43
1948	8 Sep	League	–	L37-45
1948	23 Oct	League	W64-20	–
1949	11 Jun	League	W47-37	–
1949	22 Jun	League	–	L39-45

Hull v. Ipswich

Ipswich home matches all staged at Foxhall Heath

Year	Date	Type	Home	Away
1971	6 May	League	–	L35-42
1971	7 Jul	League	L34-44	–
1971	15 Sep	Challenge	W40-38	–
1974	1 Aug	League	–	L34-44

Year	Date	Type	Home	Away
1974	25 Sep	League	L31-46	–
1975	26 Jun	League	–	L28-50
1975	1 Oct	League	L37-41	–
1976	23 Jun	League	L36-42	–
1976	7 Oct	League	–	L29-49
1977	15 Jun	League	W44-34	–
1977	13 Oct	League	–	L34-44
1978	1 Jun	League	–	L32-46
1978	6 Sep	League	W42-36	–
1979	28 Jun	League	–	L33-42
1979	1 Aug	League	W57-21	–
1980	23 Jul	League	D39-39	–
1980	21 Aug	League	–	L35-43
1981	25 Jun	League	–	L26-52
1981	15 Sep	League	D39-39	–

Hull v. King's Lynn

King's Lynn home matches all staged at Saddlebow Road

Year	Date	Type	Home	Away
1974	5 Jun	League	L36-42	–
1974	10 Aug	League	–	L36-42
1975	19 Apr	League	–	W41-37
1975	4 Jun	League	L36-41	–
1976	12 May	League	W40-38	–
1976	21 Aug	League	–	L37-41
1976	6 Oct	Challenge	W54-24	–
1977	27 Apr	League	L38-40	–
1977	16 Jul	League	–	L26-52
1978	26 Apr	Knock-Out Cup	D39-39	–
1978	29 Apr	Knock-Out Cup	–	L38-40
1978	24 May	League	W52-26	–
1978	12 Aug	League	–	W41-36
1978	18 Oct	Challenge	W41-37	–
1979	9 May	League	W56-22	–
1979	15 Sep	League	–	L38-40
1980	19 Jul	Inter-Divisional Knock-Out Cup	–	L29-49
1980	24 Sep	League	W41-37	–
1980	28 Sep	League	–	L22-56
1981	11 Jul	League	–	L29-49
1981	26 Aug	League	W42-36	–

Hull v. Leicester

Leicester home matches all staged at Blackbird Road

Year	*Date*	*Type*	*Home*	*Away*
1949	9 Apr	Knock-Out Cup	W77-31	–
1949	15 Apr	Knock-Out Cup	–	W58-49
1949	23 Apr	League	W53-30	–
1949	10 Jun	League	–	L35-49
1974	25 Jun	League	–	L27-51
1974	4 Sep	League	W42-36	–
1975	1 Apr	League	–	L35-43
1975	3 Sep	League	W43-35	–
1976	21 Apr	League	W45-32	–
1976	1 Jun	League	–	W46-32
1977	19 Apr	League	–	L35-43
1977	11 May	League	W41-37	–
1978	12 Jul	League	W48-29	–
1978	26 Sep	League	–	L23-55
1979	25 Jul	League	W60-18	–
1979	18 Sep	League	–	W40-38
1980	21 May	League	W42-36	–
1980	24 Jun	League	–	L35-43
1980	17 Sep	Challenge	W43-35	–
1981	29 Apr	League Cup	W68-28	–
1981	2 Jun	League Cup	–	L37-59
1981	4 Aug	League	–	L37-41
1981	19 Aug	League	W47-31	–

Hull v. Liverpool

Liverpool home matches all staged at Stanley Stadium

Year	*Date*	*Type*	*Home*	*Away*
1949	23 May	League	–	L34-48
1949	27 Jun	League	–	L36-48
1949	2 Jul	League	W53-31	–
1949	27 Aug	League	W54-29*	–

* The final meeting at Hedon Stadium

Hull v. Long Eaton

Long Eaton home matches all staged at Station Road

Year	*Date*	*Type*	*Home*	*Away*
1971	14 Apr	Challenge	W42-36	–
1971	20 May	Challenge	–	L32-45
1971	5 Aug	League	–	L36-42
1971	22 Sep	League	W46-32	–
1972	4 May	League	–	L33-45
1972	14 Jun	League	W50-28	–
1973	17 May	League	–	W42-36
1973	13 Jun	League	W46-32	–

Hull v. Middlesbrough

Middlesbrough raced as 'Teesside' 1971-1973
Middlesbrough home matches all staged at Cleveland Park

Year	*Date*	*Type*	*Home*	*Away*
1971	19 May	League	W55-23	–
1971	19 Aug	League	–	L35-43
1972	20 Apr	North-Eastern Trophy	–	L28-50
1972	26 Apr	North-Eastern Trophy	W49-29	–
1972	7 Jun	Knock-Out Cup	W40-36	–
1972	8 Jun	Knock-Out Cup	–	L30-48
1972	3 Aug	League	–	L31-47
1972	4 Oct	League	W46-32	–
1973	11 Apr	North-Eastern Trophy	L36-42	–
1973	19 Apr	North-Eastern Trophy	–	L38-40
1973	19 Jul	League	–	L34-44
1973	3 Oct	League	L38-40	–

Hull v. Mildenhall

Mildenhall home match raced at West Row

Year	*Date*	*Type*	*Home*	*Away*
1980	11 May	Inter-Divisional Knock-Out Cup	–	W50-28

Hull v. Newcastle

Newcastle home matches all staged at Brough Park

Year	*Date*	*Type*	*Home*	*Away*
1948	15 May	Challenge	L35-48	–
1948	16 Sep	Challenge	W57-26	–
1976	4 Aug	Challenge	W41-37	–
1977	22 Aug	Challenge	–	W41-37
1978	9 Oct	Challenge	–	W43-35
1981	3 Jun	Challenge	W51-27	–
1981	24 Aug	Challenge	–	W50-28

Hull v. Newport

Newport home matches staged at Somerton Park

Year	*Date*	*Type*	*Home*	*Away*
1974	15 May	League	W51-27	–
1974	19 Jul	League	–	L33-45
1975	29 Jul	League	L35-43	–
1975	5 Sep	League	–	L32-46
1976	26 May	League	W40-36	–
1976	16 Jul	League	–	L36-42
1976	11 Aug	Inter-Divisional Knock-Out Cup	W50-27	–

Hull v. Oxford

Oxford home matches staged at Cowley Stadium, Sandy Lane

Year	*Date*	*Type*	*Home*	*Away*
1949	5 May	League	–	W51-32
1949	25 Jun	League	W60-24	–
1949	28 Jul	League	–	L29-54
1974	8 May	League	W40-38	–
1974	26 Sep	League	–	L28-50
1975	5 Jun	League	–	L29-49
1975	8 Oct	League	W40-38	–

Hull v. Peterborough

Peterborough home matches all staged at the East of England Showground

Year	*Date*	*Type*	*Home*	*Away*
1971	8 Sep	League	W43-35	–
1971	17 Sep	League	–	W43-35
1972	17 May	League	L35-43	–
1972	19 May	League	–	L27-51
1973	16 May	League	L32-45	–
1973	18 May	League	–	L27-51

Hull v. Plymouth

Plymouth home matches all staged at Pennycross Stadium

Year	*Date*	*Type*	*Home*	*Away*
1948	10 Jun	League	–	L24-59
1948	10 Jul	League	W58-26	–
1948	7 Aug	League	W58-26	–
1948	12 Aug	League	–	L33-51
1949	28 May	League	W44-40	–
1949	9 Jun	League	–	L25-59

Hull v. Poole

Poole home matches all staged at Wimborne Road

Year	*Date*	*Type*	*Home*	*Away*
1948	3 May	League	–	L19-65
1948	7 Jun	League	–	L24-59
1948	3 Jul	League	W58-25	–
1948	11 Sep	League	W47-36	–
1949	30 May	League	–	L40-44
1949	4 Jun	League	W54-30	–
1949	13 Aug	League	W49-35	–
1974	26 Aug	League	W58-20	–
1974	28 Aug	League	–	L34-43
1975	25 Aug	League	W49-29	–
1975	27 Aug	League	–	L36-42
1976	31 Aug	League	W53-25	–
1976	1 Sep	League	–	L37-41
1977	29 Aug	League	W47-31	–
1977	31 Aug	League	–	L30-48

Year	*Date*	*Type*	*Home*	*Away*
1978	28 Aug	League	W41-37	–
1978	30 Aug	League	–	L30-48
1979	27 Aug	League	W62-16	–
1979	29 Aug	League	–	D39-39
1980	29 Jul	League	D39-39	–
1980	30 Jul	League	–	D39-39
1981	9 Jun	League	W45-33	–
1981	10 Jun	League	–	L33-45

Hull v. Rayleigh

Rayleigh home matches all staged at The Weir Stadium

Year	*Date*	*Type*	*Home*	*Away*
1949	18 Apr	League	–	L31-52
1949	6 Jun	League	W62-22	–
1949	9 Jul	League	W52-32	–
1971	29 May	League	–	L33-45
1971	4 Aug	League	W45-33	–
1972	22 Jul	League	–	L36-41
1972	9 Aug	League	W44-34	–
1973	30 May	Knock-Out Cup	W43-34	–
1973	9 Jun	Knock-Out Cup	–	L32-46
1973	2 Jul	League	–	D39-39
1973	8 Aug	League	W40-37	–

Hull v. Reading

Reading home matches all staged at Smallmead Stadium

Year	*Date*	*Type*	*Home*	*Away*
1975	28 Apr	League	–	L30-48*
1975	9 Jul	League	L36-42	–
1976	26 Apr	League	–	L36-42
1976	25 Aug	League	W44-33	–
1977	13 Jun	League	–	L36-42
1977	6 Jul	League	L31-47	–
1978	31 May	League	W44-33	–
1978	26 Jun	League	–	D39-39
1979	20 Jun	League	W51-27	–
1979	16 Jul	League	–	L35-42
1980	28 May	League	W40-38	–

Year	*Date*	*Type*	*Home*	*Away*
1980	9 Jun	League	–	L35-43
1981	15 Jun	League	–	L31-47
1981	2 Sep	League	W45-33	–

* The first meeting at Smallmead Stadium

Hull v. Rochdale

Rochdale home matches all staged at The Athletic Grounds

Year	*Date*	*Type*	*Home*	*Away*
1971	30 Apr	Knock-Out Cup	–	L31-47
1971	5 May	Knock-Out Cup	L38-39	–
1971	25 Jun	League	–	L38-40
1971	23 Aug	League	W51-27	–

Hull v. Romford

Romford home match staged at Brooklands Stadium

Year	*Date*	*Type*	*Home*	*Away*
1971	3 Jun	League	–	L38-40
1971	18 Aug	League	W47-30	–

Romford home match staged at Brooklands Stadium

Hull v. Scunthorpe

Scunthorpe home matches staged between 1971-1973 at Quibell Park, 1980 at Ashby Ville

Year	*Date*	*Type*	*Home*	*Away*
1971	3 May	Challenge	–	L38-39*
1972	7 May	League	–	W46-32
1972	10 May	League	W48-30	–
1973	16 Apr	Challenge	–	L36-40
1973	9 May	League	W40-37	–
1973	28 May	League	–	L35-43
1980	13 Oct	Challenge	–	W43-34

* The first meeting at Quibell Park

Hull v. Sheffield

Sheffield home matches all staged at Owlerton Stadium

Year	*Date*	*Type*	*Home*	*Away*
1974	10 Apr	Northern Trophy	L29-48	–
1974	18 Apr	Northern Trophy	–	L24-54
1974	9 May	Knock-Out Cup	–	L26-52
1974	29 May	Knock-Out Cup	L38-40	–
1974	15 Aug	League	–	L36-42
1974	9 Oct	League	W45-33	–
1975	16 Apr	Northern Trophy	L36-42	–
1975	17 Apr	Northern Trophy	–	L29-49
1975	28 May	League	L38-40	–
1975	24 Jul	League	–	L30-48
1975	15 Oct	Challenge	W42-35	–
1976	7 Apr	Northern Trophy	L38-40	–
1976	8 Apr	Northern Trophy	–	L32-46
1976	14 Jul	League	W43-35	–
1976	2 Sep	League	–	W42-36
1977	6 Apr	Northern Trophy	W46-32	–
1977	28 Apr	Northern Trophy	–	L24-53
1977	21 Jul	League	–	L33.5-34.5
1977	17 Aug	League	W52-26	–
1978	5 Apr	Northern Trophy	W42-36	–
1978	6 Apr	Northern Trophy	–	L32-46
1978	23 Aug	League	W49-29	–
1978	28 Sep	League	–	L34-44
1979	4 Apr	Northern Trophy	D39-39	–
1979	19 Apr	Northern Trophy	–	L28-48
1979	31 May	Knock-Out Cup	–	L48-60
1979	1 Jun	Knock-Out Cup	W81-25	–
1979	15 Aug	League	A30-12	–
1979	6 Sep	League	–	W49-29
1979	12 Sep	League	W57-21	–
1980	1 Apr	Northern Trophy	L38-40	–
1980	28 Apr	Northern Trophy	–	W40-37
1980	10 Jul	League	–	L35-43
1980	27 Aug	League	W60-18	–
1981	9 Apr	League Cup	–	L47-49
1981	22 Apr	League Cup	W53-43	–
1981	8 Jul	League	W47-30	–
1981	1 Oct	League	–	L29-49

Hull v. Southampton

Southampton home matches all staged at Banister Court

Year	*Date*	*Type*	*Home*	*Away*
1948	8 Jun	League	–	L25-59
1948	10 Aug	League	–	L28-56
1948	14 Aug	League	W45-39	–
1948	9 Oct	League	W47-36	–
1948	15 Oct	North v. South Cup	–	L43-53*

*Raced at Dudley Wood Stadium, Cradley Heath.

Hull v. Stoke

Stoke raced as 'Chesterton' in 1973

Stoke home matches all staged at Loomer Road

Year	*Date*	*Type*	*Home*	*Away*
1973	25 Apr	League	L37-41	–
1973	28 Jun	League	–	D39-39

Hull v. Sunderland

Sunderland home matches all staged at Newcastle Road

Year	*Date*	*Type*	*Home*	*Away*
1971	7 Apr	Challenge	W47-25*	–
1971	30 May	League	–	W40-38
1971	11 Aug	League	W51-27	–
1972	19 Apr	North-Eastern Trophy	W46-31	–
1972	23 Apr	North-Eastern Trophy	–	D39-39
1972	21 Jun	League	W40-38	–
1972	23 Jun	League	–	L30-47
1973	6 Apr	North-Eastern Trophy	–	L36-42
1973	18 Apr	North-Eastern Trophy	W42-35	–
1973	20 Jun	League	W43-35	–
1973	15 Aug	Challenge	L38-40	–
1973	*9 Sep*	*League*	–	*A17-29*
1973	7 Oct	League	–	L33-45

*The first meeting at The Boulevard.

Hull v. Swindon

Swindon home matches all staged at Abbey Stadium, Blunsdon

Year	*Date*	*Type*	*Home*	*Away*
1974	1 Jun	League	–	L29-49
1974	24 Jul	League	W48-30	–
1975	11 Jun	Knock-Out Cup	W46-32	–
1975	14 Jun	Knock-Out Cup	–	L31-47
1975	24 Sep	League	W43-35	–
1975	11 Oct	League	–	L36-42
1976	5 May	League	L38-40	–
1976	25 Sep	League	–	L33-45
1977	27 Aug	League	–	L32-46
1977	14 Sep	League	W41-37	–
1978	22 Jul	League	–	W44-34
1978	4 Oct	League	W49-29	–
1979	8 Aug	League	W55-23	–
1979	26 Aug	League	–	D39-39
1980	17 May	League	–	L32-46
1980	3 Sep	League	W42-36	–
1981	5 Aug	League	D39-39	–
1981	26 Sep	League	–	L14-40*

* Abandoned after 9 heats. Result stood.

Hull v. Tamworth

Tamworth home matches all staged at Deer Park

Year	*Date*	*Type*	*Home*	*Away*
1948	19 Jun	League	W43-38	–
1948	31 Jul	League	W53-30	–
1948	31 Aug	League	–	L37-47
1948	19 Oct	League	–	L30-53
1949	16 Apr	League	W43-41	–
1949	27 Apr	Knock-Out Cup	–	L38-70
1949	30 Apr	Knock-Out Cup	W61-47	–
1949	1 Jun	League	–	L30-53
1949	6 Aug	League	L37-46	–

Hull v. Walthamstow

Year	*Date*	*Type*	*Home*	*Away*
1949	7 May	Challenge	D42-42	–

Hull v. West Ham

West Ham home match staged at Custom House

Year	*Date*	*Type*	*Home*	*Away*
1972	23 May	League	–	W40-38

The final meeting at West Ham

West Ham's remaining matches in 1972 were completed by Barrow, including the home match with Hull

Hull v. White City

White City home matches staged at White City Stadium, London

Year	*Date*	*Type*	*Home*	*Away*
1976	31 May	League	–	W 44.5-33.5
1976	2 Jun	League	W43-34	–
1977	11 Apr	League	–	L24-54
1977	22 Jun	League	L38-40	–
1977	19 Oct	Challenge	W50-28	–
1978	3 May	League	W47-31	–
1978	25 Jul	League	–	W42-36

Hull v. Wimbledon

Wimbledon home matches all staged at Plough Lane

Year	*Date*	*Type*	*Home*	*Away*
1974	10 Jul	League	L38-40	–
1974	19 Sep	League	–	L27-50
1975	12 Jun	League	–	L33-45
1975	18 Jun	League	W42-36	–
1976	28 Apr	League	W46-32	–
1976	19 Aug	League	–	L33-45
1977	4 May	League	W43-35	–
1977	30 Jun	League	–	L31-47
1978	6 Jun	League	W50-28	–
1978	22 Jun	League	–	L33-44
1979	26 Jul	League	–	L36-41
1979	22 Aug	League	W51-27	–
1980	31 Jul	League	–	L31-47
1980	10 Sep	League	W44-33	–
1981	29 Jul	League	D39-39	–
1981	30 Jul	League	–	L34-44

Hull v. Wolverhampton

Wolverhampton home matches all staged at Monmore Green Stadium

Year	*Date*	*Type*	*Home*	*Away*
1974	19 Jun	League	L37-41	–
1974	12 Jul	League	–	L38-40
1975	14 May	Challenge	W41-37	–
1975	18 Jul	League	–	L36-42
1975	6 Aug	League	W47-31	–
1976	15 Sep	League	W57-21	–
1976	24 Sep	League	–	L35-43
1976	20 Oct	Inter-Divisional Knock-Out Cup	W57-21	–
1976	22 Oct	Inter-Divisional Knock-Out Cup	–	D39-39
1977	27 May	League	–	L38-39
1977	10 Aug	League	W52-26	–
1978	7 Jul	League	–	D39-39
1978	13 Sep	League	W48-30	–
1979	25 Apr	League	W43-35	–
1979	5 Oct	League	–	W52-26
1980	30 Apr	League	W41-36	–
1980	11 Jul	League	–	D39-39

Hull v. Wombwell

Wombwell home matches all staged at Station Road

Year	*Date*	*Type*	*Home*	*Away*
1948	21 May	League	–	L31-53
1948	29 May	League	W47-31	–
1948	16 Jul	League	–	L40-44
1948	4 Sep	League	W58-26	–

Hull v. Workington

Workington home matches all staged at Derwent Park

Year	*Date*	*Type*	*Home*	*Away*
1971	2 Apr	Challenge	–	L35-43
1971	28 Apr	League	W43-33	–
1971	20 Aug	League	–	W42-36
1972	16 Jun	League	–	L34-44
1972	5 Jul	Challenge	L35-43	–
1972	27 Sep	League	L38-40	–
1973	22 Jun	League	–	L33-45

Year	Date	Type	Home	Away
1973	26 Sep	League	W42-35	–
1976	29 Sep	Inter-Divisional Knock-Out Cup	W54-23	–
1977	6 May	Inter-Divisional Knock-Out Cup	–	W50-28

Hull v. Yarmouth

Yarmouth home matches all staged at Caister Road

Year	Date	Type	Home	Away
1948	24 Apr	League	W52-28	–
1948	11 May	League	–	L35-48
1948	12 Jun	League	W51-33	–
1948	21 Aug	North v. South Cup	W68-28	–
1948	21 Sep	North v. South Cup	–	W56-40
1948	28 Sep	League	–	L33-50
1949	14 May	League	D42-42	–
1949	21 Jul	League	–	L18-66
1949	16 Aug	League	–	L24-60
1949	20 Aug	League	L35-49	–

Matches against Continental Opposition

Hull v. Fredericia (Denmark)

Year	Date	Type	Home	Away
1972	26 Jul	Challenge	W55-23	–

Randers (Denmark) v. Hull

Year	Date	Type	Home	Away
1975	22 Jun	Challenge	–	L38-40

Landshut (W. Germany) v. Hull

Year	Date	Type	Home	Away
1977	2 Jul	Challenge	–	W42-36

Matches against Miscellaneous Opposition (all at Home)

Hull v. Cradley Heath and Tamworth

Year	Date	Type	Home	Away
1948	3 Apr	Challenge	W45-38	–

Hull v. Halifax Nomads

Year	*Date*	*Type*	*Home*	*Away*
1948	10 Apr	Challenge	W52-32	–

Hull v. Odsal Starlets

Year	*Date*	*Type*	*Home*	*Away*
1948	2 Aug	Challenge	W61-23	–

Hull v. Hanley and Cradley Heath

Year	*Date*	*Type*	*Home*	*Away*
1948	2 Oct	Challenge	W45-39	–

Hull v. Stars of the League

Year	*Date*	*Type*	*Home*	*Away*
1971	20 Oct	Challenge	L38-40	–
1972	16 Aug	Challenge	D39-39	–

Hull v. Barry Briggs Select

Year	*Date*	*Type*	*Home*	*Away*
1978	14 Jun	Challenge	W46-32	–

Hull v. All Stars*

Year	*Date*	*Type*	*Home*	*Away*
1978	9 Aug	Challenge	W48-30	–

*Bobby Beaton Testimonial Meeting

Hull v. Reg Wilson Select

Year	*Date*	*Type*	*Home*	*Away*
1979	10 Oct	Challenge	W50-26	–

Division Three Stars v. Sheffield

Year	*Date*	*Won by*	*Home*	*Away*
1948	25 Sept	Sheffield	–	W42-41

Individual Meetings at Hull

World Championship Qualifying Rounds

Year	*Date*	*Winner*	*Pts*
1948	17 May	Alf Bottoms	15
1949	21 May	Billy Hole	14
1974	1 May	John Boulger	15
1975	21 May	Bruce Cribb	14
1978	17 May	Ivan Mauger	14
1979	2 May	Ivan Mauger	15

Grand Prix Qualifying Rounds

Year	*Date*	*Winner*	*Pts*
1976	7 Jul	Peter Collins	15
1977	21 Sept	Ole Olsen	14
1978	17 May	Ivan Mauger	14
1979	2 May	Ivan Mauger	15

The World Championship and Grand Prix Qualifying Rounds for 1978 and 1979 were merged into the same meeting.

Northern Riders Championship Qualifying Rounds

Year	*Date*	*Winner*	*Pts*
1974	26 Jun	Peter Collins	15
1975	13 Aug	Peter Collins	15

Yorkshire Television Trophy

Year	*Date*	*Winner*	*Pts*
1974	21 Aug	Phil Crump	13
1975	23 Jul	Ivan Mauger*	Final
1976	21 Jul	Dave Jessup	15
1977	20 Jul	Ole Olsen	15
1978	5 Jul	Vaclav Verner	13
1979	4 Jul	Ivan Mauger	15
1980	2 Jul	Ivan Mauger	15
1981	1 Jul	Bruce Penhall	15

*Raced as a Knock-Out Tournament

Hull Open Championship

Year	*Date*	*Winner*	*Pts*
1971	12 May	Reg Wilson	15
1972	24 May	Phil Crump	15
1973	6 Jun	Dave Mills	14

Anglo-Swedish Open Championship

Year	*Date*	*Winner*	*Pts*
1971	23 Jun	Doug Wyer*	14

* After run off with Reg Wilson

Supreme Individual Open Trophy

Year	*Date*	*Winner*	*Pts*
1972	28 Oct	Jim Ryman	14

Colin Tucker Farewell Trophy

Year	*Date*	*Winner*	*Pts*
1973	17 Oct	Dennis Gavros	15

Pairs Meetings at Hull

Humberside Best Pairs

Year	*Date*	*Winners*
1971	9 Jun	Tony Childs/Colin Tucker

Inter-Continental Best Pairs

Year	*Date*	*Winners*
1974	12 Jun	Reidar Eide/Dag Lovaas

Test Matches at Hull

Year	*Date*	*Result*
1973	4 Jul	England 53 Poland 55
1973	12 Sept	England 44 Australasia 64
1974	17 Jul	England 69 Poland 39
1975	23 Jul	England 41 Rest of World 37
1977	24 May	England 55 Rest of World 53
1978	16 Aug	England 36 Australasia 70
1980	7 May	England 47 USA 61

Hull Speedway Track Record Holders

Hedon Stadium

Time	*Rider & Club*	*Date*
91.6	Les Jenkins (Hanley)	27 Mar 1948
88.8	Reg Gregory (Hanley)	27 Mar 1948
87.2	Alf Webster (Hull)	27 Mar 1948
85.4	Alf Webster (Hull)	3 Apr 1948
84.8	Ken Le Breton (Newcastle)	15 May 1948
84.6	Bob Baker (Hull)	3 Jul 1948
	Mick Mitchell (Hull)	17 Jul 1948
	Dick Shepherd (Hull)	31 Jul 1948
83.8	Norman Price (Odsal Starlets)	2 Aug 1948
83.4	Mick Mitchell (Hull)	9 Oct 1948
83.2	Bob Baker (Hull)	9 Apr 1949
	Mick Mitchell (Hull)	30 Apr 1949
82.8	Billy Bales (Yarmouth)	14 May 1949
82.4	Billy Bales (Yarmouth)	14 May 1949

The Boulevard

Time	Rider & Club	Date
76.4	Russ Dent (Sunderland)	7 Apr 1971
75.8	Mal Mackay (Workington)	28 Apr 1971
75.4	Peter Collins (Rochdale)	5 May 1971
	Reg Wilson (Hull)	5 May 1971
75.2	Peter Collins (Rochdale)	5 May 1971
75.0	Tony Childs (Hull)	26 May 1971
74.8	Doug Wyer (Berwick)	30 Jun 1971
74.2	John Louis (Ipswich)	7 Jul 1971
73.8	Mal Mackay (Workington)	5 Jul 1972
73.4	Phil Crump (Crewe)	12 Jul 1972
	Soren Sjosten (Belle Vue)	17 Apr 1974
	Jim McMillan (Hull)	1 May 1974
	Mitch Graham (Hull)	15 May 1974
	Reidar Eide (Newport)	15 May 1974
73.0	Jim McMillan (Hull)	15 May 1974
72.4	Phil Crump (Newport)	12 Jun 1974
72.2	Phil Crump (Newport)	12 Jun 1974
72.0	Dag Lovaas (Oxford)	12 Jun 1974
71.4	Scott Autrey (Exeter)	12 Jun 1974
70.8	Dave Jessup (Reading)	24 May 1977
70.4	Ivan Mauger (Hull)	21 Jun 1978
	Ivan Mauger (Hull)	25 Apr 1979
	Bobby Beaton (Hull)	2 May 1979
70.2	Ivan Mauger (Hull)	2 May 1979
	Michael Lee (King's Lynn)	9 May 1979
	Scott Autrey (Exeter)	23 May 1979
70.0	Peter Collins (Belle Vue)	5 Jun 1979
	Bobby Schwartz (Cradley H.)	4 Jul 1979
69.8	Ivan Mauger (Hull)	4 Jul 1979
	Bo Petersen (Hackney)	23 Apr 1980
69.6	Bo Petersen (Hackney)	3 Jun 1980
	Bobby Beaton (Hull)	3 Jun 1980
69.4	Dennis Sigalos (Hull)	3 Jun 1980
68.6	Dennis Sigalos (Hull)	23 Jul 1980